D0850357

Sod-House Days

LETTERS FROM A
KANSAS HOMESTEADER 1877-78

Written by HOWARD RUEDE

Edited by JOHN ISE

Published at NEW YORK   1966

COOPER SQUARE PUBLISHERS, INC.

Printed in U.S.A. by
NOBLE OFFSET PRINTERS, INC.
NEW YORK 3, N. Y.

Editors' Foreword

PROBABLY NO SINGLE factor has so profoundly affected American development and shaped American ideals as the West and its frontier. Its influence upon our agriculture, industry, politics, education, and literature—in fact upon every phase of institutional life—can scarcely be overestimated.

The conquest and settlement of the West by the white man was already well under way during the Colonial period. Indeed, long before the outbreak of the Revolution the mighty movement destined to carry courageous settlers over the slopes of the Alleghenies into the alluvial valley of the Mississippi, out across the plains, and ultimately to the waters of the Pacific was already under way.

The reasons for this phenomenal march westward were strikingly similar to those which impelled seventeenth-century Europeans to seek the New World. Some went West for mere love of adventure, lured on, as it were, by the unknown wilderness and the exaggerated tales of daring which found their way back to the older-settled communities. Others, not unlike the sixteenth-century European fortune hunters, went in quest of easy wealth. Still others went to escape the social, political, and religious restrictions and injustices of a crystallized and conforming Eastern or Old World society. A few went with the hope of achieving political fame. But most numerous of all were those who turned to the West, with its abundance of free or relatively cheap lands, in search of economic betterment. To the struggling Eastern farmer, dissatisfied tradesman, religious dissenter, oppressed mechanic, or ambitious young lawyer, or the zealous missionary seeking fresh spiritual conquests, the West was a sort of Promised Land, the gates of which were ever open. In other words, virtually the same motives—economic, religious, and patriotic—which inspired Englishmen to seize India and to make settlements in Australia, Frenchmen to acquire Algiers, Spaniards to plant their flag on the soil of Cuba and the Philippines, and Japan to seek a foothold on the mainland of Asia, drove Americans, during the nineteenth century, first into the trans-Appalachian country and then into the territory beyond the Mississippi. Missionary and fur trader were followed by homeseeking pioneers, greedy land speculators, gold seekers, and business men. Powerless before this onrush, the "backward peoples"— the Indians—and the buffalo herds so necessary for their existence gradually disappeared.

This volume records the experiences of one of that great army of settlers from the East and from the Old World who crowded westward during the eighteen-seventies, just after the heyday of Indian fighting and buffalo hunting. The book is doubly significant. Not only does it portray the hardships of pioneering, but it also furnishes first-hand information about the status of agriculture in a west central Kansas community, at a time when the seeds of agrarian discontent were being widely sown. In discovering and editing these letters Professor Ise has rendered a real service to students of social and economic history, and particularly to those interested in a better understanding of American agriculture.

H. J. C.
R. G. T.

COLUMBIA UNIVERSITY
IN THE CITY OF NEW YORK
February 8, 1937

Preface

WHILE STUDYING the pioneer history and life of a small community in Osborne County, in central-western Kansas, in the summer of .1928, I happened to find these letters. They were stored away in the basement of the home of Miss Ruth Ruede, of Osborne, Kansas, a sister of Howard Ruede, the author of the letters, who had died several years previously. Miss Ruede and a surviving brother, George Ruede, generally referred to as "Bub" in the letters, kindly consented to the publication of the letters in the form in which they appear here.

It has been hard to decide whether to call this book a series of letters or a diary, as most of the series were intended to serve as both. They were written by the author to his family in Bethlehem, Pennsylvania, and were later copied into blank books and stored away. It is fortunate that they were first written as letters, because the author in his letters to his family naturally tried to draw a careful and graphic picture, so that they would be able to see and understand all about his life and surroundings in the strange new country. When his people joined him and he turned from letters to a brief diary entry each day, the account lost most of its interest.

A small amount of the material contained here, it should be stated, was not in the original letters in exactly the form in which it appears here, but was published long afterward by the *Osborne Farmer*, most of it based on some of the original letters, but expanded and elaborated by the author himself, who was then working on the *Osborne Farmer*. A few of the most interesting accounts contained in this book were published in this way; but it seemed wise and proper, or at least permissible, to include them, since they were after all the work of the same author as the original letters and represented merely his more mature view of the life and conditions he describes. In a few cases it was necessary to edit these accounts, and to some extent the original letters, to eliminate purely personal matters, to avoid duplications, and to make the general picture consistent.

Acknowledgment must be made of many fine courtesies extended me in this work: especially to George Ruede, a younger brother of the author, until his recent death an official in the Internal Revenue Office at Wichita, Kansas, and to Ruth Ruede, of Osborne, Kansas, a younger sister of the author, for permission to publish these letters. Thanks are due also to Mr. and Mrs. Sabert Hampton, of Downs, Kansas, for opening their hospitable home to me while I was working on the study of pioneer life in that community, and to many others, old friends and acquaintances, many of them pioneers of the early seventies, who helped me to get the point of view needed to edit these letters intelligently. Mr. Charles Mann, editor of the *Osborne Farmer*, generously gave permission to print the letters which appeared in the *Farmer*. And, finally, acknowledgment is made of financial aid from the Graduate Research Committee of the University of Kansas, which made possible the investigation of pioneer life of which this book is a by-product.

J. I.

UNIVERSITY OF KANSAS
February 2, 1937

Introduction

HOWARD RUEDE was born in Bethlehem, Pennsylvania, the oldest boy in a family of Moravian stock—a family of exceptional intellectual endowments. Beside Howard, there were his mother and father, a younger sister, Ruth, and two younger brothers, Syd and George (Bub), the latter still a boy of some fourteen years at the time these letters were written. Howard was a printer by trade, and while the letters indicate no extraordinary wit or brilliance, they show his unusual powers of observation, which enabled him to present an interesting and accurate picture of the life of the pioneer community in which he lived. He was twenty-three years old when he went to Kansas, in March, 1877.

He settled near Kill Creek, a small tributary of the South Solomon River, about fifteen miles southwest of Osborne. Osborne had been settled in the hope that a railroad would some day be built along the Solomon Valley, but the nearest railroad point at this time was Russel, fifty miles to the south, on the Kansas Pacific—later the Union Pacific Railroad. Thus the letters picture a community without the advantages of railroad service, where all farm products sold and all products bought—lumber, farm machinery, and manufactured stuff—had to be freighted in lumber wagons fifty miles over the rough prairie trails, across the Saline River and up and down the hills. It was partly for this reason that the products sold were always extremely cheap, while those bought were generally very high in price. When eggs were selling at 5 cents a dozen, butter at 10 cents a pound, corn at 20 cents a bushel, and wheat at 35 cents a bushel, many articles of cloth-

ing and most household goods were much more expensive
than they are at the present time.

The picture presented by these letters is that of a community which had passed the stage of buffalo hunting and
Indian fighting, and had settled down to the undramatic task
of earning a living and perhaps a small fortune from the soil.
It is the hope of the editor that these letters will serve as a
corrective to the notion, so generally propagated by writers on
pioneer life, that pioneering was great fun, an interesting and
exciting adventure. The dramatic aspects of the life of even
the first wave of pioneers—the hunters and Indian fighters—
have generally been exaggerated. The life of the settlers who
followed was in most respects almost inconceivably hard,
dreary, monotonous, and uninteresting. Most of the settlers
had of course the hope of some day owning their own farms,
and this hope buoyed them on, but the conditions under which
they lived would otherwise have been almost intolerable.

Their close and invigorating contact with nature, however,
seems enticing to one who has been surrounded with the
luxuries and trivialities and artificialities of modern city life—
more enticing at this distance, probably, than it would at closer
range. Reading some of Howard Ruede's letters, one can almost feel the clear, bracing tonic of the bright fall days, the
cold of winter, the boundless, generous promise of April and
May, the burning sun and heat and the tiring, incessant winds
of Kansas July and August; one can picture the dew on the
buffalo grass of summer mornings, the diamond-glittering
frost of October, the rain and thunder and lightning. These
pioneers lived close to nature, and the modern city-dweller
will almost envy Ruede his fifteen-mile walk through the
buffalo grass and along the meandering trails to Osborne.

On the other side of the picture, we can see in these letters the hard, wearing work that these people, with so little power and so few mechanical contrivances at their disposal, had to do: walk long distances, perhaps carrying heavy loads; dig wells, perhaps with broken-handled picks; cut wood with dull axes—there were few grindstones; cut grain with cradles; hoe corn—all with poor tools and at the greatest disadvantage. Ruede says that the settlers did not work as hard as people did back in Pennsylvania, but few farmers of the present day would care to work as Ruede worked when he was on his claim.

There were other hardships, perhaps even more serious: poor food; poor and insufficient clothing and bed clothes; such crowding in the tiny dugouts that three must sleep in a bed; lack of almost all facilities for keeping person or clothes clean; unsanitary water to drink—the water in Ruede's well, as in many others, was largely surface water; bed bugs and fleas, flies and mosquitoes, which swarmed in the dugouts that had no screens. In reading these letters one senses too the slowness and tedium of the lives of these pioneers, who would walk ten miles to hear an execrable sermon, or perhaps even to read a newspaper, and would hang around the post office for hours waiting for the mail—for something to lighten the tedium of their lives. Ruede makes little complaint of any of these hardships, for he was a singularly cheerful and even-tempered man, but his letters nevertheless draw the drab picture very clearly.

The poverty of these early settlers—almost unbelievable poverty, from the point of view of present-day standards— did not seem so serious a matter at the time, since it was shared by almost all. Howard Ruede makes almost no complaint regarding it, partly because it was not his disposition to complain of anything, but partly because all were poor, and so no one felt it keenly. If some had horses, others oxen, and others no work animals at all, it was felt to be a temporary situation, and one to which they need not give too much attention. Social stratification was not yet a serious matter. Those who glory in our present standards of wealth might well study the life of these pioneers and see whether, after all, we are much happier or better in all respects than the poverty-stricken people who lived on the prairie frontier a few decades ago. If it is true that these pioneers, in spite of their poverty, were happy—perhaps as happy as we now are—because there was little economic inequality, that fact is very significant in its bearing on the whole problem of inequality. Perhaps the fact that inequality has grown as our wealth has increased is the reason why that wealth has brought so little happiness or contentment.

LETTERS FROM
A KANSAS HOMESTEADER
1877-78

WEDNESDAY, MARCH 7, 1877

BETHLEHEM, PENNSYLVANIA

After supper had a long talk on the Kansas question, and finally decided to go with Levin Brunner. Joe Weaver thinks I had better stay.

MONDAY, MARCH 12, 1877

OSBORNE, KANSAS

About 9 went to the bank and drew $75—all I had—thence to Brunner's—helped Levin pack his trunk—over to the depot for the tickets—$23.05 apiece. Everybody wishes me a safe journey and lots of good luck.

Arrived at Kansas City,[1] we struck for the Kansas Pacific train, which stood on the other side of the depot, but before we could get on board we were stopped by the demand of a brakeman to see our tickets, and when he had looked at them he said, "Emigrants lay over till 6 this evening," and there

---

[1] It will be noticed that at some points the narrative seems to take the form of a diary rather than of letters. Probably this was the result of revision at the time Ruede copied the letters—some years after they had been written. He copied them into several ledger books, and it was in that form that I found them.

we had to lay over. We didn't care much, because we were glad for a chance to walk round a little, and John was glad to hear something from home. Hen Wilhelm is also there. He has a good job at work on a grain elevator. These elevators are built of wood, the walls about 8 inches thick. The planks are about 1½ inches thick and 4 inches wide, and they lay the planks flat on top of each other and nail them with 10-penny nails. It takes a great deal of lumber to make an elevator. They have to lay the plank in such a way that when the grains swell—as they sometimes do—the pressure will come against the grain of the wood. John was to commence work the following week on a building in the city, laying brick. They struck it lucky, having been introduced to the Mayor, who is the largest contractor in the place. Now you might suppose that Kansas City was in Kansas, but it is not—it is in Missouri, about half a mile from the state line. The river that appears on maps as being part of the eastern boundary of Kansas is really east of the city. John showed us round the city, taking us to the market place and several other places of interest. There are about a dozen different makes of wagons for sale, the difference in pattern being very slight; the main difference that I could see was the *name* of the wagon. The "Kansas wagons" are made in the penitentiary. There was quite a display of agricultural machinery for sale. The sulky plows are a singular machine; the driver's seat is between the wheels, similar to the driver's seat on a reaper, and he manages the plow by means of levers which regulate the depth of the furrow. There were also gang plows—two plows, one behind the other—by the use of which two furrows are made in place of one. John said they didn't like Texas—folks there were too rough, and it was almost as much as a man's life was worth to go out on the streets after dark.

Travelers west should take care how they spend money here in Kansas City, because they have what they call "Kansas City money," which is worth only 80 cents on the dollar, and is hard to get rid of, as the people don't care about taking it. . . . There were a lot of emigrants in the depot who had arrived here at midnight the night before, and they looked as though they were pretty badly fagged. The streets were awfully dusty. They have street cars here in spite of the hills, and they are no small ones either. Kansas City is built on the top and sides of a pretty high bluff, and is a right pretty place. There is a great deal of business done here. Jim wanted some bologna, so he stopped at a butcher shop and got some, and what do you think he paid? 12½ cts. per pound. And then he got stuck—he got some of that Kansas City scrip in change for green backs. Al Ross says he intended to try for a situation as telegraph operator in Kansas City, but after we had been pretty well over town he concluded he didn't care to stay there, and at 4:30 he left for Leavenworth. He said he probably would come to Osborne, but we don't expect to see him. We have made up our minds that he will strike for Bethlehem inside of a month. About 4 o'clock the agent for the Kansas Pacific R. R. got a coach round for the emigrants, saying he thought it might be more comfortable than laying round in the depot, and a good many got in. . . . The agent, M. A. Roedelheimer, passed through the car, saying he would have another coach put on, so that those who wanted to dance could do so—but there were not two of the passengers who looked as if they cared for such amusement; they all appeared to wish they were at their journey's end. The train pulled out at 6, but at the state line we laid over for nearly an hour till the freight and cattle cars had been drilled into the position the conductor wanted them. We had come from Bethlehem to

Buffalo in a first class passenger car, and from there to Kansas City we went second class (smoking car); but from the latter place we traveled on a "cattle train" as Jim called it. Of all the slow traveling, this was the slowest. We did not average 10 miles an hour the first 100 miles. That's the honest truth. The train stopped as long as half an hour at some stations. The boys would jump off and run round. At one place they proposed to camp out. They brought in a handful of ground to show me "the first specimen of Kansas soil"; the next was Jim, who brought me a "bouquet" of dead grass, etc. Friday morning at 6 o'clock we reached Manhattan, 118 miles from Kansas City. Here a good many left the train. One man who had come from Harrisburg turned back. He said this was a God-forsaken country, and he didn't want to see any more of it—he was going back to where he came from, where he could get $2.10 a day for his work. Talk about high winds! At Ogden Station I was in the smoking car, and soon after we left that place I started for the other car, where my valise was. Just as I got to the door some one asked me a question and I turned to answer it. And that cost me my hat, for I forgot to pull it down on my head—and just as I stepped out on the platform the wind took it off. That was a costly pipeful of tobacco, wasn't it? I had to stay in the car after that, and I did not get out of it but once, when the water had been out of the cooler for about 5 hours, and we had to go back into the other car when we wanted a drink. The women in the car used up a lot of water to wash with in the morning; and what they used in that way would have lasted nearly all day for drinking. At Salina is the land office of the K. P. R.R. Co. They have a fine building there. There are also several eating houses. Over the door of one I noticed the sign: "Deutsch Eating House by J. Evert." Meals 50 cents at nearly all the stopping places along the road. Brookville is the terminus of one division of the road. Here is a round house for locomotives and an immense water tank, but not much of a town. On the tank I noticed three or four advertising boards, calling attention to Dan'l F. Beatty's pianos and organs, manufactured at Washington, N.J. I didn't think he had got so far west with his advertising. During the day we passed Fort Harker, which was abandoned in 1872. It stands on a Government reservation. I couldn't learn much about it. There was a man on the train, with his wife and two daughters, who were to meet their sons at Abilene. The boys recognized their sisters. We caught a glimpse of Fort Riley as we passed. At Ellsworth we took the caboose, as the passenger coach was taken off of the train. A surveyor got on board at Wilson, and he and another man got to talking about finding "corners" of claims and townships. He said in comparing the field notes with the marks, there was a good deal more variation than would be supposed. At one place the corner was described as being an oak tree 18 inches in diameter, and they only found a little elm. Talking about corners, some one mentioned that he had seen a whole wagon load dumped on a pile—supposed the surveying party had been surprised by Indians. . . . This soft coal burns with a flame, like wood; but that is not the only thing that is new to us. . . . At 9:30 P. M. we got out of the car at Russell, having been on the road 96 hours. Having no hat, I pulled the cape of my overcoat over my head and pinned it. There were two hotel runners at the depot—one for the Russell House and one for the Centennial House. We gave our baggage to the Russell House man, who piloted the way, and we were soon there. After taking a good wash we turned in and we slept well, in spite of the lack of shaking to which we had become accustomed in the cars. After a fellow has been in the cars three days and nights he can sleep almost anywhere.

Saturday morning when we got down stairs it was nearly 7 o'clock. I borrowed the landlord's cap and went across the street to a store, where, for $1.25 I got a good worsted cap. Our lodging and breakfast cost us $1 each. The hack driver wanted us to go with him to Osborne, but the fare was $3.50 (trunks extra) and we "could not see it." Levin looked round for a team going to Osborne, but had no luck. After awhile I went round to the Centennial stables to try my luck, and was told that a couple of teams were unloading potatoes, and would probably go to Osborne, so over I went to Moon's store, where the teams were, and made inquiry. I found that the freighters lived nearer to Cawker than to Osborne, but were willing to carry us for $1 apiece, including trunks. Jim's trunk had not arrived. About 11 o'clock we set off. The freighters' names were Geo. Shipton and John Owens.[2] The latter had been a hunter and trapper for 15 years, but settled down. The folks here think nothing of driving 50 miles a day with an empty team, and they say they have gone to Russell empty, loaded up and then got back in a day and a half. We got on first rate with our freighters. They are a good natured set and will tell a fellow anything he wants to know that they are able to inform him about. Freighting pays right well out here.[3] Geo. says he was out huckstering about 200 miles

---

[2] Both these men lived near my (the editor's) early home, and they were both somewhat lawless characters. A few years later than this, George Shipton, while intoxicated, shot a man who was working for him, and fearing arrest, hastily left the country. Owens was a man of somewhat similar character, perhaps even more reckless, and similarly left the country very suddenly and never returned. There was always much mystery as to his past history, and as to his reasons for going, and also as to where he went.

[3] It is doubtful if Ruede is correct in saying that freighting paid well. Occasionally it did, but if allowance be made for the wear and tear on

west of here last winter, and cleared $4. a day. They haul
heavy loads, too—from 2000 to 3500 pounds. Geo. says he has
hauled as much as 53 bushels of shelled corn at one load—
two horses. Jim tried to catch a prairie dog, but of course
failed. The swiftest greyhound can't get hold of one. They are
seldom far from their burrows, and they pop in before you
can count three. Levin and I had got a lot of grub at Russell
(25¢) and about 2 o'clock we stopped on the prairie for dinner and to bait the horses. Our bread was about an inch thick,
and the butter wasn't thin either. By nightfall we arrived at
the house of a man named Wilder, about 35 miles from Russell and here we stopped for the night eating what we had
brought from Russell for our supper.

As the night was cold, Mr. Wilder insisted that all five
of us should sleep indoors. We wondered how we were to be
stacked up for the night, seeing that the family consisted of
six persons and there were only four beds in sight; but the
freighters had blankets and wagon sheets and said we would
have to sleep on the floor. On entering the cabin we noted
that the beds stood in the four corners of the single room,
and opposite the door was a big stone fireplace with a wood
fire blazing in it. The middle of the room was all the place
there was in which to move around, but we were content to
sit in front of the fire and hear the freighters tell stories till
bed time.

Late in the evening the head of the family came in—he
had been attending "meeting" somewhere in the neighbor-

---

wagon and horses and on the freighter himself, and for the risk of accidents
and of theft it is very doubtful if freighters made even a modest wage. A
little farther on, Ruede states that these men lost one horse on this trip.
Freighting was a terribly hard life. Yet it was one way of making money,
and not a few of the settlers resorted to it at times. Money was very scarce
in the new country and often sorely needed.

hood—and didn't he bring the preacher with him! The
preacher's name was Clarkson, and he was of the Baptist persuasion, as we soon discovered. Mr. Wilder entertained us a
while with stories about his life among the Indians. He must
be very old, though I should say he is not over 60, because he
says he was 35 when he left Kentucky and lived 20 years on
the Verdigris, 15 years among the Osages, and so on, until
by figuring up, I concluded he must be 100 years old. I suppose he has told the story so often that he believes it himself.
There is one hitch, though. He and his wife tell different
stories about their life among the Osages. He maintains that
they treated him as well as he was ever treated in his life,
while she says they stole their horses and raised Cain generally. Well, let it go for what it is worth.

When we were ready for bed something happened of which
I had read, but had supposed was mere fiction. The women
folks had been sitting back of us, occasionally putting in a
word when the talk seemed to lag. We heard someone say:
"Gentlemen, look at the fire;" and as we considered ourselves
in that class we did as requested. Several minutes passed, and
we could hear considerable moving around; the strain on our
eyes from looking at the fire was presently relieved by the announcement that we were free to move again. The women
folks had retired. We spread our blankets on the floor and lay
down with our feet to the fire, but not until the last glimmer
from the embers had disappeared did all slumber. That was a
well-filled dormitory, surely—twelve people altogether, in
one room.

Sunday morning we turned out before sunrise; when Geo.
went to cooking pork and coffee for breakfast, John went to
feed the horses, and came back saying that one of his horses
had got loose and left. They spent a couple of hours looking

for the animal but did not find her. We boys had run out of
bread, so we got Mrs. W. to make us a lot of biscuit. She
would not set a price, so Jim gave her 50 cents. The old man
said that was too much, but we were satisfied, so she kept it.
In a few minutes the girl brought out a dish of fried eggs—
there must have been a dozen and a half—which made quite
an addition to our fare. We had fried pork, eggs, biscuit and
coffee, and what more would a man ask for? I caught a heavy
cold by sleeping on the floor, and had a raging headache all
day.

When we first sighted Osborne, about noon, it looked like
a little bunch of houses along both sides of a single short
street, with the prairie running right up to the houses, and
the main street angling off in our direction. The freighters
drove up to the watering trough near what they told us was
the City Hotel, a 1½ story frame building which looked comfortable enough to rest in for a couple of days. The home-
like appearance of the place, with its watering trough outside
a whitewashed paling, the well ten feet from the kitchen door,
the hearty welcome extended by Landlord E. Keever—all
helped to make us feel we were likely to stay more than a day
or two. "Keever," as he is called, bustled round, brought fresh
water from the well and towels to remove the grime of our
fifty miles of travel, and announced dinner, calling his guests
and boarders by ringing a large auctioneer's bell outside the
front door. The appearance of the dining room reminded us of
a farmer's home. The roast was on a big platter in the middle
of the table, and whoever happened to get a seat there was
expected to display his ability as a carver. Vegetables were
served in large dishes and passed from hand to hand, and
whole pies were set at intervals for each man to help himself.
Mrs. Keever and her assistants are fine cooks and know how

to dish up victuals in style, and the house is as neat as a pin.

There were several "drummers" at the hotel, and they had a table separate from the common herd, as they paid higher rates. Transient guests—not drummers—pay 35 cents per meal, and 25 cents for lodging, regular boarders $3.50 a week. There were not many regular boarders though, when we came.

There is one thing about these hotels that appears strange to an eastern man—that is, the absence of a liquor bar. You cannot get liquor at a hotel—they don't sell it. Not feeling well, I went to bed before supper. Had a hard night of it. Levin slept with me, and says he had to put me in bed about half a dozen times during the night. Mr. Jacob Schweitzer had heard that we were in town and came in Sunday evening to see us, but we were in bed—that is, I mean, Jim was up yet, and saw Mr. S., who invited us to come and see him.

MONDAY, MARCH 19, 1877

AT SCHWEITZER's, OSBORNE, KANSAS

Turned out at 7, and after breakfast, Mr. Hays, Col. Bear's son-in-law, called at the hotel to see us. He took us over to see a couple of claims about 2½ miles from town. They are not exactly what are called upland claims, but are between an upland and a bottom claim. An upland claim lies on top of a divide, and it is hard to find water sometimes. A bottom claim is one along a creek or river. These two claims—one of 160 and one of 80 acres—would have to be contested before we could get hold of them, and it would cost us about $50 to have it contested, and as none of us could afford that, those claims will lie open awhile yet. After dinner we struck out for

Schweitzer's across the prairie. On the way over we stopped
to talk with several men who had heard that several Pennsylvanians had arrived. The folks here are all very sociable
and like to talk. They don't work as hard by half as they do
at home. A good many have their corn planted, and others are
plowing the land for it. Talk about plowing! Here they never
plow more than 3 or 4 inches, because the ground dries out
as far as it is plowed. Out on the prairie you can scratch a hole
two inches deep, and the ground will stay in any shape you
press it into, but when it gets dry it will blow away. We got
into a dugout this afternoon belonging to a man from near
Pittsburg, who has been living here a year with his wife and
four children. The children, he says, haven't had a shoe on
their feet all winter, and none of them were sick. He had a dollar and a half when he got here.[4] A man named De Tuck, from
the vicinity of Reading, wanted to take us to the Indian
camp, about 6 miles from here, but we didn't go because we
had to see Mr. Hays. Mr. Schweitzer is going down on Thursday, and says he will take us. I will tell you about them when
we have seen them. We had quite a long talk with Mr. Dengler. He says he has always had enough to eat and clothes
don't cost much here. A man in rags is as much respected as if
he was dressed in broadcloth, provided he shows himself a
man. We met a Mr. Guiger, whose wife was one of Owen
Rice's sisters. Well, we got back to Schweitzer's about sundown. Stayed all night. Mr. S. has a nice place. He has built
him a good, substantial stone house, and did all the work himself. Anybody, with a little practice, can lay up a stone house.

[4] Very many of the new settlers came with almost no money or wealth
of any kind, many of them without even a team. An old settler I once
interviewed stated that he came with his family and a team and 25 cents
in cash, which he spent immediately for chewing tobacco.

The rock is soft and can be dressed square and hardens by exposure. We made arrangements to stay here the balance of the week. On Friday Mr. S. intends to take us to Kill Creek and Pleasant Valley, to show us places where we can get three claims near together. Kill Creek is about 8 miles from Osborne. We are all in good spirits and feel quite at home. Mr. S. says we shall keep what little money we have as long as we can, for when we are out we can't tell when we will get more. Tobacco is about the most expensive thing you can buy here, and everybody uses it. I guess by the next time you get a letter from me I will be settled on my claim.

TUESDAY, MARCH 20, 1877

AT SCHWEITZER'S, OSBORNE, KANSAS

After finishing my letter to you, we hitched up and went over to town for the baggage, which we had left at Keever's. The horses here are seldom shod except in winter or when they are a good deal on the road, or used steadily for freighting. As the hack from Russell had not yet arrived we went over to the printing office, where we had quite a long talk with the editor. He says they pay what they must and have no regular wages for a printer. At present he is paying $8 a week. Tramps are not plenty round here. . . . Our bill at Keever's was $1.65 each—35¢ per meal and 25¢ for beds. . . .

There appears to be a sort of monomania round here to become preachers. Some folks think it is laziness that induces so many to turn preachers, because then their congregation must support them.[5]

[5] Ruede later states that this is a mistake—that the preachers of the Mennonites and Dunkards did not get any pay for their preaching.

Landes' dugout is about the largest I have yet seen, and is walled out and plastered. When he gets ready to build a house, all he has to do is to take off the roof of the dugout and use the walls for a foundation. I tell you, living in a dugout is not what you folks might suppose. The ground is dry, and the wind has no show at you—it blows over instead of through the house. At any rate, it is the sort of residence we will have to inhabit for awhile. Got home about 10 o'clock and turned in. There is generally a little talk about who shall sleep in the middle of the bed, which is ended by the one who is quickest in getting there.

WEDNESDAY, MARCH 21, 1877

AT SCHWEITZER'S, OSBORNE, KANSAS

A beautiful day and very little wind, but though the sun shone brightly it was none too warm to wear an overcoat. To-day Mr. S. took us out to look for claims. We struck north-west to Pleasant Valley, but that did not suit us. It lays too high—in fact, it lays right in among the bluffs. We stopped to talk with a man named Roice, to ask the way to a place Mr. S. wished to take us. Roice's well is 55 feet deep, cut through the rock all the way down. The beauty of this rock is that no blasting is required. Let the rock be as solid as you please, by boring into it with an auger, large pieces can be wedged off. And he got good water, too. He is putting up a house of this white lime stone, which can be dressed with very little labor, and looks very neat. It hardens by exposure, but can be easily cut with a knife, even after being exposed for a long time. We arrived at the South Fork of the Solomon about noon, so we unhitched and stopped for dinner.

After giving the horses about an hour's rest we started off for Neuschwanger's near Kill Creek. Mr. N. is a Mennonite preacher. He and 4 of his children have their claims all in one body of land, and they all work together. Here are 800 acres all belonging to one family. They have the finest orchard of young peach trees I ever saw, and the trees were not set out either, but the peach stones were set out just where the trees stand. They say that setting out trees, unless the season is wet, is a bad thing, because the ground gets dry as deep as it is stirred. Trees two years from the seed are two feet high and very bushy. They plant them about 6 feet apart, and don't let them grow so high as they do at home. Mr. N. knew of no government land in the neighborhood, but said that probably Snyder, who lives 3 miles west, knew of some. So over to Snyder's we went. He said that right west of him were three quarter sections of land close together and proposed that we should drive over to see them. Over we went, and the land suited us well. It lies just one mile north of Kill Creek P.O., Osborne Co. which will hereafter be our address, as we have decided to locate there. My claim is the S. W. ¼ of section 4; Levin is next west, and Jim west of Levin, all on the same section line, and on the south slope. The land is of the intermediate grade, neither bluff nor bottom land, and is covered for the most part with buffalo grass, which Mr. S. says is a sure sign of its being good. This buffalo grass does not get more than 3 inches long, and about the middle of August turns into hay—cures on the ground, and if you pull up a bunch, you are sure to find green grass close to the roots. We got home about 8 o'clock, and, I suppose drove over 40 miles in all today, because we were on the go from about 8 this morning. There are peculiar customs here. For instance, when there is preaching at a place, all who

attend are expected to stay and eat dinner, so that till they are
through it is 4 or 5 o'clock.

THURSDAY, MARCH 22, 1877

AT SCHWEITZER'S, OSBORNE, KANSAS

The first thing on the program was a visit to the Indians.
These are part of the tribe of Omahas, who have camped on
the South Fork about 6 miles from Schweitzer's. The squaws
are tanning buffalo robes for a man named Rathburn. The
hunters, whoever they may be, were out about three months
last winter, and will probably realize $500 to $600 apiece. We
saw the hides in all the grades of curing, for they are not
tanned. When the hide is hard, they soak it in the creek till
it is right pliant, then smear it with soap and grease and lay
it away for 24 hours. Then it is brought out and stretched
in a frame like a bed quilt—only the frame is made of poles,
some of which are none of the straightest. In this stage the
work is done. First the squaw scrapes the hide with a piece
of sheet iron, and afterwards with a tin dish in the bottom of
which is punched a double row of holes. The edges of these
holes are sharp, of course, and scrape off bits of the hide. After this process has been carried on until the hide is thin
enough, it is rubbed against a rope, and worked back and
forth until it is pliant. We got inside of a tent—I can't call
them anything else, because they are made of duck. There was
a large tin kettle on a few hot coals, with a mixture in it
that I would not have attempted to eat. I think there must
have been wood ashes mixed with the corn—I don't know—
but I do know that the smell was not at all appetizing. There
was in the tent an old Sioux Indian—at least he said he was.

One of the Indians in the tent showed us a nearly finished tomahawk, and claimed to have done all the iron work about it; the head was of wrought iron and nicely polished. These men are a repulsive looking set; they have thick lips, big noses, and as their clothing is none too clean and what they have is just enough to cover their bodies, they don't present a very pleasing object to the eye. If the men are dirty, the women are filthy, for their work does not help to make them any cleaner. They asked through their interpreter whether there were any dead animals in Mr. S.'s neighborhood. They will go a good distance to fetch any animal that has died— no matter whether death was occasioned by natural causes or otherwise. I noticed two papooses tied fast to boards. One of them was yelling at the top of its little voice, but nobody appeared to take any notice of it. An old squaw—and she was ugly, too—was shaking the other one to sleep. I noticed one of the little boys—about 6 yrs. old, I suppose, had his head shaved below his ears and on top of his head, leaving a circle of hair just above the ears; and in front just above the nose, was a lock longer than the rest, and at the back of the head, just above the neck was a similar lock—I suppose those were scalp locks. I tell you it looked queer. It made me think of the picture in Harper's Magazine of the monks building the prison in Paris (the Abbeville). Only one Indian asked for "Chabak," which is something they all know how to say. All the English of which the owner of that tomahawk appeared to be master was "seven dollar" the price he wanted for it. There were some 600 Indians camped here a few days ago, but most of them have gone back to their reservation at Omaha, Neb. Some of the men wear their hair long. I saw one whose hair would have measured at least 14 inches, and black as coal. I never heard of an Indian getting gray, but I saw a couple of old squaws whose hair was decidedly gray. There was only one tolerably good-looking squaw in the crowd, and she was only about—I don't know. She was bright copper color, and looked as though she might be quite intelligent. The interpreter was a full-blood, and appeared to be the most intelligent of the whole crowd. He wears a full white man's costume, but no hat. None of them wore hats or shoes. Those who wore anything had moccasins on, and a few had a strip of red flannel tied round their heads. They cure the hides for halves. After we had been in that lodge a little while, the owner (I suppose it was he) spoke to the interpreter, who told us it was time to go. And we left. There were a good many ponies belonging to the Indians, but they were hard-looking stock, because they had had no feed except what they could pick up on the prairie, and their ribs stuck out like the hoops on a barrel. We got home about noon, and between 2 and 3 we three started for Squire Walrond's office to make application for land. We took out homesteads directly. We might have "filed" on the land, and that filing would have been good for 30 months, at the end of which time (or before) we could have bought the land or put a homestead on it. As it is, we must live on it five years. The first two years we live "off and on"—that is, we must sleep on it once in a while and make some improvements on it within 6 months, or it will be forfeited. It is to be our home, but we can hire out by the day or month as we like. A man here has three rights—homestead, filing and timber filing. By taking land under the first he must live on it five years, and at the end of five years of actual residence can "prove up" and get a deed. The second right I explained above.[6] The timber filing requires a man

[6] This second right referred to, the right to "file," was apparently the preëmption right.

to break 10 acres the first year, which he must plant with trees
12 feet apart the second year, besides breaking an additional
10 acres. The third year he must plant these 10, and break 20,
which must be planted the fourth year. Then he is entitled
to an additional 160 acres. It is a hard thing to live up to the
law on a timber filing because young trees are hard to get,
and when you have them, the question is whether they will
grow. The application and affidavit cost us $16—50 cents
cheaper than if we had gone at separate times. If we had gone
to the land office at Kirwin it would have cost but $15 but then
we would have had the expenses to and from Kirwin, besides
our meals there. We were recommended by Mr. Schweitzer
to go to Walrond.

They tell a story here about the way a certain young fellow
got a homestead before he was of age. It was perfectly legal,
too, for the law says specifically that a man has to be 21 years
old, or the head of a family when he appears at the land
office to make a homestead entry on government land. The
term "head of a family" is held to mean anyone who has
relatives dependent upon him or her, for a woman is not
barred from the homestead right. Tommy wanted a piece of
land and had had his eye on a certain quarter section for a long
time, and nobody else seemed to think that particular claim
was worth taking. It lay in a section on which there were a
couple of settlers, and a new comer would not have suspected
that it was vacant, especially as corner stones are not easily
found and the roads are mere crooked trails over the prairie.
To tell what land a man holds, it is necessary to have someone familiar with the neighborhood to point out the corners.

In this case the land was not "held by my brother-in-law,
who is coming here from Iowa soon to live on it," as was often
told a new comer in search of a homestead, when the man

to whom he applied wished to keep settlers away from a piece of land that joined his own until he could prove up and put papers on it himself. Well, Tommy coveted that piece of prairie and the neighbors didn't sic any outsiders onto it because they preferred to let him get it if he could.

It didn't keep him awake nights studying how to gain possession, but finally settlers came in so rapidly that he concluded it was time to move. He was handicapped by his age —only 19. To put a pre-emption on the land was feasible, but a little risky, because if his age was proved, the party proving him under 21 was able to oust him and he would lose all the improvements he might put on the place, unless the other fellow chose to give him something for them. He concluded to get his girl to help him, for he knew of the proviso in the law regarding the head of the family. So he saddled his pony and went over to Mary Ann's home to confer with her. She looked favorably on the project and consented to become his bride at once, so he continued his journey to the county seat and got a license to wed. Next morning he was over at Mary Ann's bright and early. She was busy with the week's washing, but took her hands out of the suds, dried them, and went with Tommy to the nearest justice of the peace, by whom they were made man and wife instanter. Mary Ann returned to her wash tubs and Tommy hiked for Kirwin, where the land office was located. The officials were not over-inquisitive, and Tommy got his homestead papers as "head of the family." At any rate that is the way the story goes.

Jim's trunk arrived by the hack this evening, and he was happy because it was not broken. Levin's had the top burst off and if he had not had it well tied, there is no saying where his property would be now. . . . I'll send you a map with my place marked on it. We expect to go out to the place and make dugouts the beginning of next week, and then look for work. There is not a great deal of work to be got until harvest and corn husking, but then there will be plenty, and if we can scratch along till then, I reckon we'll be O. K. But there is one thing we need very much—a team. And we will have one too, by hook or crook, if it is only an ox team; a team is what a man wants first here.

FRIDAY, MARCH 23, 1877

AT SCHWEITZER'S, OSBORNE, KANSAS

Mr. Schweitzer took a load of potatoes over to the railroad —or, rather, he started for the road with a load—as there is a box over there for him. Directly after he left, Jim and Monroe yoked the oxen and went to town for Jim's trunk. They got back towards noon, and then the three went hunting. It was cold, as a very cold wind has been blowing all day, and this afternoon we had a snow storm. There was not a great deal of snow on the ground after the cloud blew away, but the snow whirled round in the air so you could not see a quarter of a mile. The hunters came back and reported that they had shot a rabbit, but it was on the other side of the river and they could not get it. All they brought was a small chicken hawk. They say that these dugouts are alive with fleas and bedbugs. If we find it so, you may count on my building a stone house as soon as practicable. Just let us get a team and we will soon have the rest. Stone can be had for the asking; or by going upon government land we can get it without asking. And a man can soon learn to be a stone mason here. There is a man here named Dengler, who never laid a stone wall before, and he is putting up a little house, and it looks nice, too. I find that exercise makes me cough, so today I stayed in the house; I got Mrs. S. to make me some "stewed quaker," and it helped, but the mixture was almost too rich and nearly sickened me.

SATURDAY, MARCH 24, 1877

AT SCHWEITZER'S, OSBORNE, KANSAS

We slept late this morning, but that did not matter, for Wally hadn't had his breakfast when we came down stairs. Directly after we got up from the table, Monroe and Levin went out after rabbits, but didn't bring anything along when they came back, about 2 p.m. Jim and I stayed in the house all the morning, but after dinner the sun was pretty warm and we managed to get out a little, though we didn't go far from the house. Talk about cottonwood lumber for building. I don't want any in my house if I can get any other. It must be put in green, and when it begins to season, it warps and cracks, and draws all out of shape. And it is the meanest sort of wood to chop. You can't cut it into kindlings like pine, because when you get it as small as round your arm, it all breaks. It don't seem to have any grain.[7] There is something you will hardly believe: There is a bone here that came out of the hump of a buffalo, that is three inches longer than from my elbow to the end of my middle finger. This bone stood straight up when in the animal. I would hardly have believed it if I had not seen and handled the bone. I have been troubled a good deal with fever blisters at the corner of my mouth, but they are healing fast now. A person can always sleep here,

[7] My mother recalls some of the trouble she used to have with the cottonwood floor in her cabin. The boards were badly warped, and the floor so uneven that she had difficulty placing the bed so that all four legs would rest on the floor at once.

especially if he is out doors a good deal. These winds make one awfully drowsy.

SUNDAY, MARCH 25, 1877

At Schweitzer's, Osborne, Kansas

A beautiful day. Rather cold this morning, but by 10 o'clock it was warm. About 9 o'clock we three took a walk up to the bluffs. A man up there has put up a monument about 6 feet high. From the top of the bluff you can see Cawker City and Osborne, and for miles around till the range of vision is stopped by bluffs on all sides. We didn't go to preaching at Getz's, about a mile from here, this morning. This afternoon it was *hot*, and we were out nearly all the time. Mr. S. got home with his box from Russell just before nightfall. He had a pretty bad time of it on Friday when it snowed and blew so hard.

MONDAY, MARCH 26, 1877

At Schweitzer's, Osborne, Kansas

Bright and clear, and very mild this morning. We had hardly left the breakfast table before a man on horseback came up to the house for help at the saw mill on the South Fork about 3 miles below Schweitzer's. He wanted two hands, so Levin and Jim went. We had intended to go out to the claims today, but concluded a day's work was not to be sneezed at, and the claims might wait. I had intended to go to town for a pair of overalls, and Mr. S. said I should go with him in the wagon. He was to help Cooney Walter move. Went with them to Walter's place, a mile west of Osborne, and helped load up three teams. On the way back, stopped at Blake's store and got a pair of overalls for $1. He had some for 90¢, but they appeared to be poor goods. When we got to Col. Bear's place, to which Walter moved it was about dinner time. The Col's place is three miles east of Osborne, on the section line. Walter brought a lot of money with him when he came here, but it disappeared, and now he says, "If you have the means, go to Washington Territory. There you can get a big price for your produce and the land can be homesteaded, and there is timber on all the claims." I am not heeding any of that sort of talk. Even if I can't show a single tree on my claim, and no water as yet, just wait till I get a start. There will be a well there, provided we don't get work soon. Levin expects to get a job running a stationary engine at Russell in a short time; wages $40 a month and board. But I am getting away from the moving. They called us in to dinner, and as I thought I had earned it, I went in with the rest. Mr. and Mrs. Ruth, who helped, are a jolly couple. They live about 2 miles west of Schweitzer's. After dinner we went back for another load. On the way back we had a cow tied behind each wagon, and we had some trouble with the one tied behind Walter's wagon, so he got off and drove her, leaving the team to me. I had been moved from Schweitzer's wagon, because his oldest daughter, Vesta, was coming home, and she took my seat. It was nearly sundown when we got to the Bear place. This is a three-roomed house—or, rather, three separate shanties joined together, each containing one room. The well bucket was gone, but we had brought Walter's along, and as the teams were getting thirsty and uneasy, I went to drawing water. The old cow used up four big pails full of water, and the horses a bucket apiece, and when you think that I had to draw two buckets from the well for each bucket I gave to the stock, you may well imagine I was pretty tired. We drove home by moonlight after supper. The day had been a very hot one, and you may believe me when I say that I sweated riding along in the wagon. It was a regular scorcher for this season as Levin and Jim can testify, for they were out in the ṣun all day—Jim chopping wood. They got back about 9 o'clock, and we turned in soon after. It was rather warm in bed—in the middle—that was my place—but I managed to put in a good night. Cooney Walter is the only man I have met who says Kansas is not a good place to be in. He says people are induced to come here by means of false representations in regard to everything, and that when the little wood now along the creeks and rivers is used up, the folks will have nothing to burn. To be sure, there is coal about a day's drive from Osborne, but it costs the labor of a man and team for three days to get a load—a day to go, one to get out the coal, and one to return. He does not make allowance for the trees the people are planting every year.

TUESDAY, MARCH 27, 1877

At Snyder's, Kill Creek, Kansas

As Levin had the best paying job at the saw mill, he decided to put in another day's work, the proprietors wanting only one hand today, Jim and I concluded to go to the claims today so about 8 o'clock we started. First we settled with Mr. Schweitzer, who charged us $1 apiece for the week's board, and was afraid that was too much. Jim carried his army coat in a shawl strap and I had our dinner in the caba. We thought probably we could catch a team to carry us across the South Fork, but did not depend much upon the chance. No team appeared to be going in our direction, so we had to use our wits to get across. There was a large tree lying part way across the stream a short distance below the ford, and a lot of drift-wood was lodged against it. To this point we directed our attention, and by dint of a little climbing and balancing on a loose log, we managed to reach the other bank. It was no very easy thing to do, for besides the coat and the dinner, we had a shovel, axe and handle that we bought in Osborne as we passed through. From here to Kill Creek was plain sailing, and when we got across the creek at a very narrow but muddy place, we sat down to rest awhile, and while sitting there fell asleep. The nap didn't last long, but I felt pretty good after-wards. We kind of missed our way to Neuschwanger's and concluded to strike across the prairie to a house we saw in the distance. It was about two miles across, and if we had kept the road it would have been full three. At N.'s we stopped at the pump, which furnished the liquor and the caba furnished the solids for the meal. N. only dug 6 feet for his water, in a "draw" or gully, of which there are a good many in this part. Between the bluffs these draws serve to carry off the surplus water. We had still three miles to walk to Snyder's, which distance was gone over in a short time. Our traps were de-posited in a corner of the house, and after resting a bit, we struck out to look for "corners" which we did not succeed in finding. I tell you, we were almost lost when we got to N.'s, and almost despaired of finding the place until we saw the peach orchard north of a large rye field, and that satisfied us we were on the right track.

Snyder thought he could make room for us until we had a place to sleep in, so here we are fixed for a few days. We have good fare, too, though Syd would turn up his nose at the side meat. We have plenty of that, with horseradish, plenty of potatoes, eggs, etc. and some of the best bread I ever ate—almost equal to "O Re Bread." This is a sod house, plastered inside. The sod wall is about 2 feet thick at the ground, and slopes off on the outside to about 14 inches at the top. The roof is composed of a ridge pole and rafters of rough split logs, on which is laid corn stalks, and on top of those are two layers of sod. The roof has a very slight pitch, for if it had more, the sod would wash off when there is a heavy rain.

Perhaps you will be interested in the way a sod house is built. Sod is the most available material, in fact, the only material the homesteader has at hand, unless he happens to be one of the fortunates who secured a creek claim with timber suitable for house logs.

Occasionally a new comer has a "bee," and the neighbors for miles around gather at his claim and put up his house in a day. Of course there is no charge for labor in such cases. The women come too, and while the men lay up the sod walls, they prepare dinner for the crowd, and have a very sociable hour at noon. A house put up in this way is very likely to settle and get out of shape, but it is seldom deserted for that reason.

The builder usually "cords up" the sods, though sometimes he crosses the layers, making the walls about two feet thick, but a little experience shows that the extra thick walls are of no real advantage. When the prairie is thoroughly soaked by rain or snow is the best time for breaking sod for building. The regulation thickness is 2½ inches, buffalo sod preferred on account of its superior toughness. The furrow slices are laid flat and as straight as a steady-walking team can be driven. These furrow slices, 12 inches wide, are cut with a sharp spade into 18-inch lengths, and carefully handled as they are laid in the wall, one length reaching across the wall, which rises rapidly even when the builders are green hands. Care must be taken to break joints and bind the corners of the house. "Seven

feet to the square" is the rule, as the wall is likely to settle
a good deal, especially if the sod is very wet when laid. The
door and window frames are set in place first and the wall
built around them. Building such a house is hard work.

When the square is reached, the crotches (forks of a tree)
are set at the ends and in the middle of the house and the
ridge pole—usually a single tree trunk the length of the building, but sometimes spliced—is raised to its place by sheer
strength of arm, it being impossible to use any other power.
Then rails are laid from the ridge log to the walls and covered with any available material—straight sorghum stalks,
willow switches and straw, or anything that will prevent the
sod on the roof from falling between the rafters. From the
comb of the roof to the earthen floor is usually about nine
feet.

The gables are finished before the roof is put on, as in
roofing the layer of sod is started at the outer edge of the
wall. If the builder is able, he has sawed cottonwood rafters
and a pine or cottonwood board roof covered with sod. Occasionally a sod house with a shingle roof is seen, but of course
this costs more money.

At first these sod houses are unplastered, and this is thought
perfectly all right, but such a house is somewhat cold in the
winter, as the crevices between the sods admit some cold air;
so some of the houses are plastered with a kind of "native
lime," made of sand and a very sticky native clay. This plaster
is very good unless it happens to get wet. In a few of the
houses this plaster is whitewashed, and this helps the looks
very much. Some sod houses are mighty comfortable places
to go into in cold weather, and it don't take much fire to keep
them warm. I will have to be contented with a very modest
affair for a while, but perhaps I can improve it later.

There is a saw mill down on the banks of the Solomon—not a building but merely a circular saw and a run of chopping burrs on a big platform, everything exposed to the weather. The owner does a lot of work, too, sawing native lumber for anyone who brings logs, either for cash at a fixed price per hundred feet or for a share—usually half—of the sawed lumber.

WEDNESDAY, MARCH 28, 1877

At Snyder's, Kill Creek, Kansas

Noah staked two of the corners of my claim this morning, before he went out to herd the cattle and Jim and I followed him, looking for a place to make our dugout. We found a spot about ¾ mile from Snyders house where a patch of wild sunflowers had killed the grass. Here we began to dig, and by noon had made some progress. We laid off the ground 10 x 14 feet, and we'll have to dig it about 6 feet deep. Just before dinner I wished myself back home, and would have started for Osborne, but Jim persuaded me to say. After dinner we went back to the hole and in about two hours had dug about half of it to the depth of two feet. And then we were stopped by a shower coming up, which bid fair to keep on till night, but did not, though the clouds hung very low. We went back to the house, and Snyder fixed the handle to our ax. My dugout is at the head of the prettiest draw on my claim, and if the clouds clear off we will have it finished by the middle of next week. This afternoon Bevvy Neuschwanger rode up to see Mrs. Snyder and while they were talking we made off and put in a little more work on the claim. Talk about hard work will you? Just try digging in the ground out here two feet from the surface—oh, I should have written 6 inches from the surface. The ground is packed just as hard as could be, and it is no fun to pick and shovel it. It is damp as far as we have gone down (some 27 inches) and sticky as putty. Sometimes we can throw out lumps as big as your head. About 3 o'clock we had a little shower and then we quit work and went back to the house. We wanted a little instruction about putting the handle into the axe, and Snyder offered to do it for us, for which we were glad enough and by the time it was dark, the axe was fixed. Now our possessions consist of an axe, shovel and tincup, besides our clothing.

The prairie chickens are about as pretty a bird as you will come across. They are about as big as a half-grown barnyard fowl, and are not much shyer. The folks say they become more numerous as the land is broken up. The law forbids a man shooting them on any claim but his own, but if a poor fellow shoots a couple on somebody else's claim for food, no one thinks of having him up for it. The folks here all talk German more than English, but they can all get along, even if they cannot use the latter tongue very fluently. I talk English altogether and they may talk what they please.

THURSDAY, MARCH 29, 1877

At Snyder's, Kill Creek, Kansas

Turned out about 7, and soon after breakfast Mr. Neuschwanger and Grandfather Snyder drove up, but as Snyder and wife were at Hoot's, they did not stop long. The clouds hung very low, and we thought it best not to go to work, but instead, go to Neuschwanger's for the pick, which the old man had said we might have. The one we had been using was borrowed from Alex Blair, who lives south of Snyder's, and had to be returned. N.'s is 3 miles east of Snyder's, and we went

over and back, besides talking awhile with Henry N. and at
the house, in 1¾ hours. The road is over the prairie. Every
few minutes we heard the "conking" of the wild geese, and
we could hear them a good while before we could see
them, as it was rather foggy. We saw a couple thousand at
least, in flocks of 10 to a hundred. We got back home by
12:15, and after dinner went over to the hole and made it
somewhat larger. When we came home for supper, who should
be there at the table but Levin, who had just arrived from
Schweitzer's. He lost himself three times on the road, and
had a hard time generally. He got his dinner at Neuschwanger's. It took him about 9 hours to come over, and he thinks
he walked over 20 miles. We are about 18 miles from
Schweitzer's. This evening the entire Hoot family were up
here, and Grandfather Snyder kept meeting. I believe he is
a Mennonite preacher. They sang Mennonite and Methodist
hymns indiscriminately, and got a good deal of music out of
them too. After the Hoots had left they got after me to sing,
and I favored them with T.82 and a couple of others, and
then went to bed. There was a heavy thunderstorm during
the night, with a good deal of sheet lightning in the north.

The people here don't go to church—they "go to meeting."
Services are held in private houses. The various denomina-
tions are not exclusive, and everybody is welcome to the services whether he is the particular faith of the preacher or not.
A Roman Catholic and a Hardshell Baptist, or a Methodist
are on just as friendly terms as though both had precisely the
same creed and observed the same forms in their worship. A
visiting preacher, no matter of what denomination, is always
sure of an audience in proportion to the size of the house in
which he has been invited to hold the service, and often the
room is full and others unable to get into the house stand by
the door and windows to catch what they can of the sermon.

At whatever house the services are held all the people present are expected to stay for dinner, which follows the sermon. . . . The dinner is usually substantial and palatable. It seems to be thought no imposition for fifty or more people to take dinner at a place, and even sometimes people take offense if you attend meeting and leave without partaking of their hospitality. In some cases those who attend meeting arrive the night before, coming ten to fifteen miles to hear preaching by a minister of their own denomination. This is especially true of the Dunkards, who have a small organization east of Osborne.

FRIDAY, MARCH 30, 1877

At Snyder's, Kill Creek, Kansas

Took the pick to Blair's, and then struck for the dugout. Levin and Jim were bailing out the water that had got into the hole from the rain. We dug awhile and as I said it was near noon, started for the house. Told them I could tell within an hour of dinner time, and sure enough, it was 11 o'clock when we got to the house. After dinner we went back to the hole and Jim wanted tobacco. He thought that as he and Levin were more used to the work, I had better go to Kill Creek P. O. and get some, because I had lighter shoes than he. So I struck across the prairie and walked S.W. about 1½ miles to the P. O. (That will be our address hereafter: Kill Creek P. O., Osborne Co., Kansas.) Got back about 3 o'clock and then we dug till sundown. We got a good deal out, and expect to get the hole as deep as we want it by tomorrow noon. It will be 4 ft. 2 in. deep in front and about 5 ft. behind. The ground was wet for about 3 feet from the top, but below it is perfectly dry, and packed hard as stone, but we have not found a single stone as big as a marble yet.

SATURDAY, MARCH 31, 1877

AT SNYDER'S, KILL CREEK, KANSAS

This was a beautiful clear day, and right after dinner it was real hot work to dig, but we kept at it, one working while the other two rested, and we got through digging the hole by the time it was dark. The hole is 10 x 14 feet, and in front 4 ft. deep; 4½ ft. behind. On Monday we must look for a ridge pole and dig steps so we can get into the place. You ought to see us three at table—we have No. 1 appetites and the way the grub goes is a caution—and the grub is first-rate, too. I'm a little afraid that we might get spoiled by living so high now, and after while coming down to hardpan. As to going to Mrs. Knase for bread, why, that will be hard to do unless they come up here to the creek, for it is about 18 miles from here to Col. Bear's place, and what is more, Cooney Walter has rented that place. We have a pretty good time at work. Jim is the best hand with the shovel, though we are getting up to him by slow degrees. Towards night the wind came up strong from the west, having shifted to that point from S. E., and during the night we had a heavy wind storm. There has been but one day—last Sunday—since we are here that the wind did not blow.

SUNDAY, APRIL 1, 1877

AT SNYDER'S, KILL CREEK, KANSAS

Mrs. Snyder was afraid she would not have enough eggs "for Oshtera" [Easter], but she must have cooked about 4 dozen. Eggs are worth only 5¢ per dozen in Osborne, and the folks say it is just as cheap to eat them as to take them to town. Butter is 12½¢ in Bull City, our nearest market town, 7 miles, northwest. This morning Mrs. Neuschwanger and

Mary came up with John to spend the day. I had a little hard time talking with them, because they don't understand English. After dinner L. & J. went to Osborne to get a pick and some lumber they had earned at the saw mill. Schweitzer will probably bring it over for us. I will have to get the ridgepole and dig out the steps tomorrow. They both went because there may be work at the saw mill, and if so, one will remain to do it and earn some more lumber. The boys went with Snyder to the west line of the claims this morning. We must get a pick because it is rather far to walk 3 miles to Neuschwanger's to borrow one, and then take it back when they want to use it, whether we are done with it or not. When they bring the lumber they will bring our clothes. I need stockings, for mine are dirty, and have holes in the heels big enough to put your fist through, and that worked a blister on my heel, and the blister rubbed open, so I had to stay in the house to let it heal a little. Talking about mud, on Friday when we came home for dinner, Levin concluded that if we walked into the hole and then came out again and cleaned our shoes off, we could get the ground out a good deal sooner than if we used the shovel, because the mud is very sticky, and when you get your shoes full of it, it is no easy thing to get them clean again. It hardens in a short time, too. Bevvy says she wants that "Deutschlander" (yours truly), and we have all received invitations to call round. Whenever we make an acquaintance, they are sure to say, "call round." There are a couple of things in which I am deficient—one is a lack of Dutch, and the other is cheek. Mrs. Snyder says she feels lonesome now that L. & J. are gone. I am almost a nobody because I can't jabber Dutch, but all the family understand English. A fellow must be careful how he lights his pipe here or he will set the prairie on fire, or maybe a house. So most of the folks round here chew, and it is all plug tobacco. You can get shorts at Bull City, but I have not seen anybody except Snyder who uses anything but plug tobacco. It astonished the folks to hear that we don't raise spring wheat round Bethm and the way they thrash! Here the chaff and straw all go on one pile, and the grain comes out of the separator and thresher clean.

MONDAY, APRIL 2, 1877

AT SNYDER'S, KILL CREEK, KANSAS

First thing this morning I went over and dug out the steps, and after dinner struck for Guyer's to get a ridgepole. On the way down I met Hoot and Lapp, who said I had better go to Rook, further up the creek, as Guyer was away from home. So I turned and rode with them a short distance. When I got to Rook's, the first man I saw was Smith, Rook's partner. He had the timber for sale, and after looking at some trees struck a bargain for one 14 to 16 inches through at the butt, and about 20 feet clear of branches; get top and all—the entire tree—burr oak—for $1. And they said they would haul it, and R. cut it down, for 50¢. R. saw I was no hand with an ax, so he cut the tree down and lopped the top off 18 ft. from the butt. Then we went for the team. He, or rather, the two of 'em, have a big pair of Texas oxen, and all they want to make a good team is a little more feed. We got the log to the claim, and found there a pile of boards and slabs that L. & J. had brought over with Schweitzer's team. Loading that log was no easy work, and we almost broke the wagon loading it. It was no light load, either, so it was just tied to the hind wheels and dragged on the ground. We almost stuck going over a soft spot in the road. When I got home Levin brought out that 12 page letter from home, and I was glad to get it. You probably have not got the first installment of my diary, as no mention was made of it. Unless somebody would give Pa enough money to buy a team and enough to live on for 6 months, I would not advise him to come out now, for work is very scare, and if you expect to get money for your work, you will miss it bad. It seems more like home to me now, and I like it better every day. Tonight we had "knep und milch" for supper.[8] We are high toned here—breakfast between 7 and 8; dinner between 12 & 1, and supper about 7:30.

TUESDAY, APRIL 3, 1877

AT SNYDER'S, KILL CREEK, KANSAS

We had a heavy shower last night, but I did not find that out till this morning; and then only by hearsay, for I neither heard it nor saw that any had fallen. After breakfast made for Rook's to cut up the top of that tree into pieces handy to haul. He was breaking, and stopped to tell me that Heiser, a man from Nebraska, wanted some digging done, and he couldn't do it, and wondered whether I could. I concluded to take the job. Went on and chopped till about 10 o'clock, when Rook came for me to help fetch a pig from Guyer's. He hooked the oxen to the wagon and we got the pig home by noon. I didn't charge him anything for the help, as he had got the job at Heiser's for me. We went to see about it when we fetched the pig, and Heiser said I could have the job. So after dinner I shouldered the shovel and walked about 2 miles to Heiser's new house. The cellar had to be deepened about 5 inches, and I had to work hard to make the mattock —a broken one—go into the dirt, which was as hard as a

---

[8] "Knep und milch'—dumpling and milk.

brick. And when the dirt was loose, the greater part of it had
to be carried 10 to 12 feet and thrown out of the door. About
sundown Heiser drove off, telling me to take the harness off
the plow horses, and I could ride one home. Did so, and had
to pay for my lively canter of about two miles, for riding
bareback is not conducive to comfortable sitting on a wooden
chair. But I enjoyed the ride anyhow. Got supper about 8:30
and turned in about 9:30. Slept first rate till about 4:30, when
I was awakened by Mrs. H. rattling at the stove. About that
time you were at breakfast, for our time is nearly 2 hours
slower than yours. Rolled over and took another nap till 6,
when we all turned out. They have morning and evening
prayers, and say grace before and after meals. They both
came from Germany and have been in Nebraska (Newbraska
they call it) for the last few years.

WEDNESDAY, APRIL 4, 1877

At Snyder's, Kill Creek, Kansas

About 8 o'clock I got to shoveling the dirt away from the
cellar door and got through about 10, when I went to digging
a place in the hill to put a hen house. Here the cattle and
fowls are all put into half-dugouts—that is, part dugout and
part log, sod, or stone, with straw roofs. That was mean digging, with the busted pick and in gravelly ground. The gravel
is as firmly packed as though it had been rammed down.
Finished that about 4 o'clock and then started digging for a
well where old man Gsell said there was water. He found it
out by the use of a forked branch of a peach tree. That was
the first time I ever saw forks used for finding water, but I
have heard it said that the black shale will draw the switch
as well as water. And when you strike shale before you get

to water it is no use to go any deeper, but if you strike the water first, go ahead and make your reservoir in the shale and you will always have a supply. These two days' work were the hardest I have done in 6 months. I got $1 a day and board, so there is $1.50 earned. L. & J. were at work at the house—dugout—while I was away. I got back to Snyder's about 7 o'clock. Had bean soup for supper. It was hot today, and I worked without coat or vest.

THURSDAY, APRIL 5, 1877

AT SNYDER'S, KILL CREEK, KANSAS

This was another hot day, and we had heavy work too, laying up sod. Snyder broke a lot for us this a. m. and we began laying up the wall. It is 20 inches thick. These "Kansas brick" are from 2 to 4 inches thick, 12 wide and 20 long, and the joints between them we fill with ground. Just before sunset we got the ridgepole into position on the crotches, so that the room will be about 7 feet high. We expect to get the roof in and have the place in condition to live in by the end of the week. The sod is heavy and when you take 3 or 4 bricks on a litter or hand barrow, and carry it 50 to 150 feet, I tell you it is no easy work. We quit just before sunset. Had supper about 7:30. I could hardly walk today—the result of that bareback ride. It was awfully hot right after dinner, and Levin fetched water from Snyder's in a jug. That water tasted good.

FRIDAY, APRIL 6, 1877

AT SNYDER'S, KILL CREEK, KANSAS

Plenty of air stirring today, so it was not so hot. We finished off the gable ends of the dugout and got the boards on the rafters, ready for the straw. A lot more sod to carry tomorrow for the roof. Had jack rabbit for supper. They dress 7 lb. sometimes and I tell you they are big ones, almost twice as big as ordinary rabbits. You ought to hear the prairie roosters. This is the pairing season, and they strut around and keep up a constant humming, and you can hear them ¼ mile, and farther if the wind is right. There are lots of them on my claim.

SATURDAY, APRIL 7, *1877*

AT SNYDER'S, KILL CREEK, KANSAS

Used part of the straw on the roof, and covered the whole roof with a layer of sod, and then threw dirt on it, and the "House" was finished. We had not enough rafters, so L. & J. went to Rook and cut the balance of the top of that tree I let lie when I went to work at Heiser's the other day, and bought another tree and split it into rafters. Then they got Rook to haul the two loads of wood and a lot of straw to my claim, and for the entire job he charged $1. Cheap, wasn't it? The trades are pretty well represented here: Snyder and Heiser are coopers; Rook was a pawnbroker in England; Smith, a clerk in a store; Stevens, a gas meter maker; and then we three.[9] I have a boil on my left lower jaw, and it troubles me not a little. And my heel isn't well yet, and won't be till I am fixed better to take care of it, which will not be for some days yet—till we get a well dug at the residence.

---

[9] The diversity of trades noted by Ruede here was observed by many writers of frontier life, and the fact that so many of the settlers knew little or nothing about farming was one of the reasons for the large percentage of failures among them. Of course very many of them did not go west with the purpose of farming, but merely wished to get title to a piece of land.

SUNDAY, *APRIL 8, 1877*

AT SNYDER's, KILL CREEK, KANSAS

Turned out at 6:30—my time, now-a-days, for it is no use to be earlier, because we don't get breakfast till 7:30. Stayed home all the morning, as it was rather windy, and read several numbers of the Farm Journal. After dinner we three went about 2 miles south, to the top of a high bluff, and took a good look at the surrounding country. The view was a fine one, for we could see for miles to the north, east and west. The view to the south is shut off by high bluffs, of which there is a long range just south of Kill Creek. Levin is going to have some things sent to him in the fall, and I want a couple of blouses and a pair of overalls, and my whip. I will let you know from time to time what I want, so you can get the things ready. Since the dugout is finished—all but the door—we begin to feel right at home there. We have planted a row of gooseberry bushes on the west side of the house. We got them down along the creek. We are anxious to get into our place, for we can board ourselves for about one half what it costs us to board somewhere else. And when we work out, we get board and lodging, both being included in the day's wages. I am going to get a stove for work if I can, and I think it is possible. Tomorrow Jim and L. are going to Osborne and Schweitzer's for the well auger. . . . They will bring hinges for the door, and then we can hang the door and make the bunks in a day. I'd like to see you all, but I like this place better than Bethm and after I get you all here I'll be O.K. You would like it as much as I do if you were here. I am going to have a stone house in two years—not live in a dugout all the time, like a good many folks here. But I'll have to go in debt for breaking, I think. I'll make a bargain like this: get a man to break for me, and I will pay him in work during harvest and corn husking. I would like to have a paper once in a while. Direct to Kill Creek P. O.

MONDAY, APRIL 9, 1877

AT SNYDER'S, KILL CREEK, KANSAS

First thing this morning was to look for a second hand stove. For this I went to a man named Greenfield, who lives about 2½ miles east of here. He was not at home, not having arrived from Hays, to which place he had gone with a load. His wife, however, was home, but she didn't know whether the stove was for sale, and told me to come tomorrow. On the way back stopped at Guyer's, where I had seen two stoves, but only one belonged to them. Then I went to Rook's. He will break sod for me for $2.50 per acre, and take his pay in work. But I made no bargain. Came back by Aleck Blair's. His house is built of logs, and as the water was scarce, he dug a well about ¼ mile south, and today he was moving his house to the well. For this purpose he had five teams, and the house was only a pile of logs. His household goods were all out on the prairie. Got back to the house by 10 o'clock. Started about 8, and in all walked about 8 miles. Jim and Levin had started for Osborne when I left the house, to get the luggage from Schweitzer's to Blake's store, as Mr. Neuschwanger had promised to bring it and some other stuff the boys bought in Osborne if we would leave the things at the store. We did not look for the boys tonight, but they arrived about 10 o'clock, having ridden all the way with Guyer. After dinner I cut a lot of wood and shoveled some ground away from the dugout.

TUESDAY, APRIL 10, 1877

AT SNYDER'S, KILL CREEK, KANSAS

Went over to the dugout, and as Jim had the hinges and screws in his pocket, we proceeded to hang the door. Then we made a wooden latch to fasten the door. It is a masterpiece of locksmithing. Wanted to make the table and bedstead, but were stopped for want of nails. So we went back to the house and read the Times. Levin brought me a letter from Pa and one from Addie and those two copies of the Times, for which I was mighty glad. I had intended to write a letter specially for the Times, but as they publish my journal I won't write extra. The boys reported that they had had a long talk with the Glueckers and Huber. I made out an estimate of the cost of our house. This does not include what was paid for in work: Ridgepole and hauling (including two loads of firewood) $1.50; rafters and straw, 50¢; 2 lb. nails, 15¢; hinges 20¢; window 75¢; total cash paid, $4.05. Then there was $4 worth of lumber, which was paid for in work, and $1.50 for hauling it over, which, together with hauling the firewood, 50¢, makes $10.05 for a place to live in and firewood enough to last all summer. After dinner we struck for Greenfield's again, and did not find anybody at home. Thinking that perhaps I might be able to get meat or potatoes from Heiser for the work I had done, I went over to see him. Two young men named Bleam were digging a well, and had got into the shale. H. could not accommodate me with the articles desired. He appeared to think I was in a hurry for the money, and told me I could have it by Saturday. Levin and Jim had gone after a well auger, but returned without it. We looked for our trunks when Snyder got home, but he said that Neusch had forgotten them. We were considerably put out about it. What was to be done?

WEDNESDAY, APRIL 11, 1877

AT SNYDER'S, KILL CREEK, KANSAS

I left for Osborne at 5 a.m. or a little before. We did not know what time it was, because the clock had stopped a little before 4. It is 13 miles to Osborne, and I got there by 7:30. Rode with a man about half a mile. He said they had been in the country 8 years and there were 10 in the family. During the 8 years not one had been sick. One of the first persons I met in town was Mr. Schweitzer. I had heard he intended bringing Huber and Berger over to Kill Creek today, and started early so as to meet him and have him bring the things for us. But he was at work in town and intended to go to Russell tomorrow for a load of goods for Glueckers, so he could not bring a load over for us. Looked around about three hours for a team, and was at last successful in finding one (Dave Bleam) who would bring them within four miles of home. During this time I had quite a long talk with Mrs. Gluecker, as well as with Herman and Franz Huber. Berger had gone to the North Fork on a fishing expedition. Invested $2.40 in provisions, and about 1 o'clock we set off. Arrived at Bleam's about 4, and had dinner, after which I hired him to take my things the rest of the way. I expected to find L. & J. in the well near my ranch, but could see nothing of them when we arrived. They had started to dig, but went farther down into the draw, where they expected to get water at a shallower point. They had dug about 10 ft. down (5 ft. diam.) that afternoon, but had not yet struck water. About a mile further east there are in the same draw two wells five feet deep, always full. Bleam charged me 50¢ for bringing the things over.

THURSDAY, APRIL 12, 1877

AT SNYDER'S, KILL CREEK, KANSAS

Went to digging again. Got down through two feet of gravel, and then struck shale. Then we gave up, for it is not much use to go into shale very deep to find water. Rook dug 42 feet through shale and didn't get a drop of water; and then he struck water in 20 feet, about 15 feet from where he struck so much shale. We put off to the ranch and made a table and bed, and got back to Snyder's about dark.

FRIDAY, APRIL 13, 1877

AT SNYDER'S, KILL CREEK, KANSAS

When in Osborne the other day, I heard that Dr. Tilden, at Bloomington, 7 miles n.e., wanted a hand, so this morning Levin went over to see about it. He got back about 3 o'clock, but had not seen the Dr. though he had learned that the Dr. did not want any help. Jim and I attempted to build a fireplace, but did not succeed. I made dinner on a fire in front of the ranch. About 4 o'clock we went over to see Greenfield again. He was plowing for potatoes, and said he would not sell the stove. But he said he wanted help in a few weeks and that when he got his cane mill in operation this fall he would need three or four hands. Jim McGuire wanted a herder, and when he passed Snyder's this evening on his road home from mill, the boys stopped him, and the talk ended in their making an appointment to go over in the morning to see him. His place is 5 miles s.e. I drove a yoke of oxen this evening awhile. It goes rather slow, but I like it. We will have to wait till next spring for a yoke, for we can't go it yet.

SATURDAY, APRIL 14, 1877

AT SCHWEITZER's, OSBORNE, KANSAS

I started for Osborne directly after breakfast, and walked all the way to the South Fork. My socks hurt my feet, so I pulled them off, and then I walked easier. I had heard that Rupert, who lives in the schoolhouse 2 miles east, was going to town today, but as I did not see a team about the place, I concluded he had gone, and so did not stop. But just as I had got on the other side of the river, somebody hailed me and wanted to know why I didn't wait—and there were Rupert and Hoot, in the wagon. Rode with them into town, and after making a few purchases and getting the goods into the wagon, I struck out for Schweitzer's. On the way over I missed the road, and got about a mile out of the way; but I found the section road on the east of his place, and about 1 o'clock arrived at the house. After putting away some grub, I went with Monroe and plowed awhile with the oxen, but it did not go as well as with Snyder's. Hen Knase and Herman Gluecker were digging a well about ¼ mile west of the house, and we went over to see them. Wils Berger had helped them the day before, and in lighting a cigar set the dry grass on fire, and they had hard work to put out the fire. They struck water at a depth of 14 feet by boring, but have as yet got down only about 10 feet. The boys went fishing, but brought nothing along when they came home, about 10 o'clock.

The prairie here is covered with trails running in all directions. It does not take many trips over such a trail to make a pretty good road, and when the track gets muddy, travellers turn out to one side, making a whole lot of ruts and putting the sod in very bad shape for breaking. To turn travel onto section lines is a hard matter too, for in spite of the board set up in the trail bearing the word "Closed," some people always follow what they think is the shortest road to wherever they are going. Stretching a wire with dangling rags across the track only makes matters worse, for the travellers drive around the end of the "fence" and cut back to the old road at various angles. A furrow or two is sometimes drawn across the trail, as a warning to keep off and follow the section line.

SUNDAY, APRIL 15, 1877

At Snyder's, Kill Creek, Kansas

Went to where Glueckers are living, about a mile from Schweitzer's. The house has been empty for a long time. The rent is $3 a month. The old folks and Paul had gone to a place about 8 miles southeast that they had bought with the load of goods Schweitzer brought from Russell last night. Huber and Berger went to town. After dinner at Schweitzer's we sat round till 2:30, and then I started for home. Had walked about a mile from town when a team overtook me, and I asked to ride. The gentleman introduced himself as Rev. Bowers, who lives 4 miles east of us. Rode with him to a point about 5½ miles east of us, where he stopped, as he had an engagement to preach there that evening. Stopped at Bleam's to get a drink. It took about a quart to satisfy me. Reached Snyder's about 7 o'clock. The boys have secured places at Mc-Guires, L. for herder, and J. to work round the house—the work to be paid for in breaking, or at least part of it. The boys leave for McGuire's tomorrow morning.

MONDAY, APRIL 16, 1877

AT THE DUGOUT, KILL CREEK, KANSAS

Settled off with Snyder. His bill was $18.12; 12½¢ per meal, and nothing for lodging or breaking sod for the ranch. That leaves me $2.20 in hand and $1.50 coming from Heiser. I moved the goods we had at Snyder's over to the ranch this morning. Had to build a chimney and fireplace before I could make dinner, and when I had it made it consisted of one dish of mush. The ranch got full of smoke, too, but I did not care much because the door and window being opposite, the place was cleared in a short time. About 4 o'clock the sky was overcast, and from then till about 7 we had a heavy thunder storm. The sky turned to a pale, bright yellow-green, and a good deal of hail fell. Some of the stones were as big as hazelnuts. I lay on the bed and heard it beat against the door until I feel asleep. The storm came from s.w., and the west wall leaked a little, the water running under the sod because the bank of earth from the excavating had not been removed. The roof did not leak at all, but the rain beat in at the door so that there was about an inch of water over ¼ of the room. The wind howled like it does through the alley there at home, and that was one reason why I did not go to Snyder's. The other was that I would have got wet to the skin and I did not like that.

TUESDAY, APRIL 17, 1877

AT THE DUGOUT, KILL CREEK, KANSAS

Slept well. Turned out about 6. The mail from Russell came in last evening and I went over to see if there were any letters for us. But there were none. Was invited and stayed to breakfast. Then went back to the ranch for the water bucket, and then to Snyder's. They were at breakfast, and invited me to sit up and have some, but I had had my breakfast so I didn't take him up. Followed the breaking plow a couple of rounds, and then struck for the house to get my bucket. Made fire and got me some dinner. Bill of fare—mush and broiled ham. The meat flies have got at it, and it must be used up soon. Send me a recipe for making johnny cakes. The corn-meal here is what you call chop—hulls and all. Don't publish my diary entire. If you want any of it published, let Syd make up letters from it. I don't care to let everybody know how I live, though it might deter some from coming who would otherwise throw away their money. This is not a hightoned way of living, and I wish for some "Ol Re" Bread. If I had a stove I could do better. My sod chimney would draw all right, but the fireplace leaks badly, and I have a hard time starting fire. After the dinner dishes were washed, I shouldered the axe and went to Snyder's woodland and chopped awhile— till I got thirsty. The sky looked as though we would have rain, so I put back for the house. This wood is a mile from the house. Stopped to get a drink, and then went on to the ranch, and as I felt hungry, cooked a mess and after stowing it under my jacket I felt better. Bill of fare: Ham and beans; cold mush. The beans I soaked about two hours before I put them over. The ham I put in when the beans went on the fire; and it did not taste bad either. This is the way to find out for how little a man can live. About ½ lb. of ham, 5¢; 1 oz. beans, ⅜¢; total 5⅜¢ for a meal. There is figuring for Pa. Everything is sold by the pound here. Levin thinks the prairie is made of cottonwood—it warps so fearfully. You never saw a chimney and fireplace made of sod; neither did I till I made mine; but I had nothing else to make it of. In talking to Huber the other day, he remarked that nobody would know me if I was to go back because I was so sunburned. We have not got over the news that Ross is back in Bethm. He could not have been gone more than two weeks.

WEDNESDAY, APRIL 18, 1877

AT THE DUGOUT, KILL CREEK, KANSAS

Turned out about 6 and made fire. Forgot to put the beans to soak last evening, so it took a little longer to boil. Wind n.w., and the fire smokes a good deal, but that kills the meat flies, so I can stand it. While the breakfast was cooking I went out and cut wood so it will be drying out. Rather cloudy this morning. Levin took his ink with him, so I'll have to get a bottle when I go to town again. About 9 o'clock went to chopping again. Guess I'll have to quit, because it makes me short-breathed. Quit about 11, and got as far as Hoot's, on the way back. He was at work on a breaking plow and I stopped to help him a bit. It was raining right smart, and we had showers all day. We tinkered away at the plow till noon, and then I would have left, but they asked me to stop, so I went in and had a square meal. The meat he told me to guess at. I guessed veal, but it was coon. Learned a little about setting the rolling cutter on a breaking plow by watching him and Snyder. When I left for the ranch I bought a loaf of bread from Mrs. Snyder, and I felt as good as if I had drawn a prize in the lottery. Tried a new dodge with the cornmeal. Mixed it with a little water and salt, and baked it over the fire, and it went down a heap better than mush. My supper will be a slice of ham boiled with beans, and a slice of bread. How is that for high toned? The wind is n.e. and the room is full of smoke.

THURSDAY, APRIL 19, 1877

At the Dugout, Kill Creek, Kansas

Maybe you think I am lonesome living all by myself, on the prairie; but I am not. Today the wind is north, but not very cold. Such a day as this I wish for a paper from home, if not a letter. Well, the mail comes in tomorrow evening, and then I may get a letter. It takes a whole week for a letter to come out here. If Stuber could photo the inside of my ranch, I don't believe that there would be as many young men without money wishing to come out here and batch it. I would not want anybody to come to call on me yet. Last night I dreamed I was at home with you, but woke up to find that my overcoat had slipped off of me. It was pretty cold, too. Families coming out here should bring no luggage but clothes and bedding and a clock, but bring all the cash they can, for then they can buy a team and go right ahead. Without a team you must depend on others and pay according. We three work toward a common point, and all we earn goes for the benefit of the company. When we have enough to have a division, the things will be equally divided. Some one must stay round home to look after the trunks, etc., and I think I'll be the one for a couple of months. When you write to me send me some postage stamps. I can't tell what time it is, because the sky is overcast. The other day over at Schweitzer's well, Hen Knase wanted to know what time it was, and I said 4 o'clock. He wondered how I knew. I said by the sun. He looked at his watch, and I was within 20 minutes of the correct time. The blister caused by walking from Osborne three weeks ago is not yet well. I grease it with speck, and that appears to do it good. I am not at work just now. The boys say that somebody must be at home to see that our goods are not stolen, and as they have work, I have to look out for myself. But I will have

something to do soon, making dugouts for L. & J. and I spoke
to Hoot today to let me help him when he goes to making
his. . . . Went to Snyder's about 9:30 and from there to
Heiser's to get that $1.50, and reached there just as they were
at dinner and was asked to sit up and have some, which I did.
Schnitz and knep[10] was the bill of fare, and it tasted good,
too. Heiser had no cash, but offered some molasses. I had
nothing to put it into, so I didn't get it. After dinner went
back to Snyder's and as I had seen Hoot going over to his
claim, struck over and had a talk with him. He showed me
a place where he guaranteed that I could find water, and I'll
try there when I can get an auger. It is near the s.w corner
of my claim. Bright and warm this afternoon. Bill of fare for
supper: Boiled beans and ham and corn cakes. I take cold
water and mix the corn meal till it is too thick to run, and
fry it. I tell you it goes down. Syd need not turn up his nose
at that kind of grub, for it tastes good to me. . . .

FRIDAY, APRIL 20, 1877

At the Dugout, Kill Creek, Kansas

Turned out about 6, and after breakfast went over to Snyder's. John was shelling corn, and I turned in and helped
him. He soon left, to go and herd the cattle, but I kept on
till near noon; and I stayed to dinner to pay for my work. . . .
The man who sold that claim to the Glicker's told them there
was no more good land up here—that it was all sand hills, and
every wind shifted it. That's not true, for we have as good
land here as can be found, and the upland is better for raising
small grain than the bottom land, which is too loose. As I
have no oil, I go to bed with the sun, and try to get up with

[10] "Schnitz and knep"—dried apples and dumpling.

it, though as yet I have not done so. At Snyder's today we had visitors—Mary Lapp and Mary Shellenberger. Take good care of my journal, that none of it is lost, for I want it when one or the other comes out. I guess I will have work for one of you by next spring. The start we have made goes very slow, but I think we will get ahead so that next spring we can go to farming and not have to work round. I have a hard time with the meat flies and have taken thousands of eggs off of the ham. I have no dark or smoky place to keep it in, and they get inside of the paper in which it is wrapped. Hardly know what to do with it. It weighs 20 lb. and was twice as big as I wanted, but I could not get a smaller one. The provisions I bought on the 16th cost $2.80. I'll see how long they last. Pickled or smoked hog meat costs 10¢ per lb., corn meal $1.25 per cwt. Hope I'll get papers or a letter with this evening's mail.

SATURDAY, APRIL 21, 1877

At the Dugout, Kill Creek, Kansas

Turned out before the sun was fairly up and put the breakfast over the fire. Had bad luck and spilled the beans just as they were done to a turn. But I was in too much of a hurry to see whether there was a letter for me at the P.O., so I did not stop to boil another mess, but made my breakfast off a piece of bread and the meat, and then struck for the P.O. It took me a full half hour to go the mile and a half, as the wind was very high, and my cane came into service to help me down the hill. The wind was so strong that I had to bend far forward, and I got pretty tired. You will perhaps think it is easy walking across the prairie, but it is anything but easy, as the dry grass is very slippery, and walking tires one very soon. On the way back picked up a buffalo skull and brought it to the ranch. I'll put it on a stake at one of my corners when I find them all. The n.e. corner is in the middle of the section, and no stone was put there to mark it, but by staking off the n. & e. sides I can come very near to it. A man at the p.o. said he did not intend to plant corn today because it was too windy to work. The wind blows the seed around too much. I got neither letter nor paper, so I had to content myself by reading over an old one. Has Syd forgotten me? After dinner went over to Snyder's and read the Allentown Welt Bote, which Neuschwanger takes, and I saw in it something about Bob Peysert's difficulties. Brought a bucket of water along when I came back; and it was hard to keep the water in the pail on account of the high wind. Trimmed off the fat from the ham and fried out the grease to fry my corn cakes in. I took Mrs. S. by surprise by reading something for her in a German paper about raising calves. That is her hobby. She milks five cows, and this a.m. sent 35 lbs. butter to Russell. That is what she had left in two weeks after the household had been supplied, and they use lots of butter in the family. I expected L. & J. this evening and put off making supper on that account pretty long, and just as I got the meat boiling, the door was darkened, and there sat Jim on a pony. Levin had not come. Jim brought the intelligence that a widow over near McGuire's wants him to farm her place this season. She will furnish the teams and implements and grain for seed, and we can have half what we raise. There are 20 acres broken on the place, and a field of wheat. Then there is another place about 1½ miles from my ranch that we can get for one-third in the field or ¼ in the crib—that's what the man who rents it has to pay. I told Jim to go ahead and rent them if he thought we could do well by the operation; and the widow is looking

for an ox team, which we will be allowed to use in breaking
our land. Jim says "all the people like us," and that appears
to be true wherever we go. He was in Osborne the other day
and got the mail for me. Oh, but I was glad to see him and
the more so because he brought me news from you. He says
Barnhart, the printer in Osborne, wants me to come and see
him. That may mean a job. Here I take any kind of work
that offers. Will go to Osborne on Monday. Jim left about
dark, but after I had turned in for the night I lay awake,
thinking, for about two hours, at the end of which time I
heard someone calling me, and on looking out, there was Jim
come back to spend the night. We picketed the pony and
made up a fire in the ranch. Then we had a smoke and talked
till near midnight.

SUNDAY, APRIL 22, 1877

At the Dugout, Kill Creek, Kansas

Turned out about 5 and made breakfast. Couldn't read
Syd's letter last night by firelight, so while breakfast was
cooking, I had a good time reading it. I find that it costs me
about $1 to $1.50 per week to batch. How is that for cheap
living. . . . Made arrangements to have our trunks stored at
Snyder's till we want them, and traded the ham to him for
meat as we want it, pound for pound. Bright and very windy.
Wind s.w. Pa wrote that every ignorant man could tell me
something I might make use of. As I told Rook, I listen to
every man, and when I think his advice good, follow it, if not,
let it alone. . . . (Our household goods now include): 2
buckets, 1 crock, 1 earthen dish, 1 saucepan, 1 spider, 1 tin
dish, 3 pie plates, 3 china plates, 3 pair knives and forks, 3
spoons, 3 cups and saucers, 1 cracked china cup for salt, and a

tin cup! How's that for an outfit. Then we have an ax and shovel. That is all we have. No, there is a sack of corn meal, and a couple of ropes we found. Levin concluded the supper I made was good enough for him to live on. About 6 o'clock we went over to Snyder's, and had been there only a short time when a thunder storm blew up, and there was a little rain. We were there about an hour, and the sky looked so threatening that we concluded to go back to the ranch, which we reached just in time to get an armful of wood apiece and get under cover before the storm burst. And we had a heavy one for about two hours. The wind shifted from s. to n.w. and the water that came in at the window loosened a chunk of ground as big as my head. We managed to put in a good night's sleep, however.

MONDAY, APRIL 23, 1877

At Schweitzer's, Osborne, Kansas

Turned out before the sun rose, because I didn't want L. to go off without something to eat, and made breakfast. At 6:15 we got to Snyder's and he yoked up the oxen for us. Then John and I went over to the ranch for the trunks. Loaded up and got back safely. Stored them in the granary. The ham weighed 11 lbs. Shouldered Neuschwanger's pick and left for Osborne, where I arrived about 11 a.m. Waited half an hour for Barnhart, and then found that he wanted me to work only on Thursday's. Made a bargain to work for $1.75 a day and board myself. But if I get a job that will last a month or so, I am not bound to help him. Then put off for Schweitzer's. Had some dinner and a rest. The proprietors of a saw mill below here are moving the machinery. They had four yoke of big oxen attached to the wagon on which the boiler was. Just about dark Jim came over, so we had quite a housefull of boys, as Wils. Berger and Frank Huber were also there.[11]

TUESDAY, APRIL 24, 1877

AT SCHWEITZER'S, OSBORNE, KANSAS

Didn't turn out till 6. Made an arrangement to stay at Schweitzer's every Wednesday night and get three meals for 50 cts. Also offered to work for my board today and tomorrow, as I don't want to walk back and forth more than I must. He put me to work chopping firewood, but after a while Huber came over from the well for help at the windlass, as it was too heavy for one to pull up the bucket. I helped at the windlass till 4 p.m., and we struck water at about 12 ft. Went to town after supper. I spilled my ginger, so I stopped in at the drug store to get some. I put in a good word for Billy's cigars. The proprietor wants to know what it will cost to express them from Bethlehem to Osborne, and wants samples. Maybe I can make a sale that way and get some scrap for my trouble. They have a brand called "Old Style," some of Catlin's (St. Louis) cheap rotgut tobacco, and from that price up. Tell Billy to send the samples to me at Kill Creek by mail. It is raining right hard tonight, and we got a little damp coming home from town. In coming home from the well this afternoon, we found a jackrabbit's nest with 6 or 8 young ones in it.

[11] In Mr. and Mrs. Schweitzer we see pioneer hospitality at its finest. Ruede was not the only one who stayed with them on his arrival in the new country. Everyone was welcome at their table, or to stay over night. Many of the young bachelors who, like Ruede, were building their own "soddies," used the Schweitzer home as a sort of headquarters whenever they had no other place to go. As Ruede says later in his letters, the Schweitzers were often imposed upon.

WEDNESDAY, APRIL 25, 1877

At Schweitzer's, Osborne, Kansas

It rained all last night, and stopped this morning about sunrise. Helped Mr. Schweitzer quarry rock for the well, and after dinner Wally and I took charge of the windlass, while Mr. S. dug the well a little deeper. The water came in fast. We had to dip out a lot before he began digging, and we dipped out 32 buckets full while he was at work, and that was not all the water that came in. You may believe I put away a lot of grub at supper. Smeary is the word that best expresses the condition of my overalls when I got through at the well. In the stone quarry, this morning, I noticed that the rock was full of cracks at some places, and Mr. S. said that was the result of freezing. When they get wet and then freeze, they crack into small pieces.

THURSDAY, APRIL 26, 1877

Osborne, Kansas

Turned out at 5:30 or somewhere thereabout and had break-fast. Then, as it bid fair to rain, I borrowed an overcoat and put off for town, with my dinner under my arm. Mrs. S. put up enough grub to make dinner and supper on a pinch such as I am in. Got to the office and set up one of the Washington Correspondence Bureau letters and began on another piece of copy before dinner. Type setting went a little slow, and no wonder, because I have not worked at case since March 10. Barnhart was very much interested in my letters that were published in the Times, and complimented me on my "close observation." Reckon I'll sleep here in the office tonight. It is noon hour and raining like all-gitout. That is what we want to make the corn grow. But there may be so much that it will not. Hope not. The wheat and rye is heading—no, not yet, but it is 6 inches high; up on the creek the small grain bids fair to excell this around the city. . . . You remember I wrote that Hays wanted some of us to contest Joe Sharp's claim when we first arrived. Now a man named Joy has put on file at the land office at Kirwin a contest on that very piece of land. I divided my supper, so I'll have enough to make a slim meal tomorrow morning. I think it will be too bad for me to travel tomorrow morning. This letter is for Ma's birthday present. . . . There were only half a dozen teams in town today, and no business was going on in town. . . . Old batchelors are at a discount up on the creek, and I don't believe you could sell one for a quarter because nobody would bid. After Barnhart comes back from supper I am to help him strike off a few copies of the paper for the mail. I don't know how working at a hand press will agree with me, but if it is no harder work than the windlass at a well, I can stand it. . . .

The river will be up too high for me to get off tomorrow, and the mud is too deep. I'll try to get more work in the office, if only for my board.

Much love to all from

How.

He gave me $2 for my work, because I helped him with the forms after supper. He said I worked well and satisfactorily. (Ahem.)

FRIDAY, APRIL 27, 1877

At Mrs. Pixley's, Kill Creek, Kansas

Turned out before 6, and took the papers to the P.O., and as the p.m. was not about, hung them to the door knob by a string. Then I concluded that a good hot meal would not

hurt me; for that I went to Keever's and had a hearty breakfast of meat and potatoes. As the rain had stopped, I concluded
to take the road to Mrs. Pixley's, because I had promised Jim
to go. If it had not been for that promise, I would have taken
the back track to Schweitzer's. The road between Osborne and
the river was very bad on Monday, so I took the road south
and crossed on a footlog near the ford. When I arrived at a
place about three miles from town, it began to rain in a steady
drizzle, but I thought I might as well push on. Had to inquire at a good many places in order to keep the road, but
managed not to lose myself, though the houses were few and
far between, and the road a strange one. The storm kept getting worse and worse, and the way the wind blew was a
caution. The last place I stopped at to ask the way was 1½
miles from my desired haven; the rain had turned into snow
and hail, and the wind being n.e., traveling was not the most
pleasant occupation. I got into the gumbo bottoms, and the
way that gumbo stuck to my shoes made walking anything
but nice. Gumbo is a very sticky clay in which nothing grows
except wild rye, which stays green all winter, and gets greener
and furnishes pasture early in the spring before the other grass
comes out. The gumbo sticks to your shoes till they are twice
their legitimate size. Arrived at a place about noon that I
thought must be Mrs. Pixley's—and it was, to my great satisfaction. My overalls were wet and muddy up to the knees,
and the right side of my coat was pretty wet. Just before I
arrived the hail cut my face so badly that I almost had to
put my handkerchief round my head. Mrs. Pixley is a woman
of a thousand. Her husband died last fall, and she is running
the place, besides taking care of three children. She is a very
nice sort of woman, by all that I can see and hear. She recognized me directly, and called me in. My shoes must be full of

mud. They were wet through. Did a few chores, but the most I did was sit by the fire. Everybody says this is the hardest storm they have seen since they were in Kansas. It has rained, off and on, for the last 48 hours, and looks as though it might continue. I am almost ashamed to carry so much mud into the house, but they say "It can't be helped," and they all bring in lots. Jim left here yesterday morning, and has not been seen since. I told Mrs. P. that it seemed as if she was bound to have one of us all the time. She thought it was a real Godsend to have me come, because, she says, otherwise she don't know how she could have got some wood chopped.

SATURDAY, APRIL 28, 1877

AT MRS. PIXLEY's, KILL CREEK, KANSAS

It succeeded in clearing off by night. Jim put in his appearance by noon. He and L. have spent the last couple of days on the west side of the bluffs. Mrs. P. sent me out this evening to milk the cows, and it made my hands rather tired. A good many folks have had their cattle scattered during the storm, and now they are going round trying to find them again. Jim McGuire lost 45 head yesterday.

SUNDAY, APRIL 29, 1877

AT MRS. PIXLEY's, KILL CREEK, KANSAS

Bright and clear, but cold this morning. I had to milk this morning. The cow and a fresh heifer together gave only about 2 quarts of milk. We intended to go to Wismer's to meeting this morning, but one thing and another delayed us, and we did not get started till noon, and then went only a mile, and turned back. After dinner Jim and I went over into the bluffs to see Levin, who was herding for McGuire, as the latter was out after the cattle that got away for him the other day. He got the biggest part of the runaways. Will Paris was here this afternoon and told us to come over to see his cattle, and maybe we could make a trade. A man named Towne has offered us a yoke of well broken oxen for $120, on 30 days. Maybe Paris will wait longer. I leave that to Jim to decide. Hoot has been talking to the boys about buying 40 acres of school land with timber on it for $3.25 per acre ($130), part cash, and the balance on ten year's time. We four are to go shares on it. I have not much notion that way. One of the reasons given for "going for" me on the question of publishing my journal was that "we don't want to make a show of ourselves; if folks want to know how it is out here, let them come and see." I know if I had been told how I would have to shift round, I would have fixed myself differently, especially in the clothing line. My shoes have a hole in them and ought to be mended. The prairie grass is hard on them. Everything is "awful" good, bad or indifferent with Mrs. P. That is her favorite expression. We did not have any supper this evening, as Mrs. P. did not get any ready.

MONDAY, APRIL 30, 1877

At the Dugout, Kill Creek, Kansas

I tell you it was cold this morning. We had a slight frost and ice ⅛ inch thick. The ponies had pulled up their picket pins, and we had a pretty good walk to find them. After a breakfast of slapjacks (I ate 17) Jim and I struck out. Mrs. P. threw up her part of the agreement about the farm, so we left her. Went to see Paris' oxen. He wants $100 cash by the 1st of August, and though Jim was in favor of making the attempt to earn it, I gave him good reasons for not buying. And when we got to Neuschwanger's the old man told us that we had better earn $120, as for that sum we could buy a team of horses. We had dinner at Snyder's, and afterwards ground the axes and went to chopping cord wood for him at $1 a cord, wood 3 feet long. On our way to the ranch for supper we saw Greenfield, who wants us to chop about 12 cords of oak for him—he to pay us in breaking at the rate of three cords for an acre, equal to about 75 cts. per cord.

TUESDAY, MAY 1, 1877

AT THE DUGOUT, KILL CREEK, KANSAS

Went to chopping at an elm butt—the ugliest sort of wood to split. We had to spawl off pieces from the sides before we could split through the heart, and we used up two mauls in doing it. Jim made another out of a young elm which lasted pretty well. After dinner he cut down an oak, and we went to trimming out the top. That was soon done, and we had to go at the large limbs. The trunk was to be saved for a saw log, as it was a nice straight one. Chopping and splitting oak is easy compared to elm, and the first cord was soon filled up. I struck for the ranch to make supper, and Jim went to the P.O. and brought me a letter from Pa and the long one from Syd with the office boys' tintypes in it. Pa's letter I read by fire-light, and you may imagine my surprise when I read that he intended to start for Kill Creek on the 14th. We didn't turn in till late, talking on the prospects of getting a team, and laying plans, which, I reckon, may be spoiled.

WEDNESDAY, MAY 2, 1877

AT SCHWEITZER's, OSBORNE, KANSAS

Chopped all the morning. We turned out before 5 and got to work by 8. Would have begun sooner, but I had to read Syd's letter, and that took a half hour, and making breakfast took another so that we didn't get to work so very early. We quit about 11 o'clock, in order to get dinner ready, so I could start early for town, to work tomorrow. Got off between 1 and 2 p.m., and made pretty good time the first 5 miles. My shoes I had trodden away on the inside of the foot, so that the rest of the way was hard traveling. Just before I reached the crossing at Kill Creek, where it crosses the road in a northerly direction, I saw two children at the side of the road; a woman was lying on the grass with her head on the little girl's lap, and when I came closer, she raised her head and spoke to me. To my surprise I recognized Mary Neuschwanger. She told me they had been to town for some goods, and the horses ran off, running over her. A little further on I came to the team. The old man had borrowed one from a man living in the neighborhood, and had loaded the wagon with the contents of his own, which stood in the road with a wheel off. He told me the horses had broken the doubletree and cleared out. The cause was a very nasty step which was washed out directly across the road by the rain, about 18 inches deep, against which the front wheels struck, throwing the old gent out forward, and the wagon passed over him, skinning his face and bruising him badly. Mary jumped out, but did not escape, for the wagon ran over her too. The two children and Bevvy were thrown out but were not at all hurt. The doubletree broke and set the horses free, and they made a short cut home. When I got to the river, I found it too high to cross on the fallen tree, and so I had to walk about a mile and a half out of my road in order to get to the footlog below town. Arrived at Schweitzer's about 7, and had hardly got into the house before Mrs. John Fettee spoke to me. I did not know her, but she asked if I was "one of Mr. Ruede's boys" and of course I replied in the affirmative, but told her she had the advantage of me, as I did not know who she was. Then she introduced herself and we had a little talk. But I came just in time to get a good hearty supper. Got Mr. S. to mend my shoes. Had a narrow escape from cutting off my left foot this morning. The axe glanced from the log, and in turning struck my shoe, out of which it cut a slice.

(The following letter was written "extra" in answer to several I had received on reaching town.)

MAY 2, 1877

AT SCHWEITZER'S, OSBORNE, KANSAS

I will first tend to Pa's case and answer his questions. I think that the medicine idea is a good one, as doctors are few and far between. The nearest is Dr. Tilden, and he lives at Bloomington, 7 miles off, and charges $5 and $6 a visit. As to teaching school, there is a good show for a good hand at it. As to where you will land: when you get to Russell, there will be hotel runners at the depot; go to the Russell House (and mind you bring lots of provisions with you—if you have too much, we can clean it away in a short time). Stay over night. In the morning go to the livery stables and inquire for teams that will go to either Osborne or Kill Creek. If one is there that is going to Bull City [now Alton], it will go through by Kill Creek P.O. If you fail in going with a freighter, don't take the hack, sooner stay at Russell than pay $3.50, trunks extra, but wait till night and inquire for the

Bull City mail carrier. He stops at Kill Creek P.O. on Monday night, and probably will be able to bring you and your trunk to the P.O., from where it will be easy to get to our dugout. If you come to Osborne, just make yourself easy till Wednesday night, when I will be in town, and you can go home with me on Friday. I will manage to get your trunk over. Now for the articles: Syd's shawl will be good, if Ma don't need it; a tick for straw bed and pillows, quilts, blankets (if you can get them in the trunk), a pair of scissors, a jack-knife (a big one for me—I lost mine), my tobacco (Jim's aunt will probably want to send some tobacco, and perhaps money, to him), and the other articles I mentioned—except the bread. Old papers would not be worth the trouble, and the books would be hardly worth it. Half a ream of writing paper is better than printing paper, and packs better. Ink I have. Bring your pen along. Postage stamps you can get here, if you have the cash, of which bring as much as possible. Then we can get some kind of team and go to breaking, so as to sow rye this fall. Horses you can buy from $120 a pair up. But all kinds of teams are hard to get now, as the breaking season is here. The mail is brought from Russell to Kill Creek direct; the balance comes via Osborne and Bull City, reaching the Creek Friday night.

Last Friday was an awful day to travel, but I went over to Mrs. Pixley's anyhow, traveling s.w. with the wind on my right side, and got pretty wet in my 10 mile walk. On Sunday Jim and I went to see Levin, who was herding for McGuire that day, and when got back to Mrs. P.'s she told us she had concluded not to get a team, so there was no job for us. We left on Monday morning, and in the afternoon we went to cutting cord wood for Snyder at $1 a cord, the wood being only 3 feet long. Snyder will plant potatoes for us for cutting. Greenfield will break an acre for every three cords. I have worked up a pretty good sized blood blister on one hand from using the maul, and have a big crack inside the thumb on my left hand. The folks think I look healthier than I did when I came out, and I feel first rate. We didn't eat much breakfast this morning, and were hungry as wolves for dinner. Jim thought we ought to have some molasses, so we got ½ gallon (25 cts.) from Snyder, and the corn cakes went down "wie g'schmiert." I think three years is too long to wait. If things work as I expect, you will be here this fall a year. About the old clothes—take all the old man and Uncle Geo. give, and take care of them; they will come in mighty good. You might send my other shirts with pa; if they are good for nothing else, they will do to tie up cuts, etc. . . . For fear all your questions are not answered in my journal, I'll tell you the creek is 1½ miles south of my claim, and wood is worth from 30 to 60 cts. a load for driftwood that comes down in freshets. Green wood is higher. Coal there is none inside of 20 or 30 miles, that I know of. Be sure to have pockets in the overalls. The colored shirts I will not need. Had a hard time coming over today, as I was tired when I started, but $1.75 is not to be lightly spoken of by me, as I am the only one of the "company" who can get cash for his work, and we must live on that. You recommend greasing my hands. Send a chunk of tallow with Pa, and I will. I'll be glad to have him here. If he can't do anything else, he can help us make the dugouts and quarry stone this winter for the houses. I am going to move my ranch to my s.w. corner, so as to be near Levin and Hoot. I got Mr. Schweitzer to mend my shoes, as that is cheaper than buying another pair. Let Pa bring his boots (all that are fit to wear) and his shoe nails, for the prairie grass is awfully hard on sole leather. I had to go about a mile out of my way in order to cross the river coming here, and had 15 miles to walk anyhow, and every step made me more tired, but I had to go it, so there was no help for me; you may believe I was glad to get here. Hope I can make another $2 tomorrow at the office. Then I'll buy a blanket; our overcoats are hardly enough. Jim and I laid close together and threw our two army coats over us last night, and we slept well. We turned out about 5 this a.m. and I had a good time reading that 8-page letter. Pa's letter I read by firelight last night. As to how the dugout is furnished; you have my list of household goods. The bed (this is high private) is a wooden frame with boards across instead of rope, and we sleep on a pile of straw, with our overcoats over us.

MAY 3, 1877

OSBORNE, KANSAS

I want Pa to come to Osborne—not to the Creek. Barnhart wants me to work for him a couple of weeks, while he is away. Wages $5 a week, and my board bill paid. Good enough. That is enough to keep the four of us a month and a half. It's cold today. Don't start Pa without an overcoat and gloves. In putting up his grub give him boiled ham and butter-bread-sandwiches, boiled beef and biscuit. That will be enough if you fill that satchel of his—the oil cloth one, or the stiff one with the handles. You might send ¼ lb. tea along. . . .

THURSDAY, MAY 3, 1877

OSBORNE, KANSAS

Turned out about 5:30 and after breakfast made for the office. Walking went rather stiff on account of my feet being so awfully tired from yesterday's walk. Worked at case all day. Barnhart said he wanted me to work a couple of weeks for him while he was in Iowa on a visit, and wondered what I would charge him. Told him what he paid Emmons. He wanted to know how much that was, and I said $5 a week and board, to which he agreed. He made arrangements with Mrs. Reasoner of the Solomon Valley House to keep me. It is a first rate place to live at too. Plenty of good grub, and only three boarders. I am always the first at table and last to leave it. Whether I eat so much more than the others I cannot say, but I do know that I eat a good deal and much faster than they. . . .

SATURDAY, MAY 5, 1877

OSBORNE, KANSAS

Was lazy this morning, and did not get down stairs till 6:20; but it did not matter, as breakfast was not ready till 7:30. Set about 1½ columns, and then went to work on a circular asking aid for the building of a Congregational church here in town. Had type for only half of the matter, and so had to make two forms of the job. Now see here: I don't want this diary published. I'll write extra and give the Times a letter once in a while. The boys don't like it if my diary is published. I think they are very foolish about it. They say I may write for publication our "ups" but not our "downs." The "downs" are just what the people who think of emigrating don't hear of, and therefore have an altogether wrong idea of this country. We had a shower before daylight this morning, and then about noon it began again and we had a shower that lasted till 6 o'clock. Barnhart wanted to know whether I needed money, but I told him I thought not. I have $2.15, and about 50 cts. of that is owing to Schweitzer for shoe mending. It will not push me with work to run the paper if no job work comes in, and I don't think any of much account will be wanted. If I was to come back now, you would think I had had nothing to eat for a month. I eat an awful lot. Why, this evening, I would be willing to bet I ate as much as the other two fellows together. I began before they did, and was at the table about ten minutes after they left.

SUNDAY, MAY 6, 1877

OSBORNE, KANSAS

Lay as long as I could this a.m., but came down by 6:45. Didn't get breakfast till 8:30, as the other boys were lazy, and Mrs. Reasoner got vexed and told me to go ahead. For breakfast I ate about ½ lb. steak, a plateful of fried potatoes, 5 fried eggs, two rounds of bread, a slice of cake and two ginger cakes, and washed it all down with two cups of coffee. So you see my appetite is good. Went over to the office and read awhile. Had dinner at 2, but did not load up so heavily. Afterwards, as the day was fine, went to walk and fell in with Charley Herzog, the merchant, and had a long talk with him. He is a Moravian from the Vaterland, and knew Rev. E. de Schweinitz in Philadelphia 25 years ago. He set up the cigars, and then took me over to Rader's for supper. He is a nice man. Made an appointment to go with him to see Glicker's the next fine Sunday, he to furnish the horses. We will be pretty good friends. When I told him I was a Moravian, he said "That is right." The roads are nearly dry now. The wind was pretty strong all day. That was the first cigar I smoked in six weeks. It came from a factory in Leavenworth, and— "en g'schenkter gaul gookt mer net in's maul."[12]

MONDAY, MAY 7, 1877

OSBORNE, KANSAS

Up at 5:30 and over to the office and did an hour's work before breakfast, which event occurred at 7:30. Barnhart left on the stage, after delivering into my keeping his hogs.

SUNDAY, MAY 13, 1877

OSBORNE, KANSAS

My diary is not very full so I'll keep it awhile longer. The tobacco the boys brought with them. Snyder will sell his 4-year old oxen for $75. I think we can get them for $65 cash. They will be cheaper than horses. We have a good friend here in Osborne—Charley Herzog, a Moravian from the old Vaterland. In talking with him the other night, he said he was ready to give a lot if the church members ever got ready to build a chapel or church. Oh, but this is farming with a vengeance. There is a pretty good show for Levin to get a job here in town. Charley will use his influence, and that is a good deal. . . . The weather has been fine all the last week and that brought the country folk into the stores. A good many teams pass through town on their way to Washington Territory and Oregon, five on Wednesday and more on Thursday. . . .

[12] "One does not look a gift horse in the mouth." The German spoken in this community of settlers from Pennsylvania was "Pennsylvania German."

Last Thursday night there arrived on the stage from Russell a clerical-looking gentleman whose phiz looked to me as though I had seen it before. But not until the next morning did I learn that he was a Moravian minister from Northfield, Minnesota, and that his name is Steinfort. He is looking for a good location for a number of families who will come if they can be suited. . . .

I swept the office after I got through work on Friday and there was about ¼ peck of dirt. The folks seldom even try to clean off their shoes, and when it is muddy the houses get in an awful condition. . . .

There is a farm for sale situated about 5 miles s.e. of this place, on which there are 45 acres of breaking (that includes two or three years cultivation for part of it) which will be sold for $30—about one-third of what it is worth for breaking prairie. And I suppose there is a house and well, and perhaps stabling of some sort. . . . Yesterday the rain came down heavy from 9 a.m. till about 7 p.m. and the street was a sea of mud with here and there a puddle of water, and to cross it was no nice thing, but I waded it half a dozen times, and by so doing got my shoes wet through, and they are not dry yet. I gave up wearing socks about four weeks ago, as we have no water to wash dirty things up at the claim, and we could not afford to pay for having them washed. . . . For $25 I could have bought a No. 8 cook stove, with a spider, two iron kettles, a griddle, tea kettle, and a big tin wash boiler that had been used only a couple of times. . . .

Sunday is a day of rest here, but you can get into any of the stores if you wish. There are as yet no churches here to be disturbed by it. "How is this for drouthy Kansas" is an expression that I have heard for the last two days till I am tired of it. It is in everybody's mouth. The mud on the street is two inches deep. The printing office is the public reading room. All who want to read the papers come here, and once in a while when a man leaves, the paper he has been reading leaves with him—but he generally asks for it first. . . . When a Moravian arrives in town, Charley Herzog is the man to go after him and try to get him to stay in this neighborhood. If those families from Northfield come and settle within 15 miles of this place, we can start a little congregation of about 20 members, and when Levin gets his folks out here and I mine, and H. Weinland comes, we can perhaps raise enough to support a minister and put up a chapel. That's Charley H.'s plan. And he is pretty well off, too. He and his brother have a store here, and do a good business. You see with that $100 (if you can spare it) we'll buy us a team and a stove, and if L. & I can get work Jim will farm for all of us. I can make enough if I have only one day's work in a week to keep us in provisions the entire week. An ox team will be best for us now, because we need buy no feed. They can live and work on the grass, of which we have plenty to last all summer, and can make enough hay in the draws to last all winter, whereas if we had horses, we would have to buy corn, which is now worth 55 cts. per bushel, and that is a big price; and even at that it is hard to get. Wheat is scarce, and flour is $7 per hundred at Russell. There is very little if any to be had here in town. At Bush & Whitney's mill it was $4 a week ago, with the prospect of being raised to $5.

The other day Henry Hoot came and asked me to get him a sack of flour, said he was entirely out and had no money and the neighbors couldn't loan him any, for they had not enough to see them through till threshing time. The mill dam at Bull City was washed out a couple of weeks ago and so the mill was idle and flour was hard to get. I searched all the stores

in town and found that C. Herzog and Co. had practically a
corner on flour that day. Their stock consisted of two 48-pound
sacks, and the price was $2.80 per sack. They were not par-
ticularly anxious to sell it either, for while they had sent
August Kaser to Cawker for a load of flour, he was caught
somewhere down in that vicinity by high water and there was
no telling when he would reach Osborne. Hoot thought that
by the time he had used the one sack he would be able to
help himself, and he would return the flour as soon as he
threshed a small field of spring wheat then ripening. So I
got the flour at the price asked. Herzog Brothers did not make
a big profit on the article, as flour is selling at $7 per cwt. at
Russell, and the freighting costs 40 cents per hundred pounds.

This afternoon (I had dinner at Rader's with Charley) we
went to meeting at Brobst's schoolhouse about 3 miles away.
Ch. furnished the team and took me and Geise to hear Rev.
Bowers preach. He has the true German opera sing-song, and
uses the terms "we find," "look around and about you," "and
so on," profusely; and the sermon consisted mainly of these
terms, which made it rather poor; but as it was the first
preaching I have heard since I left Bethlehem, I could ap-
preciate it.[13] The thermometer marked 74 this afternoon. The
river was up pretty high, and at the ford the water came up
to the wagon box. There was a Russian right in the way, and
we drove round him and went through the river first; and
then because we didn't hurry in order to get out of his way
(he was right behind and heavily loaded) he showered choice
maledictions upon us. But we were not obliged to hurry to
suit him. He might have gone across long before we reached
the ford. I'd be ashamed to go to service with overalls on in

[13] My mother used to hear Mr. Bowers preach, and remembers that he
could read only with the greatest difficulty. Not a few of the pioneer
preachers were poorly educated, and a few actually illiterate.

Bethlehem, but here we go with or without, with pants in the boots or outside—it don't matter. There were 7 women (one a mulatto) and 13 men. The singing was execrable.

SATURDAY, MAY 19, 1877

OSBORNE, KANSAS

Corn is beginning to come up. Some of that planted before the rainy spell (the first week this month) has not yet made its appearance, and it is thought some of it has rotted. Mr. Steinfort left on Wednesday morning, but his cousin, Adolph Geise, has bought a team—mules, wagon and harness for $300. Levin was on his way to Russell after a job at boiler mending. Maybe he can get a sit as engineer; $20 a month would be a little fortune for us; but if I put in the cash the others will have to put in the work. I have no doubt that they will. . . . The grasshoppers have nearly all disappeared, and the farmers are jubilant over the prospect of good crops, unless hail comes. . . . Frank Lubrick spoke to the driver of an extra stage which left here Thursday afternoon, and the result was that Levin got a chance to ride to Russell, the driver agreeing to wait for his pay until Levin could raise the money. Wednesday night the south wind was so strong that after I got to bed I could feel the house shake— and it is not a small house, either. We haven't had any washing done yet, because we had nothing to our credit, and we would not go in debt. $100 will buy us that yoke of oxen and a stove, and what I have earned will keep us in provisions for awhile. . . . The folks here have no shoe scrapers and consequently the houses get pretty dirty in wet weather. As to my catching cold and being sick—why, if I catch cold one day, the wind takes it away the next. I can stand more wet feet here than at home, and can sleep in an awful drafty room without taking cold. Underclothes I don't wear. I quit that about the middle of April; and socks there are none to wash, as they also have been discarded. My heel is getting well now, and don't trouble me much. Those receipts will come good when I get the necessary articles to make the victuals, but till then I must wait—I must eat what I have. Wheat or rye flour is scarce at $4.50 to $5. There was only 1 cwt. to be found in all the stores in town the other day, and that was not for sale. A fellow don't need to tax his strength here because you needn't work so hard; they don't expect it. Couldn't you send one of the blouses by mail? If it costs more than ten cents, don't send it. How would you like to have me come to Russell with an ox team to fetch you to the Creek? I reckon we could make the 40 miles in 1½ days. Hackerott made the distance in ten hours with his ox team, and they are much heavier than Snyder's (ours to be). Snyder has offered us the job of stripping and cutting his sorghum cane this fall, for half the molasses. I don't know how much he has, or whether it is up yet. My thumb has not troubled me since I am here, and that's a good thing. Yes, half a dollar a week would pay; but who would pay $2 a month for pasture when they can put their stock into a herd, and have no bother with them, for 20 cents a month? The case is reversed, as I have the pasture and no cows. Why, there is grass enough to last a dozen or twenty cows a year; but the buffalo grass is too short to make hay of; the blue grass, however, makes good hay, and we have a good deal of that between us. The reason I want an ox team is that it will cost us nothing to feed them this summer, and but little hay next winter, as they can pick a good deal on the buffalo grass, which is green all winter. Levin was up to Bull City to visit Fetters on the 12th. John

has a good job—to be paid in cash for three days and the balance of the week in provisions. Well, as for the shelter for
women, I don't ask Ma and Ruth to come and live in a dugout. I don't want them to come till I get a decent house for
them to live in, and that can be done in a couple of years—
maybe by the fall of 1878, who knows? This homestead law
is a good one, for if a man dies, his heirs get the land; if he
is single, it goes to his parents. How does Bub like the idea
of coming out here? I'd like to hear from him—what he is
doing, etc. Wonder how he'd look driving a yoke of oxen.
That is a profitable team, because if they are well kept, you
can work them two or three years and get as much as you
paid for them—and you have most of the work for nothing.
This coat of mine is a fraud, especially in rainy weather, because it gets wet through without much rain. . . . Raising
good mules pays here. Four-year-olds bring $300 a pair. I
had a little talk with Gussie Knase the other day; she says
she does not like this part of the country, and would like to
go back to Bethlehem; but Vessie Schweitzer says that Gussie's talk is all talk, and that she does like it here. . . . When
I get to the creek again, I'll get Hoot to cut my hair; the barber here charges 25 cents, and that is a big sum for me now—
too big to pay for hair clipping. The other evening it was
tolerably breezy, and Adolph wondered whether it was always so windy here. We told him "that was nothing" and
proceeded to inform him that when it was windy it blew
much harder. He concluded that his hat had been blown off
much oftener that one day than it had been for the last six
months in Wisconsin. If Bub comes, give him two good strong
suits—they need not be Sunday clothes—and two pair of overalls, and a couple of blouses. Underclothes will not come amiss
this winter, but they can be bought here about as cheap as

there. Clothing and provisions are cheap—the latter can be bought for less money than at home. Some of the folks here will no doubt be sorry I'm going to leave town; but the fact is, I'd rather be up on the claim than in the city. I have got right well acquainted since I arrived here two weeks ago. Barnhart said he had no money for me tonight. Told him all right; pay when he could—the sooner the better. I gave Levin $2.50 to help him along, and kept $2.30 so Barnhart only owes me $7.70. I begin to feel rich on the $10 I have earned, and I reckon I'll get Mrs. Hoot to do some washing for me. This morning when Ed. Garrigues went past the office with his bucket of milk (the men milk here) I yelled out, "Give me some!" and he came in and I drank about a quart. It was first rate, sweet milk, too. Much love . . .

SATURDAY, MAY 19, 1877

OSBORNE, KANSAS

As I was going to mail that letter this evening Ed. Garrigues hallooed at me, saying that if I'd milk a cow for him, he'd give me all the milk I wanted to drink, so I went to the corral and helped him, and on my return to the house I had about a pint of the fluid and a big piece of cake, and he wanted me to take more, but I couldn't have put away another bit.

The people who keep cows here in town hire a man to herd their cows for them at 35 cents per month per cow. There is a corral in town where the cows spend the night, and apparently when the corral gets so muddy and nasty that it is hard to get to the cows, they just move the fence a few rods, and so the trouble of moving the manure is avoided. Every morning and evening you can see milkers coming to the corral from all parts of town with their buckets on their arms. As a rule the men do the milking, but in fine weather there is a sprinkling of women and girls.

That dramatic entertainment did not draw me a bit. My "quarters" are of more account to me than to fool them away that way. I went to call on Fritchey, and talked business till 9:30 when I turned in. Harry Humphrey wanted me to go with him to spend Sunday, but I wanted to wait for the mail, and then the chance of riding was gone. But he said I should come out some other time and bring the others.

SUNDAY, MAY 20, 1877

AT GSELL'S, KILL CREEK, KANSAS

A beautiful day. We had quite a shower this morning. Being Sunday, I rolled over and over, and slept just as long as I could, and when I did roll out, it was only 6:30. Had breakfast about 8, and left Osborne half an hour later. Some one had the kindness to fix the footlog so it is easier to cross. At the ford, or rather right above it, an emigrant family had camped overnight. The man was taking care of the baby, and the woman was after fish or something further up stream. Made pretty good time, but I got awfully tired, as I am no longer used to walking. My foot hurt me, and this evening I borrowed a knife and peeled the hard skin off and then it felt better. I am afraid it will turn out to be a corn. Got to the ranch about 2 o'clock, as I had to sit down and rest about a dozen times in the last five miles. Everything in the place was wet, as the rain beat in through the roof during the last week. Got the overcoats and let them dry. Presently Jim came up the draw, and after a little talk we went over to Snyder's. Had a little talk with the folks there, and then we went to old man Gsell's. Jim had been nursing him through a spell of

sickness. Mrs. Pixley's cows came to the corral just before
dark, and we put them in and milked them, so they will not
go dry for her. I'm glad to be back here on the Creek again.
Must go to town on Wednesday, though, for Barnhart wants
me to work on Thursday. Don't send me any more smoking
tobacco. I have enough to last awhile, and I can't afford to
keep the whole neighborhood. I have to keep Jim in chewing
tobacco, as he is out of cash.

MONDAY, MAY 21, 1877

AT GSELL'S, KILL CREEK, KANSAS

Didn't turn out very early. After breakfast went up to
Hoot's and had my hair cut. There was no charge. I couldn't
go a quarter for John the barber to cut it for me. Then to the
dugout and got the dirty clothes, and took them to Gsell's
and washed them, as well as some of Jim's. Did you ever see
a bull whip? The handle is about a foot long, and the lash
from 4 to 7 feet. The lash is about 1½ inches thick at the
handle, and tapers to the popper, and a good hand will make
them crack like a pistol. After dinner went to the ranch and
planted a lot of corn on the sod that was broken for the dugout. Then we run off a line to plow by. I got awful tired today
from walking so much. Went to the P.O. on the way back
to Gsell's for the mail. It was not in, so my four mile walk
was for nothing. But it worked à blister on my left heel. So
now I have two sore heels instead of one. Had bread and milk
for supper.

TUESDAY, MAY 22, 1877

At the Dugout, Kill Creek, Kansas

Up before 6. The dew here is like a small shower of rain on the grass. There is no trouble about going to sleep, for even if the day is roasting hot, by the time the sun is down a fine breeze is stirring. Milked the cow and watered the pony, and by the time I got to the house again my shoes were wet through. Then we had breakfast. Between the three we managed to eat 14 eggs, besides bread and meat. Then Jim and I started for the ranch. . . . Hurrah for our well! We have five feet of good water in it. That's the place we struck shale. The water in the well may be all rain water; but it may come from the vein of water we missed on one side. If the latter is the case, so much the better for us. As soon as I can, I am going to get a cow for the keep. You know there are some folks who make no butter, and they turn their cows into the herd. One of these I can get, because it will be cheaper for the owner to let us have the milk for the keep than to pay a herd bill of 20 cts. per month for her keep. After dinner we three went to the woods to chop and Levin to Snyder's to write a letter. We did not get more than ½ cord cut, because it was so awfully hot. About 5 o'clock I went to Gsell's and got my satchel and the wash, and went home to the ranch, stopping at Hoot's for a loaf of bread, which I got on account. Mrs. Hoot says if we get flour, she will bake for us, and she is a good baker. Tried to get eggs, but could not. Morris gave Levin some money and he went to the P.O. with the bucket and got a gallon of milk for 10 cents. We made a hearty meal of bread and milk—and the milk was all drunk. Made a rousing fire in the fireplace to dry out and warm the place a little before we slept inside, and about 9 o'clock it was right comfortable, whereupon I lay down. We all slept in the one bed.

This morning, on the way through the big draw, Jim stepped over, and I nearly trod on a big bull snake. We let it go, because it is harmless and destroys gophers, which alone is enough to prevent me from killing it. It was yellow with brown spots. I don't think Mrs. Snyder will like it that Mrs. Hoot got the bread baking for us, but I don't care. As Levin says: "H. is a brick" and much more accommodating than some I know of round here. Levin brought me Ma's letter, and it was read while we were lying on the grass over on his claim.

WEDNESDAY, MAY 23, 1877

AT SCHWEITZER's, OSBORNE, KANSAS

Rather cloudy this morning. Turned out about 6. Breakfasted on bread and molasses with water for a beverage. Morris and Jim went to call on Gsell, who wanted to see that man from Pennsylvania. There was a story going that Levin's brother had come—but they meant Morris. I stayed at the shanty, because I had to go to town this afternoon, and 13 miles is not to be sneezed at by a fellow with sore heels. Levin started for McGuire's for an order on Rook to do some breaking for us. The other night I was with you in my dreams and just as I was in the midst of calling on the folks and having a good time, I got awake and found it was time to get up and milk the old man's cow. There was a very heavy dew this morning, and in going to the well for a bucket of water I got my shoes pretty well wet through. Levin wanted to go to Solomon City to look for work, but I blocked that game. My time is broken up, so that if I furnish the money for us to live, he must stay home, and he and Jim work more than I. He may get an occasional job with the blacksmith in Osborne. He agreed to my plan. Morris said he wanted to go to the city this afternoon with me, and I waited for him till 2 o'clock, and as he did not come, I started off without him. I made good time, though it was awfully hot. The road never seemed to be shorter. Got to the footlog below the ford, and found that the river was up so far that I could not get across. Mrs. Proctor, who lives on Charley Herzog's place, told me that the river had been on the rise for only an hour. It had raised over two feet in that time. We saw the storm last night drawing along the river north of us, but I had no idea it would take 24 hours for the water to reach this point. I also learned that Charley's team was on the same side of the river, so I made for it and waited till he got ready and came over to town with him. The water stood two inches in the wagon box when we were in the middle of the stream. Looked in at the office and saw there was no paper wet down. Didn't think much of that, as I saw Mr. Schweitzer drive on the hay scales opposite, and concluded that as I could ride, I'd go home with him. He would be in a bad fix if he had no oxen, because his horses have the epizooty. Hiram Crist, lately of Allentown, works for him. We got to the house about 8 o'clock, and after a hearty meal and a good smoke, we turned in.

THURSDAY, MAY 24, 1877

OSBORNE, KANSAS

Don't know what time I got out this morning, but I do know that I had breakfast and walked 3½ miles to town, and then it was only 6 o'clock. Began work about 6:30. There have been no through trains from Kansas City since the end of last week on account of high water—consequently the paper had not arrived on time. . . . I send this from Osborne because I

will not get to the Creek—perhaps till Saturday night. Levin
was told by the man at Russell that he didn't want him to
come; he wrote for L. to come and then would not pay L.'s
expenses to Russell. L. says he won't go back even if the man
sends for him. The folks here—those I am acquainted with—
seemed glad to see me again. If I stay till tomorrow night,
I'll stay till Saturday and try to buy a stove at Dimick's sale.
Maybe I'll spend Friday night with Harry Humphrey, a
cousin of Dr. Humphrey of Bethlehem. He is a stone mason
and a jolly good fellow—a bachelor. Much love to all . . .

SATURDAY, MAY 26, 1877

AT SCHWEITZER'S, OSBORNE, KANSAS

The river is up over its banks and I am fast here in town.
It's real cold, and looks like rain. Everybody who could get a
horse, pony or mule, was down to see the high water. As I
could not get one, I stayed in town. The bridge across the
ravine between town and the river is washed away, and all
the ravines and low places are full of water. I laid round all
morning, waiting for Dimick's sale to begin, but it was post-
poned till afternoon, as very few folks were in town. Had
dinner at Rader's, by invitation of Charley Herzog. Attended
the sale, and bought a pick for 60¢. They are worth $1.50 at
the store. We need one for digging our wells. The stove, for
which I most wished to remain, was started at $6.50; I made
it $7; then a man bid $15; at this point I left, as I heard of a
stove one size smaller that I could buy for $16. It was sold
for $23. Went home with Mr. Schweitzer, as it will not cost
so much as to stay in town. Barnhart is about sick, and says if
he feels no better he'll give me three or four days' work next
week. Mr. S.'s idea is that after a bit B. will want me to work

all the time. I know where to get a lot of meat now. Flour is
$5.50 per cwt.

SUNDAY, MAY 27, 1877

At Schweitzer's, Osborne, Kansas

I never know what time it is when I get out of bed, because
clocks are like angels' visits—few and far between. After
breakfast Monroe and I went over to Morgan's, stopping on
the way at Wentzler's, as I wished to have a look at the stove.
It is a No. 7, rather small, to be sure, but it will do till we
are better fixed and the cash is more plenty. With it are a big
cast iron boiler, two iron pots, two griddles, an iron tea kettle,
a gallon coffee pot, a couple of pans and three joints of pipe—
all for $16. We can cook all we want to on it, but the oven
is so small that only two loaves of bread will go in at a time.
I forgot to mention two "spiders" that go with the outfit. Oh,
how I wish I could see you all! I am perfectly satisfied, and
don't want to come back to Bethlehem to remain, but I'd give
a month's work—every day in the month—to be with you a
week. But it's no use thinking about it, so I just have to go
ahead and "grin and bear it." Rode back part of the way with
Wentzler, and laid round the house all day. From noon on
the sun was out and a light breeze stirring, so it was very
pleasant. The water was standing all over the bluffs, and in
places, especially in the ravines, there was a good deal of
running water. Mr. Foster's rain gauge indicated 4½ inches
as the amount which fell on Friday night. Everybody says
there has more rain fallen this spring than during any previous
spring for 6 years. All the small grain looks splendid, and
corn only needs a little sunshine to make it grow as fast as the
weeds. When I heard it rain so hard the other night, my first

thought was "How much water will get into the ranch?" but
I was too sleepy to make an estimate. Berger and Huber had
a notion to go east during harvest, and I had a long talk with
them on the subject, which, I believe, had very little effect on
them. Don't send that box—if you send a box—until we tell
you, because we would rather fetch it with our own team
(when we get it) than to have someone bring it to Osborne,
and have to pay 40 cents per 100 pounds for freight between
Russell and Osborne. We must learn the road to Russell anyhow. I suppose you are in church at this time. I would like to
hear a real good sermon again. I would not go to Landes' to
hear Henry preach, this morning, because their peculiar customs (they are Dunkards) together with his lisping, would
have excited my risibilities to an uncontrollable degree, and
that would never do.

MONDAY, MAY 28, 1877

AT SCHWEITZER'S, OSBORNE, KANSAS

After breakfast went over to town, and had to run the
gauntlet through myriads of mosquitoes, on the prairie, especially in the draws. The wind came up pretty strong at times,
and then they would leave. Barnhart was sticking type at a
lively rate when I got in. He told me I might go to work if I
wanted to, and my coat came off in a hurry. They brought the
mail across the river in some sort of a boat yesterday, and sent
it to the hack on the other side the same way this morning.

TUESDAY, MAY 29, 1877

AT MORROW'S, OSBORNE, KANSAS

No work today. I am awfully tired of staying in town.
While in the blacksmith shop this afternoon, Joe Morrow said

he wanted me to work for him tomorrow. Hurrah, no more loafing this week.

WEDNESDAY, MAY 30, 1877

AT MORROW'S, OSBORNE, KANSAS

About 6:30 I began hoeing in the corn patch, and in a few minutes Franz Huber put in his appearance. Together we hoed 65 rods. We had gone across the field twice when a thunder gust blew up, and for 5 minutes we had a heavy shower mingled with a good deal of hail. The ground was too wet to work, so we had an hour's rest. The storm did not touch Osborne. It only extended half way (1 mile) to that place. And when we went back, we were not to work long, for another five-minute shower drove us back to the house. This evening had a friendly discussion on baptism with a Dunkard preacher who stayed at Joe's over night. Last night we were down at Kaser's to meeting. There was an Evangelical preacher there, and he was a preacher! He would begin in what he called English but it was so awfully murdered that no one would call it by that name; by the time he got warmed up, he would spit out Dutch as fast as he could work his tongue, and that went at a 2:40 rate. While at work this afternoon we speculated on what was taking place in the Decoration ceremonies about that time. How little we thought, last Decoration Day, that I would be hoeing corn in Kansas today. And we don't only have to hoe around the hills, but all over the piece, because it is very weedy and entirely too wet for a horse to be used.

THURSDAY, MAY 31, 1877

AT MORROW'S, OSBORNE, KANSAS

Went to town with Joe this morning, and when I wanted to go to work Barnhart said he did not want me; so I went back to Joe's and into the cornfield. At noon we had a heavy shower, so we had little to do this afternoon, because the ground was too wet. The river is too high to cross as yet, so I have to stay on this side. I have no idea how the boys are getting along; have got no letters or papers this week, and don't suppose I'll get any till I get back to the Creek. Didn't work a lick this afternoon. Went to town for the mail, and spoke to Wentzler for the stove. He must get one before I can have the one he has now. He will give me notice this week. Well, no teams have crossed the river today, and I am still in and around the City. Much love to you all.

FRIDAY, JUNE 1, 1877

AT MORROW'S, OSBORNE, KANSAS

This morning the ground was too wet to hoe corn, so we patched up the roof of an old house here. When that was finished we went into the corn field. By 3 o'clock we began hoeing sorghum, and that tired our eyes. It is only an inch high and looks like the grass, so that we had to get on our knees sometimes in order to find it. Last month I earned about $17, of which I paid out about $3, so you see I have almost earned the stove, besides getting my board. You can see by my diary how many days I worked. I have not yet received all the cash I have earned, but can get it when I need it. At noon Mrs. Morrow told us to "let our dinner settle" before we went to work again, so we rested a full hour. We work about eleven hours a day. She makes me think of Mrs. Brunner.

Talk about mosquitoes! After a rain, if you go across the prairies, you are surrounded by a swarm, and they bite like mosquitoes only can. They can bite through an ordinary shirt, but mine is too thick and loose. Where you have one we have a thousand. If you don't believe it, come out and count them. A man named Milne has lost about $3,000 by the high water. He had built a mill and dam, and the freshet washed away everything, besides about an acre of ground. Nearly all the mills in this vicinity (within 16 or 20 miles) have been more or less damaged. At Bull City the river makes a bend just above the mill dam, and when the river rose so high it went round the dam instead of over it, and made a new channel, leaving the dam high and dry. The miller will have to put up a new dam. Aug. Kaser went to Cawker last Friday for a load of flour, and was bound by the high water, so that he arrived in town this evening.

SATURDAY, JUNE 2, 1877

At Morrow's, Osborne, Kansas

Fixed up the interior of the old blacksmith shop this morning and then finished the sorghum. After dinner went into the potatoes and hoed about a half. Quit work earlier than other days. Huber and I have long talks about Bethlehem and the folks there while we hoe. He has had an offer of work at $9 a month, but says he can make more than that this month in harvest. The easiest way, and one much used here, to get rid of mosquitoes in the evening is to make a "smoke fire" before the door and let the smoke blow into the house. It's a good way, but some folks can't stand it. I can stand a good deal of that—more than the others. Their eyes are affected directly. The river is down now so that folks can cross at Bloomington, though not on the direct road between Osborne and Kill Creek. John Rupert came down from the Creek today, and stayed over night at Morrow's. He reports that the dugout has collapsed. The exact amount of the damage I can't learn. . . .

SUNDAY, JUNE 3, 1877

AT MORROW'S, OSBORNE, KANSAS

Cloudy and a little shower before noon. About 1 o'clock we started for the schoolhouse in Pleasant Valley, about 5 miles north of here, to attend Dunkard meeting. There were about 40 persons present. What tickled some of them was Bro. Henry Landes' singing. He has a very strong voice, very rough, and when he sings he puts the "ah" on, which made me think of "Brother Sodom." He sings this way:

> The temple—ah—'s veil in sunder rent,
> The solid marbles break—a——h.

It does sound too comical to one not used to it. When he talks he does not put the "ah" on. He preached about 30 minutes, and in that time he hardly stopped to breathe. His language was good (he preached English) and the way he quoted from the old and new Testaments shows he is pretty well posted. He has been preaching only about two years. Bro. Dave Brumbach gave us a regular "Brother Sodom" talk, as far as the "ahs" were concerned, and used up his stock of breath in a short time. Bro. John Fuller made a few remarks, and the meeting was over. We went to Ed. Humphrey's for supper. We had one of his horses and one of Joe's, and Ed's wagon. He has a splendid mule colt two weeks old.

MONDAY, JUNE 4, 1877

OSBORNE, KANSAS

At hoeing again this morning, and finished by 2 p.m. It was hot, but occasionally we had a breeze. And the latest news is that Herman Glicker and Will Landes have run away. They started yesterday, on their way east, so look out for them, for I have no doubt they will be in Bethlehem inside of a month. Henry Harp was cultivating corn with a riding cultivator today. There is an axle and pair of wheels, behind which is the seat, and the shovels are attached to the handles, so that when the machine is on the road they can be lifted up and hung on hooks for that purpose. The seat is between the handles, and the driver rides. Went to town to find out whether Joe wants me to work any longer. Levin was in the shop, at work on a reaper, and had brought Pa's letter of May 20th and 26th, besides a lot of Daily Times, for which I was mighty glad. But what "struck me all of a heap" was the announcement that Pa was to start on the 4th—tonight. It took my breath away—it did, indeed. I don't like to travel with so much cash about me, but the work up the Creek is all to be paid in breaking, so that we can wait till after harvest, and then horses will be cheap. And we'd rather have horses than oxen, though the latter are good. Barnhart says I shall work tomorrow. Levin says that the other night the bedbugs carried him out of bed, and in trying to push him through the wall wakened him. And there were about a dozen mosquitoes on the old man's back, and when he buttoned his coat they just flew away with him into a tree.

The people who live in sod houses, and, in fact, all who live under a dirt roof, are pestered with swarms of bed bugs. ... The vermin were not brought here by the immigrants; they grew on the trees along the river and creeks before the first settlers arrived. The bugs infest the log and sod chicken coops, too, in countless thousands, or, if you wish to measure them in a spoon, you can gather them up in that way from between the sods in the wall. I have heard chicken raisers complain that their fowls are killed by the bugs getting into their ears. Whether or not that is the cause of the fowls dying, the bugs are blamed. Where the sod houses are plastered the bed bugs are not such a nuisance.[14]

You don't have to keep a dog in order to have plenty of fleas, for they are natives too and do their best to drive out the intruding settlers. Just have a dirt floor and you have fleas, sure. They seem to spring from the dust of the earth. Coal oil and water are sometimes used to sprinkle the floor, but that abates the pest only for a short time, and oil costs 35 cents a gallon. People who have board floors are not bothered so much with these fleas.

Another nuisance here is what people call "Kansas itch," which attacks nearly everybody within a short time after arrival here; few are immune. Not all are affected alike; some scratch a few days, other are affected for months. It is not contagious—at least not all who come in contact with those suffering with it take the disease. There is only one way in which a sufferer can get relief—scratching; and that aggravates the itching and sometimes produces raw sore spots. But those are easier to heal than it is to get the disease out of your system. Change of water is sometimes given as the cause; bed bugs and fleas are sometimes blamed, but it seems as if the itch has to run its course in every case. It disappears as mysteriously as it came.

[14] Ruede is correct in saying that bed bugs were a terrible nuisance in the sod houses, in fact, most people were bothered a great deal with them, no matter what kind of houses they lived in; but the bugs that infested the cottonwood trees were of another sort, and not bed bugs, as many people believed.

TUESDAY, JUNE 5, 1877

AT LANDES's, OSBORNE, KANSAS

Slept in the office last night. Went to Herzog's for something for breakfast, and Gus would not give me anything till I had gone to Rader's for my breakfast. Worked in the office. This afternoon Henry Landes came in and had a long talk with me, which resulted in my going to work for him for six months on the farm at $12 a month. He is to do 8 acres of breaking for me soon and furnish me with meat, flour, etc., and the amount of $35 or $40 in cash. Went home with him.

WEDNESDAY, JUNE 6, 1877

AT LANDES's, OSBORNE, KANSAS

After breakfast we pulled a lot of sunflowers out of the wheat, and in about an hour Mr. Wentzler came, and we drove a mile to a house Henry bought, which we expected to move today. Got one wagon under by noon. The house was frame, poorly put together. The other wagon we had in position soon after dinner, and then we started off across the prairie towards where he wanted to place the building. We had to stop to fix up the house while on the road, and while thus engaged, John Sears said we had better make tracks for the stable, as there was a storm brewing. We did not start at once, but when we did, it was at a lope. I had the good luck to be first at the stable, and only got a little damp. Sears and John Walter were pretty thoroughly wet. The rain came down in torrents, with some hail. Just after the worst was over, we saw Henry running towards us. He reported that the house had been blown off the wagons and the pieces were scattered over the prairie. The storm lasted about fifteen minutes, and Henry and the two other men were wet to the skin. After the storm I jumped on one of the horses and fetched Schuyler from school. The ravines were full of water all along the road. It was a storm of thunder, lightning, wind, hail, and rain, and tore up trees and unroofed houses along the river. Direct my mail to Osborne.

Love to all.

THURSDAY, JUNE 7, 1877

OSBORNE, KANSAS

By special arrangement I worked in the office today. Rode in with Landes, who wanted spokes for a wheel that had been broken when the house fell off the wagons yesterday. Got through at the office about 8:30. Slept in the office, as it was too far (3½ miles) to walk. I was very tired and did not want to go to Delano's performance at the town hall. Wrote a postal to Pa, directed to the Russell House, saying he should come to Osborne. I hope he will get a job at home. If it pays $35 a month he'd better stay, because I don't know where to put him if he comes.

FRIDAY, JUNE 8, 1877

AT LANDES'S, OSBORNE, KANSAS

Up before 5 and walked to Landes' before breakfast. Got my shoes wet going through the grass (which had a heavy dew on it), and water on the low ground east of town. Took the hoe and tried to hoe corn, but the ground was too wet. Helped draw nails out of the pieces of the house. Loaded the wagon, and by the time he had gone to the house and come back, a cold rain had set in, so we quit work. After dinner we went to pulling sunflowers out of the wheat. Made two spells of it; and I had a chance to read part of the N. Y. Sunday Sun which I got from Barnhart.

SATURDAY, JUNE 9, 1877

At Landes's, Osborne, Kansas

Turned out about 4:30 and got up the floor of the wrecked house. Then Mr. Getz drove up on his way to the North Fork, and Landes went with him. I cut rye out of the wheat all day. When they want clean wheat for seeding they generally have to cut some rye out. Rader has a "volunteer" crop of rye that looks as though it had been sowed broadcast. The seed was knocked out of the ears last summer by hail. About 4 p.m. I jumped on one of the horses and rode into town for the mail, and to see if Pa had come. Didn't get any mail and Pa had not arrived. Had a long talk with Crist, and got back home by 8:30. It was light enough to feed and do the chores. Afterwards I went to Schweitzer's for awhile. Got to bed by 9:30.

SUNDAY, JUNE 10, 1877

At Schweitzer's, Osborne, Kansas

Sunday I had my first trip to Bull's City. When Christ first came he was, like a lot of the rest of us, not overburdened with luggage, principally because he did not know how long he would stay. It took him only a few weeks to decide that he liked the country well enough to stay longer than his limited stock of clothes would last, so he sent word for his folks to forward his belongings, and they did so when John

Fetter came. John settled near Bull's City, so Christ had to make the trip there to get his stuff, and Sunday morning he got Monroe Schweitzer to take him up where Fetter lived, inviting me to go along. I got up to Schweitzer's about 5:30, and we started about sunup, in a farm wagon without a spring seat. His wagon is of the "wide track" kind, and while the wheels on one side ran in the rut all right, the opposite wheels wouldn't, and one side of the wagon was generally tilted up several inches higher than the other. The team had worked all week and couldn't be driven out of a walk, so you may imagine that the twenty mile drive was a rather drawn-out affair. Passed through Bloomington on the road. It's a wonder they don't call that a city.

We arrived at Bull City and went through the place—which consists of a log store, in which is the post office, both of which are tended by General Bull, a hotel with all but two windows boarded up, a blacksmith shop and half a dozen dwellings. We had to inquire where Fetter lived. Oh, yes, they all knew him. He was working for J. M. Babcock and lived in the log school house across the river, about three miles west; it would be easy to get there. After crossing the river at the ford south of town we got off the trail and recrossed the stream to the north side, striking a trail which led to another ford. We didn't see any buildings and hardly knew whether to cross the river again or look around for another road, but we imagined we heard voices on the other side, behind the timber, and concluded to risk the ford, which appeared to be deep.

The approach was narrow and steep and when we got started down into the river there was no turning back. In the ford the horses struggled as if their lives depended on getting across as soon as possible, and the water came up into the wagon box. The brutes knew more about the matter than the driver, for he supposed it was merely a muddy ford, but, as we afterward learned, it was really a dangerous quicksand, and the ford was not used by those who knew the country. There was a good ford a short distance south, but we had followed an old trail and turned into the river too soon. Altogether we went about five miles farther than there was any need of.

We finally found Fetter about noon, had dinner, and about the middle of the afternoon chucked Christ's bundle into the wagon and started back. The recent high water washed a new channel on the north side of the Bull City dam about 30 feet wide, leaving the dam dry. They will have to work smart to get the mill running by harvest, and then have to run day and night to supply the custom.

On the way back we stopped at Bull City for some crackers, but the store was locked, so we couldn't get any. At Bloomington we stopped again with the purpose of spending our money —we had exactly nine cents altogether—for some crackers. We stopped at Cy Tilton's store, which was locked up for Sunday, but we were hungry and pounded on the door. Cy poked his head out of the window upstairs. "What d'ye want?" "Crackers." "Crackers? Ain't had any in the store for months." And down went the window. A mile farther east we tried at a farm house to get a loaf of bread, but the pleasant spoken woman who came to the door said they had just arrived the day before, and she hadn't had a chance to bake any bread. We tried at several houses; and at last succeeded in buying a loaf of bread, which was our supper. There wasn't a crumb left. Got to Schweitzer's about 10, had something to eat, and then threw the buffalo robe on the floor and went to sleep on it.

MONDAY, JUNE 11, 1877

At Landes's, Osborne, Kansas

Reached Landes' by 5 a.m.; had breakfast and helped bring the lower floor from the ruin, and put it in position. Presently Robt. Wentzler, a former Bethlehemite, came with his team to help put up the building. He is a carpenter and millwright, and has work almost all the time. He is soon going to Hays to build a mill for the Russians. I took his team home and went to hoeing corn. About 3 p.m. I noticed some one was coming, but didn't look particularly; but my curiosity was aroused, and I looked again, and there was Pa! He had gone to Kill Creek with a freighter instead of coming to Osborne, and came down on a team this morning. He brought your letter of the 27th of May, which had been at the P.O. Oh, but I was glad to see him. He did not recognize me at first, when he was off a piece—not till he got close. We had quite a talk till I got my row finished, and then we went to the house. I read the letter while he talked with Mrs. Wentzler. Now, Syd, I am glad you did not send that money with Pa. He had $30 snatched from his hand at Toledo. A man asked him for change, and he got it out, and just then the man grabbed it and jumped from the car. So that was gone. Now anybody who travels and has money ought to keep it in his pocket, and not allow a stranger to make him get it out, either. He has only 50 cents left. . . . As for Bub's coming out, we'll see what can be done. After supper we went to Schweitzer's, where Pa stayed over night.

TUESDAY, JUNE 12, 1877

At Landes's, Osborne, Kansas

Pa went to town with Mr. Schweitzer this morning and I went to Wentzler's to hoe corn. It's very windy today. This afternoon we had a slight shower, and a little hail, but not enough to hurt anything. After supper I had a smoke of Kansas tobacco that Wentzler raised. It is rather stronger than Connecticut leaf. Slept on a buffalo robe on the floor. I'll try my level best to have it so that Bub can come this fall. Let Syd take care of those $40, and if they are not needed in the family they can go for the interest on the house. You ought to see me drink milk here at Wentzler's. The water is not good and so I drink little except milk, over a pint at a time, about twice in the morning and twice in the afternoon. I was awfully sold on that coat. It is ripping fast, and one pocket is entirely torn out. My shoes are well ventilated at the toes, and the spring-bottoms are all kicked out of my pants. What makes Ruth so quiet? No message from her for a month. The girls evidently don't like my way of corresponding, as they have not written to me yet.

WEDNESDAY, JUNE 13, 1877

AT LANDES'S, OSBORNE, KANSAS

Bright and warm today. Hoeing goes good if I keep the hoe sharp. Did not drink a drop of water all day. But you'd better believe the milk pans suffered. I guess I drank about three quarts between times, and coffee for every meal.

Most people out here don't drink real coffee, because it is too expensive. Green coffee berries sell at anywhere from 40 to 60 cents a pound, and such a price is beyond the means of the average person. Even Arbuckles Ariosa at 35 cents a pound takes too much out of the trade when eggs sell at three to six cents a dozen and butter at six or eight cents a pound. So rye coffee is used a great deal—parched brown or black according to whether the users like a strong or mild drink. To give the beverage a ranker flavor, what is known as "coffee

essence" is used. . . . This essence is a hard, black paste put up
in tins holding some two ounces, with a red or yellow wrapper
on which is printed in bold black type the figure 5000. What
that stands for I never heard; reckon it is a trade mark. Directions for use are also on the wrapper, but I never saw anybody follow 'em. The women folks use "about so much" for
a pot of coffee, and often they have to use the stove-lid lifter,
or a hammer, or anything else that is handy to pound with, to
break the hard paste before they can get it out of the tin. It is
probably made of bran and molasses. When rye is not used,
wheat is sometimes used for coffee, but is considered inferior.

THURSDAY, JUNE 14, 1877

AT LANDES'S, OSBORNE, KANSAS

Up at 4:30. Got through hoeing by 2 p.m. High wind today, from the south. Stopped at Schweitzer's on the way down,
and got a lot of the Daily Times, which afforded me a great
deal of enjoyment. Hoed a little at some sweet corn before
I did the chores.

FRIDAY, JUNE 15, 1877

AT LANDES'S, OSBORNE, KANSAS

Followed the cultivator and "erected the corn up" all day
long, and cut out the weeds. After supper went to Schweitzer's
and had a long talk with Mr. S., who had been to Cawker
for lumber. He told me that Parker the storekeeper paid 25
cents per bushel for corn, and then had all he bought dumped
into his hog pen, where he has about a hundred hogs. He does
the same with all the rye he buys. Now the story is that

Berger and Huber have bought a claim for $100 and intend to stay; but they change like the wind—one day they are going east for work, the next they will stay. I don't know what to think of them.

SATURDAY, JUNE 16, 1877

At Landes's, Osborne, Kansas

An awfully hot day. Out in the cornfield again. Hoed awhile and then took charge of the cultivator till noon. The cultivators require two horses and are entirely different from those in use around Bethlehem. After dinner hoed potatoes. On Monday we propose to go up to the creek and break 8 acres on my place, which will take till Friday noon, if everything goes well. We expect to go into the harvest field next Saturday. All the farmers are getting their reapers in running order. I will probably be a little irregular in my correspondence through harvest, because I will only have Sundays to write.

SUNDAY, JUNE 17, 1877

At Landes's, Osborne, Kansas

I went to Schweitzer's last evening to see if Monroe would go to town with me, but he and Crist were going fishing, so I started alone, and had gone about two miles when I met Mr. S. coming home. I concluded that I'd go back, because I did not know whether I would get a chance to ride if I did not take this. Went home with him; that's the reason the letter will be mailed so as to leave here Wednesday morning. You will probably get it Saturday. The folks here store up ice in the winter so as to be able to make ice cream, and by all I have heard they make a great deal of it during the summer. It hardly pays to make butter, for it is worth only 7 to 8 cents a pound at present. Some make butter now and pack it away till winter, when it brings a better price—sometimes as much as 20 cents. Does Syd send a paper to Ad when my diary is published? I'd like him to. The folks have all gone to meeting over on Twin Creek, and will not be home till late, I reckon, because what with the sermon, dinner, etc. it takes up a good while. If I was to come to Bethlehem now and go up Main street, there would be lots of acquaintances who would not know me, for I am awfully sunburnt. . . . From what the folks say, Pa has an idea of putting up a house this summer yet. But he won't if I can help it. I am not going into debt. I am clear now, and intend to keep clear. I have nearly $9 coming to me now, that I earned before I began working for Landes, and that will keep the four of us about four weeks. I tell you we are having some hot weather now. But that does not prevent sleeping well at night, because as soon as the sun goes down it gets cooler, and by morning a pretty heavy cover is not uncomfortable. And talk of dew! why, it is like a small shower of rain, and it does not require much running through the grass to get your shoes pretty well soaked. The Moravian calls me "one of the pioneers" and says Pa will "stay to help me gather my first crop"—which will be potatoes. I wish you would save a lot of peach and plum stones, and the cherry pits of some of those big black cherries at George's, so that you can send them with H. Weinland. They will make a fine orchard in a few years. Mr. Neuschwanger has peach trees five feet high that were raised from seed planted three years ago. Yesterday morning we had a heavy fog, and when the sun broke through, there was a "fog bow" in the west—a perfect semi-circle, and as white as snow. Will Landes was reported to have been at Glicker's last Sunday, but we have not heard anything from him since. I never saw so many sunflowers in one place as I did near Bull City last Sunday. There were two patches—one about four and the other six acres, where there was nothing but sunflowers as high as a man's waist. And sand! the corn fields round the "city" are fairly covered with it. I wouldn't swap my claim for two up there. Tomorrow we expect to go up to my claim and break, and when sowing time comes, I intend to have five acres put in wheat and five in rye by next spring. I hope I'll be able to stay at home most of the time. I propose to break 25 or 30 acres on the three claims to plant corn. I am much stronger than I used to be, and feel much better than when I worked in the house. I had a good sweat yesterday while I was cultivating corn. This afternoon I was at Schweitzer's and they fetched out a freezer of ice cream, and I had a big saucer full—not one of your little saloon saucers, but a regular table saucer, and there was enough in it to cool the hottest man in Kansas. This has been a "roaster," I wonder if you had such a hot day. The other day (did I tell you already?) Al. Wilson brought some strawberries to the office—the first he or anyone raised in town. They looked nice, and no doubt would have tasted nice, but Barnhart let them dry up on his table. On the North Fork some grain was so badly cut up by the late hail storm that it had to be made into hay. No grain round here has suffered. Today for the first time since I am in Kansas I took a shave. You ought to see the fierce moustache I have left standing. You wouldn't recognize me. We had a tolerable heavy thunder storm this afternoon about 4 o'clock that lasted an hour, and a good deal of rain fell. Corn is shoulder high and growing fast. You can almost see it grow. I can eat onions like a good fellow now. The folks here use a good many. Rye bread and butter, with a big onion constituted my supper tonight, topped off with a piece of Schnitz pie, which I eat, not because I like it but to get it out of the way so we get fresh pies.

SUNDAY, JUNE 17, 1877

At Landes's, Osborne, Kansas

The folks got home by about 9 o'clock. I had tried sleeping in the dugout, but could not succeed on account of the closeness of the room, so I took a quilt and slept on the floor in the house. And I slept good, too.

MONDAY, JUNE 18, 1877

At the Dugout, Kill Creek, Kansas

Up bright and early, and soon after breakfast hitched up, and, after getting some things together, we started for Kill Creek. It looked as though someone was moving, for on the wagon we had a long pole, the breaking plow, axe, hatchet, monkey wrench, the halters and picket ropes, an old wash boiler full of provisions, a lot of Henry's clothes, and some bedding. We stopped in town to have the plow-lay sharpened. And then the file mysteriously disappeared. It was in its place on one of the plow handles when the plow was lifted from the wagon; but when we took hold of the plow to put it back, the file was missing. We finally got started, and arrived at my place about noon. Stopped at Bleam's on the way and bought a ham, for which I paid 10 cents per lb. It was just sweltering hot, and we hurriedly put up a tent by stretching the wagon sheet over the long pole. Had dinner and then paced off a plot of six acres. Henry went to breaking, and I talked with Pa, who had come up from Hoot's. By the time the team had made two rounds, they were covered with foam and sweat. The heat was awful, and there was very little air stirring. . . . We went to old man Gsell's palatial (part log, part stone, one story) residence on the other side of the creek to get the pick and shovel, as well as my valise, as I feared what proved to be the case. As Mrs. Hoot afterwards expressed it, "Sie waren all vergroatzed,"[15] and I'm afraid the coat and pants are about spoiled. They were in the ranch when the washout occurred. That dugout is a complete ruin. The cause of its falling in was that the walls slanted inward. If they had slanted the other way I don't suppose the ruin would have been so complete. I handed the valise and its contents to Mrs. Hoot for an overhauling. . . . When I got back to the tent Henry was making supper. We had ham and fried eggs, radishes, bread and butter and cheese and coffee. . . . We stretched the sheet over the wagon and fixed up a bed under it. But the mosquitoes were too much for Henry, and he went into the wagon box. I had a quilt, and, rolling myself into it, covered my head and went to sleep in spite of the pests. I never slept better than there on the prairie. I can sleep anywhere now, but prefer a place where there is draft enough over me to blow skeeters away. Today it is three months since we arrived in Osborne.

TUESDAY, JUNE 19, 1877

At the Dugout, Kill Creek, Kansas

Pa and I began digging for Levin's dugout soon after breakfast, but by 10 o'clock had to quit, as it was too hot. We have struck a place where the "prairie lime" is plenty— sometimes lumps half as big as your fist. I suppose it would

---

[15] I have been unable to get a translation for this Pennsylvania German.

be called hydrate of lime by scientists. We took about four hours for nooning, and then went back and worked till after sunset, as the moon was shining very bright. After supper Pa went to Hoot's, and in a short time Jim came hallooing across the claim. We talked till near midnight, lying on the grass. Tonight Levin performed on the cornet at a concert at Osborne. Jim does not like the idea of buying an ox team. Without my help he can't get any team and I don't want a team of horses now; they cost more than we can pay, and go in debt I won't, so he will have to let me do as I please. Breaking went very hard, as the sod is very dry and tough.

WEDNESDAY, JUNE 20, 1877

At Landes's, Osborne, Kansas

By 5 a.m. Pa was up on the claim, and we shouldered the pick and shovel and struck for the dugout. Worked till about 8, when we had breakfast. Then back to work till 10, by which time the sun began to pour his rays in a way we did not like, so we quit work and struck for the tent. Henry said the ground was too dry to break, so after dinner we loaded up the traps and started for Osborne. Stopped in town on the way to Landes. I invested 30 cents in a straw hat that Sam Young in Bethlehem would charge 15 for. It was quite dark by the time we got home because the sky was overcast. There was a fine breeze blowing all day.

THURSDAY, JUNE 21, 1877

At Landes's, Osborne, Kansas

Directly after breakfast the word was, "Howard, you take the hoe and go over to Fraley's place and clean out the sunflowers between the corn." And that was my work for the day.

It was awful hot, too. My shirts will not be blue very long. They fade fast when the sun gets at them right. The one I have on is more red than blue, on the back. John Walters was cultivating the corn, and I changed off with him, he taking the hoe and I the corn plow.

FRIDAY, JUNE 22, 1877

At Landes's, Osborne, Kansas

The calculation was to go into the harvest field this morning, so the canvas was put in position, and the harvester put in running order. Then Sears went for his team, Henry's team meanwhile being hitched to the machine. Henry drove and Sears and I were to bind. The binders ride on the machine. The grain is delivered by an elevator, from the canvas on which it falls upon a table in front of the binders, who need only make the bands and bind the sheaves. Did I write "only?" Well, that "only" means hard work, and quick work, too, for when the grain stands thick it takes all that two men want to do to keep the table clear. I have not got the "hang" of the thing yet, but I'll soon be able to bind tolerably fast. We went round the field once, and then they concluded the rye was too green. So I had to take the hoe again. I guess by the time this season is over I'll know how to hoe corn, even if I learn nothing else, for I have done more at that since I am here than at anything else. This evening we killed a small hog, as meat is beginning to get scarce.

SATURDAY, JUNE 23, 1877

At Schweitzer's, Osborne, Kansas

The same program as yesterday—hoeing corn. About 4:30 p.m. the clouds began to come up thick and fast, and I

expected to see the wind change suddenly; and if the wind
shifted, I knew we would have rain. So I took the nearest
road for home. There I found Mr. and Mrs. Kamey, who
had been to mill on the North Fork with a load of grain and
were on their way home with the flour. Henry took the family
to town this morning, so I had to get my own dinner. The
folks were getting supper. Kamey was making ice cream. That
was tip top. Had plenty of eggs in it, and was well flavored.
After supper I went to Schweitzer's, expecting to get my mail,
which he promised to bring me; but he had been cutting
wheat, so my mail had not left the P.O. Stayed there, talking
with Christ, a good while, and finally stayed all night. There
must have been a hail storm somewhere, for it was real cold
sleeping out, but we managed to get a pretty good night's
rest. Schweitzer has water on his place. He and Crist dug and
walled out a well 10 feet deep in two days. There is about
three feet of water in it, and good water, too.

SUNDAY, JUNE 24, 1877

At Landes's, Osborne, Kansas

Got home by the time the folks were at breakfast, but as I
had had mine, I didn't want any. The women folks got at
me on the subject of baptism, but could not make any head-
way with me because I would not enter into a lengthy discussion on the subject. If they think they can proselyte me, I
reckon they'll find themselves coming out of the little end of
the horn. There was meeting at Getz's this morning, and one
of the inducements held out for me to go was the promise
of a good dinner. I suppose they saw how I felt when I told
them. I didn't go to meeting in order to get my dinner; it
seemed too contemptible for anything to suppose I'd go to

hear a man preach merely to get a good square meal. And I
don't care for fresh pork now, and they had roast pork for
dinner, I know, because they got a big chunk on Friday when
we butchered. Pa is fixed all right, as I dare say you will find
out when he writes, which will occur, probably, next Sunday.
We expect to begin harvesting tomorrow in earnest, and go
right ahead. There are 120 acres that we have to cut. They
charge 75 cents per acre for harvesting here.

SUNDAY, JULY 1, 1877

AT LANDES'S, OSBORNE, KANSAS

After getting through writing last Sunday, I started to
walk to town (3½ miles) to mail the letter, so it would leave
Monday morning. Going past Getz's, Joe Morrow asked
whether I intended going to town, and said it was too hot, and
that I should go and get his pony and saddle and ride. True, it
was hot, but not bad enough for all that trouble; but, nevertheless, I did as he said. . . . Monday morning we began harvesting in earnest. Our costumes are the lightest possible: straw
hat, shirt and overalls. We wear no shoes or stockings. Henry
put me to driving while he and John Sears, the owners of the
machine, bound. Had gone two rounds when a sheaf that
John had dropped opened as it touched the ground, and he
got off the machine to rebind it. In doing so he stepped directly over a rattlesnake. He called for the whip, and soon made
an end of the reptile, finishing by cutting off the head and
punching it into the ground. When I say "driving" it means
that I had to take mighty good care, because if the horses get
too close to the grain it will leave some standing, and that is
to be avoided, as well as at the corners. This last is harder to
learn than anything, because you have to enter the field at the

corner with as square a cut as possible. We got through with those 12½ acres by 10 a.m., Tuesday, and then began shocking. This was hard on my finger ends; they were pretty sore by noon. But the work was occasionally enlivened by a little fun; we chased up three young jackrabbits, and caught them too, after a pretty sharp chase; we ran them across the stubble, and they could not get away so easy as if we had run them along the drill furrows. They weighed about a pound each, dressed, and when they were fried they were not bad to eat. After dinner we went into Getz's rye, and made a cut on two sides of his east and south hedgerows, which made two miles, the hedgerows being half a mile long each. His wheat being riper than the rye, we left the latter and began on the wheat. It was steady work for 2½ days to cut the 20 acres. The wheat was very heavy, and had got rusty, which made our eyes sore, and our clothes were covered with the rust, which is of a red-brown color. We made four or five rounds with each team and changed, so as not to bring too much work on either. By the time were were done with those 20 acres, I was able to drive straight across the field. The harvester cuts a swath about four feet wide, and the wheat was so heavy that we could not take more than two or three feet at once, and then the grain was delivered on the table in front of the binders so fast that we had to stop two or three times on a side to enable them to get the table clear. The advantages a Marsh harvester has over the other machines is that when you have driven around the field, all you have to do is to follow the machine and shock the grain, while the other machines drop the grain on the ground, thus making it necessary to have four or six binders, while on the harvester only two are required, but when the grain is heavy they have all they can do. When you work for somebody in the harvest field you may count on getting No. 1 board. They set a first rate table then, and the way the good things disappear is a caution to boarding house keepers. In making the last round on Getz's wheat we got three rabbits, two of which were nearly full grown. John threw the hammer at them and struck them stiff. They don't stick them, but cut the head clean off. Got through with the wheat before noon on Friday, and after dinner went into a 4-acre piece of Sears' wheat, which was very heavy. Had a staving good supper—fried rabbits, bread and butter, onions, radishes, pie, and coffee ad libitum. Made a few rounds after supper, before sundown. Henry got me to help him bind one round, and when John wanted to take a turn binding with me and let Henry drive, the latter affirmed that it would kill a man in three hours to bind with me, because he would have such awful big bundles. But what can he expect? He did not let me bind when the grain was thin, and he cannot expect me to keep up my end when the grain is heavy, and as much as two first rate binders can do to keep the table clear. When we got to the house we found Horace was making ice cream. After putting away the team and feeding them, I went back and had about a pint of the luxury. It was as good, if not better than Ranch's, because they did not spare the eggs. The only fault they found with it was that there was not enough of it. Yesterday morning I went to work hoeing the peanuts as Horace was driving on the harvester. After dinner we went to town. I expected to get a letter, or at least some papers, but was disappointed and got neither. I suppose you directed them to Kill Creek, in which case I may not get them for a month. I don't expect to see Pa inside of that time, as I will be too busy to go up to the claim, and he will be in the same fix, most probably. This morning Schuyler was making a nuisance of himself, and stayed in my way while I was at work, in spite

of repeated warnings, till finally I hit a clip with a brush—
that settled him. But he took to crying and throwing stones,
till I warned him that he would get some more of the same
sort if he did not desist. He stopped. I have not had any
real hard work yet, notwithstanding all the talk I have heard
respecting the hard work that comes in harvest time. The
folks have all gone to meeting; they don't ask me to go with
them when they go any distance—oh, no! If I am not good
enough to go with them when they go some distance, I'll
do as I please when the meeting is near home. I would not
have got to town yesterday if I had not made it a point of
business to see Joe Morrow in relation to those $3 he owes
me. I did not expect to get the money, so I was not disappointed. Laid in a little of the "weed," as I have not yet seen
the first of that that was put in the box. Let Syd keep account
of what he spends on me, so that when I get far enough
ahead I can make it up, for I don't expect him to keep me in
tobacco or anything else. There was some talk of Huber and
Berger buying the Elmer claim for $100, but it is stated in
this week's paper that DeTuck has bought it. Wheat is worth
$1.25 a bushel now, and there is something of a crop on the
place.[16] His share of it will bring the price down to $25 or
$50. Cheap enough. I am very well satisfied with the place
I have; have made a month now. I'm getting to be a "horny-
handed granger" very fast—especially as far as the "horny-
handed" part is concerned. But what "gets me" the worst is
short wheat stubble on my bare feet and ankles. I have two
sore places on one foot now, so I guess I'll have to wear shoes
this week and get them healed up, though I'd rather go without. The shoes are somewhat better than none at all, though
they have holes so that the toes stick out, and the gum is tear-

[16] The high price of wheat at this time was due to the Russo-Turkish war.

ing out. But that is nothing. Holey shoes are common here, and it's too warm to wear whole shoes now. I got a N.Y. Sun in the office yesterday, and had a good time reading it this morning. My eyes are pretty sore from the rust which comes off of the wheat, but they will be all right as soon as we stop cutting that. The rye is not rusty. Corn looks very fine. We had a very heavy shower on Tuesday night just before midnight, and nice cool weather all the week; there were only two or three half-days when it made us sweat. I'd give $5 to see you. . . .

SUNDAY, JULY 15, 1877

At Landes's, Osborne, Kansas

Sunday night we had a shower that lasted all night and thoroughly soaked the ground, so that it was too wet to go to cutting grain next morning. I pulled weeds till noon. Henry and John went to see a selfbinder at work. They got back by noon and concluded we might go to cutting right after dinner. After fixing the machine so that we could start, we had dinner and then put off for the field. Got through cutting John's wheat on Tuesday a little before noon, and then went to Wentzler's. We caught five rabbits in John's wheat and took them along for Mrs. W. to fix for us in a pie. Tuesday night we stayed at Wentzler's, as it was pretty far to go. We were stopped during the afternoon by a pretty heavy shower, but went to cutting again after supper. Wednesday morning I heard Mrs. W. come downstairs. Presently somebody remarked: "I won't wake him." Then I knew that Pa was at the door, and I turned over and sat up. It was 20 minutes past 4. He had come down the day before. He brought me your letter of July 1st and the bottle of ginger. He reports things o.k. up on the creek. The box has arrived, but he has not yet opened it. . . . As for Bub, he will have to stay in Bethlehem till we get our house on the creek built, and that won't be till about Christmas, because I will not get away from Landes' till 1st November or perhaps till 1st December. I intend to make the house as large as I can without going to too much expense. My only expense will be the roof (shingles) and the floor and windows and door. The stone work we intend to do ourselves. The reason that a stone house costs so much is because the work is all done by a regular stone mason which drives up the price. It seems queer to me for Pa to come to me and say, "What is the plan? Shall this be done first?" I'm boss and he is hired man; it is easier for him that way. I tell him this must be done, and when that's finished, why there's something else. A man named Quigley, on Little Medicine, has three yoke of cattle for sale, and I intend to take a look at them before I buy. If I can fix it, I want to stay on my claim after I get back to it this fall. Then next spring I'll break some eight or ten acres for corn, and that can be put into small grain in the fall. I know there will be enough work for me up there next spring and until harvest to keep me in provisions, and what more do I want? I owe $1.45, but then I have $6 coming to me. . . . I tell you harvest hands get fed good. The turkeys, ducks and chickens have to furnish meat, and the gardens are drawn upon for the best they can furnish. Tell Bub to sell his coins if he can get what they cost him. There is no market for such things here, and the money he can invest in a pig or a calf or something like that, which will pay him good interest in a short time. We came home Wednesday night, but went back to W.'s before breakfast next morning, as we had a little more to cut. Finished by 10 o'clock. We got a good-sized rabbit and two little ones in this field. Pa says they got eleven in one field up the creek the other day. We are close together in comparison to what we were two months ago, but still it is 20 miles to my claim. But 20 miles is only half a day's walk, and that's not much. After dinner on Thursday I hitched up the team and went to cutting a piece of very thin wheat, and threw the sheaves loose on the ground, as Henry concluded it would not pay to bind it. I got through with it on Friday morning, and then Henry said I should bind it; that it bound first rate. But I noticed that he did but very little of that first rate binding, and if it had depended on him to do the binding, it would not have been done. But I learned to bind on that piece, which took up all of my time Friday afternoon and all of yesterday. When we get to cutting Wentzler's spring wheat tomorrow I bet I'll have to bind on the harvester. The balance of that wheat which is yet unbound will very probably remain unbound, because this next week we will have enough to keep us busy without going at that. I killed a big bull snake yesterday. It was over three feet long and about two inches through. Last evening I went to Schweitzer's to get my mail. He had not been to town, and consequently I got nothing. They put up two stacks of grain yesterday. They have four stacks, and say they will have three or four more. We talked till near 10 o'clock, and then it looked so much as though it would rain that I concluded to stay over night in preference to running the risk of getting wet going home. This morning I was out at sunrise and went down. There had been a heavy wind storm last night, and it beat the corn down to the ground at places. The only thing I don't like at this place is that when I do a job of work, Henry never says whether it is well or ill done. If he would tell me whether a thing is done right, I am sure I would feel the better for it. Today I had

a good reading spell—all day; the first time since I am in
Kansas that I got hold of something that would last. It has
been thundering pretty hard all day, but we have had no
rain. The folks went to Twin Creek to meeting. I may go
with them next Sunday, and if I do you will not get a letter
as soon as if I stayed home and wrote. I don't know where
the next meeting will be held. Maybe it will be in the neighborhood. If it is, I will write in the afternoon. You can't
imagine how I long to see you at times, especially Sundays
when I have nothing to do. . . . Remember me to anybody
who thinks me worth inquiring after, and tell them I'm not
at all discouraged or disheartened. I'd like to be at work
on the claim, but this summer's work here will teach me
more about the running of a farm than I could learn in a
year if I was to work round and make more money. That's
one reason why I took the job. Pa appears to be in better
health than he was, and the sun and wind have not made
his complexion any fairer, you bet.

SUNDAY, JULY 29, 1877

At Landes's, Osborne, Kansas

I know you will forgive me for not writing last Sunday
when you know that the reason I did not was because I went
up to Kill Creek to see Pa and get some other clothes. I
asked Henry for the horse to ride up, and he appeared to
be unwilling, and wanted me to go with somebody else; but
I was determined to go on horseback, and borrowed a saddle
of Joe Morrow, and on Sunday morning saddled up and
started. I had to walk the horse all the way, as he is a heavy
farm horse and not much account for riding. I could have
walked up in the same time I rode up, but I would have

been more tired. Got to Hoot's about noon. Pa was up at Hackerott's, and as Levin came in with a large lot of wild grapes (which Mrs. Hoot made into pie) I concluded to go to see Pa and have a talk with him. Hoot let Levin have a horse, and together we rode up the creek about 3½ miles. Found Pa; Ellie Hoot had gone with him, and as we wanted to talk, we put Ellie on my horse and she and Levin rode ahead. Pa said he had as much as he wanted to do helping the folks stack grain, etc., and seems to be very well contented and happy. Old man Gsell wanted to rent his place to Pa, but I told Pa not to think of it, because the old man wants somebody with a family to take it, and he will board with the lessee. I wouldn't have you live there in the bottom among the bedbugs, fleas and mosquitoes for any consideration. The beforementioned "animals" are quite plenty on the high prairie, but they swarm along the creeks and rivers.[17] Pa intends to get a pig or two, and Levin intends to get one; and all will be put into Hoot's pen, which will make quite a nice lot. By the time we got to Hoot's it was full time for me to start for Osborne. My blouse and the blue overalls I wrapped round the smallest box of tobacco and mounting my steed I started. When I got to Neuschwanger's I stopped a bit to talk to Barbara, and she said she'd ride along if I'd wait till her horse was saddled (Chris was going for it) as she

[17] Here Ruede expresses a common notion of Pennsylvanians who came to Kansas—that second-bottom land was a better place to build a home than the creek and river bottom land. Accustomed to hills, these Pennsylvanians often filed on the higher land, even where the more productive bottom land was still open to settlement. The summer of 1877 was a very wet summer, and even the higher land yielded fairly well; but when later dry years came, the bottom land of course produced much better crops, and the bed bugs later ceased to be a nuisance. It is true that in very early years there was some malaria in the lower lands, but for some reason this soon disappeared. The settlers from Iowa always took the level bottom land where it was available.

did not like to ride alone. I was in the same fix, so I waited. You better believe I didn't talk Dutch to her, because I found out she could talk English. One of the colts followed us, so B. turned round and ran it back. She is taking care of the housekeeping arrangements for an old widower named Eldred, about three or four miles from her old folks' home. She is just like all the other girls I know—when you get 'em started they can talk well enough. I got home about 10 o'clock by moonlight, and I was pretty hungry, too, having had nothing since noon. The folks were over at Getz's, and the house was locked, but I managed to get in and get something to eat, after which I went to bed. . . . We had a heavy shower Friday afternoon, and it came just when I wanted it to. We had got all the prairie hay stacked, and John Sears had just finished stacking when the rain came. Last Sunday I rode over 40 miles, and Monday night I rode about 5 miles in the moonlight to notify the men who were to help us thresh on Tuesday that the machine would not be at Landes. I let the horse take his own time, and stuck my hands in my pockets to keep them warm, for the dew was falling pretty fast. I woke up Ed Humphrey to tell him he was not wanted. Talked awhile then went to Morrow's. They were in bed too. And when I came past Getz's I had to rattle the door a good deal before I managed to wake them. This morning I started for town, as when I was there yesterday I heard that Steinfort intended to hold services. Had gone about half way when Mr. and Mrs. Gruger caught up with me, and I rode with them the rest of the way. Mrs. G. says she thinks she remembers you; that she remembers Aunt Addy distinctly. Mrs. Steinfort was Miss Freeland, and taught in the Boarding School for quite a long time. She is a very nice woman, and I like her pretty well, even if I have not been long acquainted. We had a very pleasant meeting, and though the Rev. Charles did not preach a regular sermon, but merely made some remarks, I enjoyed the meeting, especially the singing. Had dinner at Fritchey's and then rode home with the Gruger's. Mrs. Steinfort appears to be a very energetic woman, and talks as though we would have a church inside a couple of months. . . . Mrs. Steinfort says I shall tell you to be sure to come, and she kind of blames me for taking a claim so far from Osborne, but I tell her that if I had a team, 15 miles is nothing to drive to meeting. We will have services in the school house next Sunday. I write this at Gruger's. I began at Landes', but the young ones bothered me so I could not write as fast as I thought I could. . . . R. G. Hays expects to go to Bethlehem this coming week. I suppose you will see him with Col. Bear's folks. He has red hair and whiskers. When you come I can tell you more in half an hour than I can write in three. Yesterday I saw a monster bull team—one of the animals would weigh about 1800 lbs. It was the biggest bull I have seen since I arrived here. Well, I must talk awhile now, or I might not be as welcome another time. I didn't get a letter yesterday.

FRIDAY, AUGUST 3, 1877

AT LANDES'S, OSBORNE, KANSAS

Tired? You better believe it. We have been threshing three days, and it is no easy work. Threshing here is different from what it is in the East. The machine is put together so that the grain is fed in at one end, and the straw is carried out at the other, while the clean grain comes out at one side of the machine. The horsepower requires ten horses to run it.

Threshing machines here thresh as much as 500 or 600

bushels a day, when they do not have to travel too far between jobs, which is not often, for these machines sometimes pull ten miles between jobs, and jobs are not very big because most men's acreage is small. Some days the thresher will knock out several jobs without being much richer, even though the price is five cents a bushel where the quantity is a hundred bushels or more. When there is less than a hundred bushels it is a "set" job, and costs the grain raiser $5, besides board for the machine men and their teams and the neighbors who help.

The machine owner furnishes three teams for the power and the farmer supplies all the other teams needed as well as the helpers. Cooking for the crowd is no little work, but the woman of the house always has enough help, for on such occasions most of the men who help bring their families along, and the women folks have a real good visit while preparing the meals. . . .

When the machine pulls in to a set all the neighbors have been notified in advance—for they go with the machine while it is in the neighborhood. Every man gathers up all the sacks he owns and takes them along, for the grain being sacked when it is taken to the granary, many sacks are in use for a short time and no one man has enough for the occasion. After the rounds are made, it takes a lot of sorting to get each man's property out of the pile, often considerably the worse for wear.

A threshing crew, besides the machine men, consists of two or three pitchers, generally three. The sheaves are bound with straw bands. Three boys are put at the end of the ten-foot carrier to pitch the straw away from the machine, and it is no snap, for the straw rolls out fast enough to keep them very busy. Then there is the measure man, who sees that the grain does not slop over the edge of the half bushel measure. The grain comes out of a V-shaped sheet iron spout slipped through the wheel, between the spokes. The measure man has to keep his wits about him, to keep track of the bushels. He has a bit of board filled with gimlet holes on each side of the machine, and with little pegs keeps count of the number of bushels. There are four rows of holes, ten in a row. The upper row is for half-bushels: when the peg has been moved, a notch at a time, from the left end of the row to the right, five bushels have been tallied and the peg in the right hand end of the second row is stuck in the first hole on the left, marking five bushels. The same process is used in the other two rows of holes, only in the third row a tally stands for 50 bushels, and in the fourth for 500.

The measure man has an assistant, whose duty is to hold sacks for the grain—considered an easy job. . . . The grain hauler has an assistant too, because the granaries are small and unhandy to fill. When the bin is nearly full the sack emptier has to wriggle along on top of the pile of grain and empty the sack as best he can, which under the circumstances is no easy task.

The band cutter, an important member of the crew, stands on top of a pile of sheaves placed at the table on which the bundles are pitched. Sometimes the grain is stacked, but when it is not, two pitchers are needed in the field, to pitch the sheaves onto the wagons, and two men with a wagon each.

We had nine teams and thirteen men at work—five teams attached to the horsepower, three hauling grain from the field, and one hauling the clean grain to the granary. . . .

It took two days threshing to get all Henry's grain away, and we threshed nearly 1000 bushels altogether. The oats averaged 62 bushels per acre, and if we had not fed any from

the sheaf, it would have averaged about 70. I worked on
the straw stack, and that was hot work, and dusty, too. The
dirt got into my eyes so bad the first day that I borrowed a
pair of goggles of Horace, and they helped me so much that
I sent to town for a pair, and yesterday when we worked at
Wentzler's, they came in mighty good, for the wheat was very
smutty, and Crist, who worked on the straw stack, got blacker
than any nig—"colored man" I mean—that I ever saw. He
had a clean shirt on in the morning, but by night it was
black as a coal. You have no idea how smut will blacken a man.
It's just like charcoal. We got home by 9 o'clock awfully tired.
Fuller was nearly bitten by a rattlesnake. It was right between
his feet, and if the snake had not been blind (they are slough-
ing now), he would not have got off so easily. He killed two
yesterday. It was too hot to wear a shirt, so I pulled mine off,
and wore nothing but my blouse and overalls. The overalls
I bought here have an awful hole in the knee, and the blue
ones you mended so nicely and which I brought from the
creek the other Sunday have a hole in them also. I split them
the first time I wore them; they are too small. Sometimes
I have serious thoughts of leaving this place and going to
work on my claim. The idea with me now is to build a house
18 feet square, and roof it with cottonwood boards, and then
put sod on top of that. By making the house that size there
will be enough place for two rooms.

SUNDAY, AUGUST 5, 1877

At Landes's, Osborne, Kansas

It rained all day Friday, so I had a chance to write. I did
not work any on Friday morning on account of the rain. In
the afternoon Henry marked off a couple of "lands" for me

to plow, and yesterday I was plowing all day. Henry went off to Rooks County yesterday morning, and may be gone till next Wednesday. There were several buffalo wallows in the land I plowed yesterday morning which were partly filled with water, and you should have seen the appearance I presented when I got through with them. My feet (I was barefoot) were literally cased in mud, and the fringes on my overalls (caused by the hem being worn off) were decorated with mud beads. It was cloudy all day, but did not rain. Last night I went over to Getz's for my mail, but was informed that no mail had arrived, as the Saline was too high for trains to cross the bridge. I tell you one reason why it is not desirable for Pa to take a claim. If he puts a filing on it, he has to go to work and put up a house and get you out here directly. If he homesteads, you would have to be here inside of 6 months; a married man is required to have his family on his claim, even though he is away at work. That is a good reason for Pa's not taking a claim, is it not? And then 160 acres are enough to support six of us, when there are much larger families living on farms smaller than that in the East. As for the stove, it is still in the hands of the man who had it when I was to see it. He has said nothing to me, or I to him in regard to it, because I have not been at home for some time to stay, and then I don't need the stove—and if he don't say anything, I will not, but get a bigger one. I never was so much surprised as when I got Aunty Clauder's letter a couple of weeks ago. She tries to make me out a hero, but for the life of me I can't see anything heroic in coming out here to do farm work—do you? Isn't it very prosy when it is put into words? It is rough on Mr. Schweitzer that all the Bethlehemites go to him. Some stay a good while and never offer to pay him. I know of a couple who stayed there off and on, for about 4 weeks, and never thought it took provisions to feed them. Talk about vines! Why there is nothing in the world equal to breaking to raise watermelons, cantelopes, cucumbers, and all such vines. I know where to go for watermelons when I want them. Several folks have invited me to help them get away with their crops.

SUNDAY, AUGUST 5, 1877

At Gruger's, Osborne, Kansas

Here I am at Gruger's again. We have just got back from meeting, which was held in the schoolhouse. There was an audience of about 20 present. I don't like the Sankey songs, or, rather, the tunes, for our meetings, and told Mr. Steinfort so. Mrs. S. wanted us to go home with them. . . . There were about 80 Pottawatomie Indians here on Tuesday. The Gruger's rode in the procession to town. The Indians camped just below town, and some of the folks took Mrs. Bollinger to see them. She says she will never get done telling the old ladies about her Kansas trip. These Indians are partly civilized. They live in Jackson Co., southeast of here, among white folks, on a reservation. . . . Pa intends to fix up the dugout to live in when he has no work. I can't cut any more wood, so I intend to pay Greenfield for the breaking he did for me, and the others may settle for what he did for them. I ought to be up on the claim now, but I guess I'll have to go through the flint mill, as Pa calls the place I have. He is sorry I took the job, and so am I, but next year I won't take any such job, if I can possibly avoid it, and I think I can get enough work up there to do without. I have my plan for the house; it will be big enough. At any rate, we can live in one room about 15 feet square for a time; lots of folks have no

more room, and many haven't as much. Oh, we'll be fixed
o.k. If you can be comfortable in such a place, we may be
satisfied with it for awhile till we can sell our property in
Bethlehem and build a better house. Then I'll use this pro-
spective for a granary, or something else. Mrs. Steinfort
laments over the fact that my claim is so far from town.

WEDNESDAY, AUGUST 8, 1877

OSBORNE, KANSAS

[Postal card.] Syd, I have left Landes, and am on my
way to Kill Creek. Will work in the printing office today. Send
my mail matter to Kill Creek hereafter. We intend to fix
up the dugout and then go at the stone house.

SUNDAY, AUGUST 12, 1877

AT GSELL'S, KILL CREEK, KANSAS

I am back to the Creek again. This is Sunday morning, and
I had intended going to Lapp's, but we had a heavy shower
last night, and that swelled the creek so we could not get
across. The way I came to leave Landes was this: I have not
been satisfied to work there ever since Pa came out, and when
he came down on Sunday we had a long talk and again on
Monday night, all of which had the result of making me
finally conclude to leave, whether or no. Pa wanted me, and
I wanted to go to work on my claim, and I told Henry so
on Tuesday night when he came home from Rooks Co.,
where he had been to meeting since Saturday morning. He
concluded that he couldn't let me go till he got another hand,
and I told him I'd stay till Saturday (yesterday). On Wednesday morning at breakfast he said I might go then if I

wished to: I took him at his word and left. For pay I got three acres of breaking and 11½ bushels of wheat, and $5 in money. He evidently thought it was not enough and was a bit ashamed, for he threw in 4 bushels of rye afterwards. When I got to town, I went to the printing office for some papers, and Barnhart offered me a day's work. I took him up, because I had only about 50 cents in my pocket. I cleared 90 cents by the day's work. Thursday I looked for a Kill Creek team till noon, and then started off on foot. The river was up, and I had to pay a dime to be ferried across. Got to Neuschwanger's about supper time. They were busy threshing. Jim and Levin were helping. I was invited to supper, and of course accepted. There was not much variety, but there was plenty of what there was, and I enjoyed it. Directly I put off for Jakey Gsell's where Pa was staying. There I found Messrs Brunner and Albright and Theo. Vogel, so that now there are eight of us who sleep here. Jim and Levin always come here to sleep.

Jakey Gsell's house is of a composite style of architecture, one half of it being log 14 feet square, and the other half stone 14 by 16 feet, only one story and with a dirt roof. Before we arranged to stop with him he lived in the log part, and used the other as a brooder room for about a hundred little "pee-pees," as he calls his pets—a flock of chickens; but when he decided on opening a "hotel" he had to banish the fowls. All of us who stay with him contribute to a common stock of provisions. Jakey has a six-year old heifer, a few pigs and a lot of chickens, and furnishes the eggs and milk for the crowd, in addition to the bread, which a neighbor woman bakes. Every Saturday night Jakey bestrides his "colt" and brings the bread home. The bread baking is done on the cooperative plan, thus: Jakey furnishes the wheat and a neighbor Shellenberger hauls it to mill at Bull's City, bringing the flour home and receiving the bran and shorts for so doing; then his wife, who is a fine baker, turns the flour into bread, her share of the proceeds being one-third of the product. Jakey is asthmatic and deaf as a post, but he dearly loves company and willingly gives room to anybody who will stay with him.

How do you suppose Jakey Gsell can accommodate such a bunch of men over night when he has only one bed in the house? He wants to sleep in it himself, and if anyone could sleep with him, wheezing and snoring like a house afire, he ought to be as deaf as old Jakey himself. There is only one who is able to do the trick—old Mr. Brunner. . . .

The rest of us have improvised a bed by bringing a few bundles of sheaf rye across the creek and spreading in one end of the stone house, covering the straw with bed quilts, and making a very comfortable place to lie. Of course, it is not luxurious or downy, but tired men don't lie awake long, and aren't we roughing it only temporarily? The bed is easily disposed of when we turn out in the morning; we just take a fork and shove the straw into one corner. To make the bed the operation is reversed. When the straw crumbles, there is more to be had for the fetching.

The principal groceries we furnish the old gentleman in return for his contributions of green corn, potatoes, bread and milk, are coal oil at 35 cents a gallon, sugar—heavy brown sugar at that—costing 18 cents a pound, and plug tobacco at 60 cents a pound. Meat is the hardest of our supplies to get. Bacon costs 10 cents a pound, and at that price is easier to get than the necessary ten cents with which to make the purchase. So we are often vegetarians perforce, unless Mr. Brunner, who has his fowling piece with him, is fortunate enough to shoot a cottontail of an evening about sundown. This does not happen often, and even when we have a rabbit, it hardly makes a bite apiece among so many.

Jakey's cow is a "self milker." Her nose has been pierced and a stick sharpened at both ends thrust through the opening to prevent her stealing the milk we want, but sometimes she manages to slip the stick out and then we are minus milk for our coffee. When we want butter, which is seldom, we have to go to the neighbors for it, as there is no churn in Jakey's outfit.

Last night while we were all asleep in our nest, a heavy rain came and the old sod roof, which was all right in a dry time, began to leak, and in a few minutes the water was dripping on us to such an extent that to lie there longer meant that we might as well jump into the creek and expect to remain dry. Fortunately morning soon came, and then the clouds rolled away and today is a lovely Sunday, but nobody can get across the creek to go to meeting.

You may publish as much of my letters as you see fit. Syd, what would you be willing to pay per month to get Bub out of the way at home? Sealed proposals will be received at Kill Creek P.O. for the next 30 days. On Friday morning Pa and I went up to the ruins of the dugout, and after taking a good look at it we concluded that—(we have just got through eating a lot of watermelons, and none of them were fully ripe, but they were good)—it was too much fallen in to fix up, so we spent nearly the entire morning looking for a site for another dugout in which to live till we can get our stone residence ready for occupancy. We settled on a place near the southwest corner, and after our dinner began at it. It will be 14 x 16 inside, as that is the largest we can make it and use the ridge pole we already have. By Saturday night we had uncovered the entire surface, and made quite an excavation in one corner. In front (east) the sod will be 4 feet high, and behind it will be 2 feet—the rest will be under ground. We will have put this place together better than the other. The edges will not be so likely to fall in so easy as the old dugout, as they are cut in a tough buffalo sod. If we feel good for work tomorrow, and it is not too hot, we will get through digging, and then we will have to get somebody to break a lot of sod for us so that we can go to building as soon as the hay is made. Hoot will cut for us on Tuesday, and the stacking will be done by Wednesday night. We make it on Gsell's place and get ⅔ of the hay. I want that dugout finished as soon as possible, so that we can go into it. Then we must bore for water and dig a well. I will not build before I get water, because I don't want to be forced to haul water like Mr. Schweitzer. The creek rises very fast—as much as 6 inches per hour—and if it does not fall till tomorrow morning we can't work on the dugout. Levin and The. made themselves pipebowls of the stone which is so plenty round here, and then went up the creek a piece for some box elder, of which they made the stems. They finished them off right neatly. The folks at the camp meeting down the creek at Wismer's are supposed to be blockaded by the high water. When the new dugout is finished I want Bub to come out, because there is a prospect for my getting a couple of months' work in the printing office this fall, and I don't want Pa to be left alone; he will get the same way he was at the mines. Then, too, it will not cost so much to keep Bub if he is here as it will in Bethlehem, and he will have a chance to earn something once in a while. Don't let him build too much on that, for it may be some time before the house is finished. I want to get it finished as soon as possible, so as to get away from Gsell's and on my claim.

It will probably take a week or two to get fixed, get a stove, etc. so as to be ready to live in the dugout. Here at the old man's we (7 of us) sleep in one bed; that is, we throw down a pile of straw and cover it with coats, quilts, etc., and that makes a good bed for us. Jim has hired out for a month to Blair, at the P.O. The corn that Pa and the boys planted on the three acres that Greenfield broke for me looks nice, but it will hardly make corn, though it will most probably make fodder. In about three weeks I will have a week's work in the office. That will be a good help to me. I don't intend to go to the office for less than three days' work at a time. Eugene Brunner, with Smith and Weaver, went back to Russell, where Smith bought a claim. I understand that Weaver intended going back east, and Eugene also thought of it. The creek rose till the middle of the afternoon, and then did not show any signs of going down. This morning I fried three rabbits that Mr. Brunner shot last evening. I had no lid to cover the spider with, and the meat was not thoroughly cooked, but we were all so hungry for meat that that did not prevent our eating it. That was the first meat I had since Tuesday. Butter, eggs and bacon are scarce. Butter can't be had for less than 10 cents a pound, and is hard to get for that price. The camp meeting is what makes butter and eggs so scarce.

MONDAY, AUGUST 13, 1877

At Gsell's, Kill Creek, Kansas

Didn't get to work at digging till near 10 o'clock, because we stopped at Hoot's to get a loaf of bread, and afterwards at Snyder's to see if we could get butter, and were gladdened by the information that we could get a couple of pounds every week if we desired. At noon Pa went to see Henry in regard to cutting grass this afternoon, so I was left alone to eat my dinner of bread and butter and water, as well as to dig alone. Quit digging about 5, and on the way to Gsell's took the butter from Snyder's. Levin made some griddle cakes, which were a welcome addition to the meal. When I went to call Pa to supper I crossed the creek on a new foot log. The bank was very slippery, but I managed to get across. But when we were coming back, I attempted to recross, and had gone only about two feet on the log when my shoes, which were full of sticky, slippery mud, gave way, and I was the victim of an involuntary bath in Kill Creek. I tumbled right over and got completely soaked, with the exception of my right shirt sleeve. Luckily the water was warm, and as I changed clothing immediately, I only suffered a little inconvenience. The bath did not hurt me. I put a brown patch on my overalls to cover that hole. It didn't matter what color patches are, but I am afraid that putting a new patch on an old garment will make the rent worse. Make me three colored shirts, and charge it to me. I don't know now when I can pay you, but—what's the use of promising. Make the shirts to open in front.

TUESDAY, AUGUST 14, 1877

AT GSELL'S, KILL CREEK, KANSAS

Up a little before sunrise, and fixed the potatoes and corn for breakfast. We live principally on roasting ears, potatoes and bread, with now and then a mess of fried eggs. . . . We had potatoes, corn, bread and butter and coffee. About 9 o'clock the dew was pretty well dried off, and so I went over to Greenfield's to get a horse and the hay rake. I sat at the well about an hour before he came from camp meeting, and

just as he drove up Pa arrived. I suppose he thought I had
got lost, so he came to look for me. I wanted to throw up
my part of the wood chopping and pay for the breaking he
did for me, but he refused to let me off, so I'll have to chop
nine cords of wood, and build my dugout, besides helping
Hoot a little if he wants me—all before the 1st of September.
Went to raking up the hay, and by night had it all raked
and "bunched"—that is, raked into piles. Took the rake home
and asked what his bill was. We had the outfit about ¾ day.
He wanted to put me off by saying, "Oh, we'll fix that some
time," but I told him that's not business, and he finally settled for 50 cents. Mr. Albright was cook today. We were
hightoned as regards supper. When we got up from table
it was quarter to nine. Old Don Pedro, as the boys christened
Jacob, had not put in his appearance, so I had to do the milking. When he came back we tried to make him believe the
cow was not yet milked, but he said, "Oh, I knew he (pointing
at me) could milk and wouldn't let the cow go unmilked."
Mr. Brunner has had two days' work for Lapp, and has some
prospect of having to help with Rupert's house this fall. My
eyes bothered me a little tonight, and as we have no shade
on the lamp, I put on my goggles, which helped me a good
deal. Pa makes up the bed with the pitchfork—a rather easy
way, isn't it? Mrs. Hoot succeeded in getting my clothes into
good order, but the shirts are ruined. They are stained badly.
The overcoat was in the mud only with one of the skirts,
and she didn't have to tend to that. . . .

WEDNESDAY, AUGUST 15, 1877

AT GSELL's, KILL CREEK, KANSAS

Today I had a hard day's work with pick and shovel, finishing digging, but did not get quite through. Towards evening

I uncovered the old dugout, and got the covering material— boards, rafters, etc.—together so it can be easily loaded and hauled to the place where we are building. Rook helped Pa haul hay and stack it, and had intended to break sod for the dugout this evening, but did not get through hauling hay. Pa estimates that our ⅔ of the hay will be about three tons. Rook offered to plow the ground and put in my fall grain. I guess I'll wait a little—maybe I'll get a team in time for sowing. I want that brown coat that I used to wear to the office; in spite of the mending it is infinitely more respectable than the one I have now, which is getting very shabby and torn up.

THURSDAY, AUGUST 16, 1877

AT GSELL'S, KILL CREEK, KANSAS

This was a showery day, though not much rain fell. Finished digging out the ground, and by that time Rook had finished breaking sod; so we all went to the old dugout to fetch the lumber, etc. By the time that was transferred it was noon. I had my dinner with me, but Pa had not. After stowing away my provisions, I went to Blair's to see if I could get his wheelbarrow for a couple of days. They would not lend it, so I had to go back without it. About 3 o'clock I was played out. Concluded to go to Don Pedro's and rest. Hoot came past with his wagon, so I rode with him. This evening Mr. Brunner shot a rabbit. I have not had a mouthful of any kind of meat since Sunday morning, and as I have a chance to go to town tomorrow I'll have to lose a day's work—but meat I must have, or I can't work. And I want to get those letters and papers that are in the Osborne P.O. for me. The way I put the corn and potatoes away this evening was a caution to dyspeptics. The dog did not fall in for much of the corn tonight. The hay is all stacked now, and I'm glad, because Pa can be with me at the dugout. If there is anything I hate, it is to have to work alone—without a human being or animal in sight.

FRIDAY, AUGUST 17, 1877

At Gsell's, Kill Creek, Kansas

Up pretty early and went to Hoot's, as I had heard that he and Rupert intended going to town, and I wanted to go to get some meat, if it could be obtained. But I found he had left word he would not go, as he was afraid the river was too high to cross, but he would certainly go tomorrow. So I had to retrace my steps in order to let Pa know, and get some more to eat, as I had not eaten enough to last me all day if I worked. Mr. Brunner had the good fortune to shoot a couple of rabbits, and that little meat set us up wonderfully. In going to the dugout (2 miles) our shoes got wet through; the dew was so heavy. We made first rate progress laying up sod, and hated to quit work, but as Levin was boring for water I thought I'd have to cook supper, so we quit at 5 o'clock. When we got to the house we found the men were all ahead of us.

SATURDAY, AUGUST 18, 1877

At Gsell's, Kill Creek, Kansas

Up a good while before 5, and after breakfast fixed up in my "good rags," and then we went up to Hoot's, where, after waiting a little, we got on board Rupert's wagon and after an uneventful ride reached town a little before noon. I immediately went to the P.O. and received your letters of the

5th. . . . As for borrowing $600, or any other sum, Syd, to be used by me to improve my claim, it is of no use to think of it. I will not go in debt for 1 cent. You would like it here, I have no doubt. If you were to come here on a visit next spring, it would cost you not less than $75 in cash, and what would Ma do if you were to leave? She couldn't earn her living, and so that thing must not be thought of till I am ready for you all, and that will not be till at least a year from now. So make up your mind to be contented and work along, always being careful to be on the right side of the old man till I am ready for the family—then I don't care, and it don't matter so much if you do get discharged. In regard to hunting and fishing, there is nothing of the latter; of the former there is a good deal in the rabbit line. Don't send Pa any money to buy pigs; he has enough coming to him to get a couple without any help. He has made about 30 days' work since he arrived, and did not hurt himself either. We bought a hatchet ($1), an axe ($1.50), 1 lb. coffee (35¢), pound of tobacco for the old man, and a couple boxes of matches. I had dinner at Fritchey's, and Pa was at Steinforts. About 4 o'clock we went to Gruger's, and as they were at Dewey's, helping to thresh, we went there for our supper. Got acquainted with Mrs. John Dewey; she has been afflicted with paralysis for the last 6 years. About dark we got back to Gruger's. Getz's had bad luck. There was a heavy rain and hail storm round here Thursday, and the water in the ravines got up so high that a lot of their chickens were drowned. This evening they burned their straw pile. That's the way the folks get rid of their straw here. On Twin Creek the storm on Thursday cut up the entire corn crop for some men. Some of the hail stones were bigger than hen's eggs. We on Kill Creek saw the storm, but it did not get to us. About 2½ miles west of town we noticed a cornfield that was pretty badly used up by the hail. I would like to be with you for the next 24 hours; maybe I couldn't talk Kansas! Tomorrow we expect to effect an organization of the church members, but I am afraid it will be no go, as some are disaffected.

SATURDAY, AUGUST 25, 1877

OSBORNE, KANSAS

[Postal card.] Was in town today to get a stove, and a lot of other things, but could get no team, so did not buy what I wanted. Could have got Steinfort's team, but he was not very willing to let me have it, and I would have had to bring it back this evening and walk up to the Creek, so I did not get it. Got your letter of the 12th, which was in the P.O. a week. The dugout is finished. Send Bub with H. Weinland. I will write instructions and send them with the mail from the Creek on Saturday next.

SUNDAY, AUGUST 26, 1877

AT GSELL'S, KILL CREEK, KANSAS

You have received the postal in regard to Bub's coming, the first chance he gets, with some one with whom you are willing to trust him. Yesterday I was to town to get our housekeeping goods. At dinner time not having found a team (waited till near 1 o'clock) going up the creek, I went to Steinfort and asked him to hire me his mule team. He hemmed and hawed, but finally, after dinner, said that if I could not get a team by the time my things were ready, I might have his team. So I went in and bought a number 8 cook stove and outfit for $24.25. The regular price was $25, but he took off 75¢ because

I paid cash. I'll give the inventory after I get it down, before the end of this letter is reached, so I'll go on with the story. Got the team and loaded up, and about 4 o'clock started for the Creek.

TUESDAY, AUGUST 28, 1877

At the Dugout, Kill Creek, Kansas

Hurrah!! we moved into the dugout this morning! Heiser was on his way to mill at Bull City, and he brought our goods from Gsell's. The dugout looks pretty large; in fact, it is pretty fair sized for a dugout. It is 14 x 16 inside, and nearly 8 feet high in the middle. The sod roof is pretty heavy, but is not thick enough yet. We intend to put on hay and ground yet, and then we think it will shed all the rain. If the rain gets through a sod roof it makes things all dirty by carrying with it some of the dirt from the roof; but it is not often that the water soaks through. I dug some potatoes out of my patch. Nobody need tell me now that the upland is worth little for raising potatoes, as I got some that weighed over a pound apiece, and would make enough for a meal for two. I took inventory this morning, and give it for your benefit: (It's awful hot, and the sweat runs off of me, and some of the drops wet the paper; so if you can't read it, you'll know the reason.) Stove, tin wash boiler, 2 iron pots, teakettle, 2 spiders, 3 griddles, 3 bread pans, 2 tin plates, a steamer, coffee pot, coal oil can, gridiron, 4 tincups, wash basin, pepper box, and 2 lb. nails for $25.40. . . . Then I got ½ dozen knives and forks, and a dozen spoons, which amounted to $2.35; lamp and chimney, 75¢; bucket, 25¢; salt, 10¢; rice, 25¢; ½ dozen china plates, 85¢; 2 bowls, 24¢; 2 store boxes, $1; sugar 25¢; soap, 25¢; coffee,

35¢; coal oil, 20¢; I forgot baking soda and a dish pan, which will have to be bought the next time I go to town—next week. This week I must chop wood for Greenfield. The "Harmony," as you delight to call the partnership, has ceased to exist for at least a month. When the boys began to earn something for themselves, I saw they did not want me to have any benefit of it, so I told them I was going out of the partnership. I took what I had bought and left the balance for Jim, who had paid for them.

WEDNESDAY, AUGUST 29, 1877

AT THE DUGOUT, KILL CREEK, KANSAS

Yesterday Heiser went to mill and brought us 100 lbs. flour. Then we went to the woods to cut some for Greenfield. Worked awhile and then came back. Pa went to see if Mrs. Hoot could let us have bread, and while he was gone I tried my hand at biscuits, and succeeded, very much to our satisfaction. It was good I made the biscuit, for Pa came back without bread. For supper we had steamed potatoes, hot biscuit, a few roasting ears I managed to secure in my patch, and coffee. It was about 9 o'clock when we had supper. Tried sleeping out on the prairie. Mosquitoes awful bad. Rolled round for a couple of hours, and then went into the dugout and managed to catch about 5 hours sleep. Turned out about 5, and after seeing that the fire was all right we went to the well on Hoot's place and took a good wash. Then came home and made more biscuit, so that we'd have enough for breakfast and dinner, after which we took our axes and put off for the woods. By 10 we had a cord of wood piled up (including what we cut last evening), and then we came home. Come to think of it, Bub had better stop at the Russell House in Russell, and if he can't get a chance to ride with a freighter to the Creek, he had better wait for Babcock, because if he goes to Osborne it will only make additional expense to get his trunks or box up to the claim; we can get Babcock to bring it up. It is right on his road to Bull City. Pa complains about his stomach, and thinks he has got the "pepsy," but I reckon he can pull through. Don't worry, because it is not much.

THURSDAY, AUGUST 30, 1877

At the Dugout, Kill Creek, Kansas

Up by sunrise, and after breakfast went to chopping again. We made our breakfast on bread and butter and coffee, but we find that it costs too much to eat light bread. Flour at $3 per cwt. and baking at 5¢ per loaf (40 loaves to the cwt.) makes the bread cost about 12½ cents per loaf, and we eat a loaf at a meal. Now with 3 tincups of flour (about a pound) and a little butter I can make enough biscuit to last three meals—so that we expect to make biscuit a standard. About 10 we quit chopping, and I came home to bake, while Pa went to Hall's, about 2 miles from our place, to try to get eggs. That was the last I saw of him till 2 p.m., when he presented himself with 3 dozen eggs. I don't know which I was most glad to see—him or the eggs. We cut a big oak nearly through, and then the wind blew it into the creek. That disheartened Pa, who said we'd beg off cutting at any price. I gave him $8, and he went to see Greenfield. This chopping is not the most pleasant occupation when the weather is so hot. We have two cords cut. . . . I write this while waiting for the water to boil in order to make coffee. It's getting dark, so I'll quit writing and take a smoke before supper. It is generally 8 or 9 o'clock by the time supper is ready.

[Later.] Pa came home with the welcome news that we need not cut more wood, but could work out the $9 some other way; but we will forfeit the wood already cut.

FRIDAY, AUGUST 31, 1877

AT THE DUGOUT, KILL CREEK, KANSAS

Started for Osborne at 6:15. At old Neuschwanger's had to go in and eat a melon, and was then allowed to go. Arrived in Osborne at 10:30 and had hardly got into the office before Barnhart offered me 50¢ to work off the edition for him. Told him all right, and had it off by noon. Took dinner at Keever's (25¢). The hottest weather this week was 108° in the shade and 128° in the sun. Can you beat that? I am going to tend a couple of masons in Osborne next week at $1.25 a day.

SATURDAY, SEPTEMBER 8, 1877

AT THE DUGOUT, KILL CREEK, KANSAS

Pa finished his letter yesterday afternoon. That was all he did after dinner. I finished the sod house for the potatoes, and then it was time to make supper. Sometime ago Pa and I agreed to take turns in writing, each to write his letter, but in alternate weeks, so that the news would be regularly forwarded and not two letters one week and none the next. This is my week. Pa uses my gold pen exclusively. He says his is too hard. Last night I went to the P.O. after supper, as the mail from Bull City comes in on Friday nights. When I got to the P.O. the mail carrier had not arrived, and that made the P.M. grumble not a little. About dark the mail came in, and I anxiously watched the old man (the p.m. is 72) sort out the various papers and letters from the lot of loose mail matter in the bag. There was a Times for me, which was all I expected. Put it in my cap and made tracks for home, a mile north, across the prairie. The supervisor was at the P.O. and informed me he wanted me to work on the road on Monday and Tuesday. That is to pay my poll tax. We are to work on the section road that is my southern boundary line. This afternoon it is raining, so I have a chance to write. This morning before breakfast Pa went to Hoot's for a loaf of bread, as Mrs. H. had told him she intended to bake yesterday. He came back without the bread because Mrs. Hoot had been called on to cook for Rook, who had a lot of threshers at his place. Pa brought word that Rook wanted both of us to work today, so directly after breakfast we went down to see about it. The result was that he stayed and I came back home and washed a couple of towels and baked a lot of biscuit, and then it was dinner time. The way I make biscuit is: 3 cups of flour, enough water to make a stiff dough, a lump of butter as big as a walnut, and a teaspoonful of salt. On Tuesday I was over at Snyder's for butter (15¢ per lb.) and got a cupful of buttermilk, which made better biscuit than water does. And I don't believe that I ever regretted so much that I hadn't a revolver, because there, not ten feet from me, sat a rabbit that would have made a splendid dinner for us. There were no stones handy, so I threw my pocket knife at the varmint, but only succeeded in frightening it. . . .[18] Told Pa to give you a description of the ranch, but he neglected doing so, so I will try. We made it 14 x 16 feet inside, digging into the ground on the west side to the depth of about

[18] In several places Ruede tells of getting so near to rabbits as to be able to kill them with almost any missile. It appears that rabbits were much less afraid of men than they later learned to be. This is of course the history of most wild animals and birds.

3 feet, and in front (east) about 20 inches. The doorway runs out on a level with the bottom of the draw in front of the house. Then we built up with sod, so that under the eaves, inside, the height is about 6 feet. In the middle, from the top of the ridgepole to the floor is a little more than 7 feet. The roof is pretty heavy. First come 6 pair of rafters, on which we nailed all the boards we could get together, filling out the vacant spaces between them with round sticks and sunflower stalks. On this we put a layer of hay, and sod on top of the hay. When the sod was all on, a layer of ground was thrown on the roof, and leveled; then about an inch of long grass was put on like thatch, and then two inches of fine ground thrown on, and the building was completed. The interior is arranged as follows: 1, door; 2, window; 3, a pile of potatoes; 4, stove; 5, boilers, etc.; 6, the trunks; 7, sack of flour; 8, 9, valises; 10, bed; 11, Pa's box, on top of which is a store box converted into a cupboard. Pa spent about 4 days banking up the north, west, and south sides of the house, finishing them off on top with nicely raked ground, so that, if the weeds do not come too thick, we may perhaps make a garden on the south side of the house.

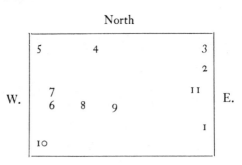

SUNDAY, SEPTEMBER 9, 1877

At the Dugout, Kill Creek, Kansas

As usual, we were up by sunrise. After breakfast Pa went out for a walk, and when he came back we started for Shellenberger's, where Bishop Neuschwanger held forth to a small audience. We did not stay to dinner, but rode with Hoot as far as Lapp's, where we were invited to stay to dinner. Accepted the invitation, as a matter of course. About 3 o'clock we went to where Lapp is building and had a couple of watermelons, and when we left he loaded us with half a dozen muskmelons and a handkerchief full of tomatoes, for all of which we were very thankful, though it was no handy thing to carry so much truck on our arms over a mile. Morris has about one day's plowing to do yet, and expects to have 20 acres of wheat sowed by next Sunday. We have lots of these black crickets in the dugout, but I don't expect they will do any damage. There is also a little toad living with us, and it is really an interesting sight to see the "baste" climb up the sod walls. It tried to do so this morning, but fell back when about half way up. We revel in roasting ears off that piece of sod corn that Pa planted after he got here. There is a good deal of sweet corn in it, I believe. I intend to draw a map of the neighborhood so you can see how the different claims lie, and to whom they belong.

MONDAY, SEPTEMBER 10, 1877

At the Dugout, Kill Creek, Kansas

According to request (he did not order me to come to work on the road) I was at the appointed place before 8 o'clock and waited for the supervisor to put in his appearance, but as he was rather slow about coming I went up to Mrs. Hoot and asked her to take a loaf of bread along for me when she went up to their claim to give the threshers their dinner. She informed me that she intended to take possession of my house for the day, as it was too far for the threshers to go a mile for their grub. I had walked that mile through the grass, and as the dew was very heavy and the grass high, I was wet through up to the knees. And my feet felt as though water had been poured into my shoes. I gave her the key; and after loafing round for about half an hour Morris came along with his team. We waited a good while, and then drove down the road. On the way back Greenfield notified me that he wished me to begin stripping sorghum as soon as possible. Told him I had two days' work on the road before I could do anything else. We were finally relieved from our suspense, about 10 o'clock, by Supervisor Taylor putting in his appearance. We chopped down a tree and shoveled a wheelbarrow load of ground, and then went down to the creek to try to fix a ford. The rest of the time before dinner was occupied in getting out drift wood in order to lower the level of the water in the creek. They got back from dinner about 1:30, and then we hauled a few loads of stone, getting through the days work before 5 o'clock. On the way home I stopped at Snyder's for butter, for which I had to pay 18 cts per lb. Butter has advanced in price. Pa had helped finish Rook's threshing, and finished out the day helping Hoot. When I got to the house the supper dishes were nearly all washed, but I got something to eat, at any rate. Old Mrs. Neuschwanger admired the stove, and Mrs. Snyder thought the house was very nice. When Mrs. Hoot left she told me I had to cook breakfast for the men,—she had left provisions enough.

TUESDAY, SEPTEMBER 11, 1877

At the Dugout, Kill Creek, Kansas

This morning I thought, after I had fried the potatoes and heated the beans, that I had not enough for 8 men, but that was all there was, and they managed to make out on it. Mr. Lapp mentioned that he was going to Russell on Thursday, so we instructed him to look out for Bub. He promised to do so. Your letter received last night, was duly appreciated, and I do believe if you happened to miss a mail day Pa would feel it very much. He is always more cheerful on Monday nights, when we read the letters, than any other night in the week, though he never is "blue" or apparently discouraged. He helped finish Hoot's threshing this morning, and then went to Guyer's to cut sorghum. That name is pronounced as though it was spelled Gweer. It is a Swiss name. Levin and I put in a day on the road. We did as Taylor said; "Do not work too hard." Pa did not get home till 8 o'clock.

WEDNESDAY, SEPTEMBER 12, 1877

At the Dugout, Kill Creek, Kansas

Turned out before 5 and went to Greenfield's, arriving there at 6 or a little after. After breakfast (when you go out to work, here, you generally get three meals) we loaded the cane mill on the wagon; that was a job, for the mill weighs 1400, and it was all that three men and Mrs. G. wanted to do to get the thing on the wagon. When that job was done, I was instructed by Greenfield how to strip the leaves from the sorghum. It consists in breaking the leaves from the standing cane with a hay fork, and goes pretty fast; but you can't get the leaves all off, because the cane is very tall—some will measure 10 to 14 feet from the ground to the top of the seed plume. This afternoon we got thirsty (Charley Stevens was at work with me) and as the water was not handy, Charley went and got a watermelon which, though not by any means ripe, we stowed away. It quenched our thirst, at any rate. I got entirely off the road coming across the prairie this evening. It was twilight, and I had been looking round for a road to avoid the draw, and in so doing I missed my nearest road. By good luck I met Pa, who was on his way home from Shellenberger's where he had been helping thresh. He thinks this was the last day for him at that business for this season. Greenfield wanted me to stay all night, but I knew Pa would come down in the morning, so I came up this evening to tell him he is not wanted, and so saved him the trouble of walking six miles. It is three miles from here to Greenfield's.

THURSDAY, SEPTEMBER 13, 1877

AT THE DUGOUT, KILL CREEK, KANSAS

Arrived at Greenfield's about 15 minutes before breakfast was ready, and then learned that I would have to go to Williams' to help thresh. I wished then that I had brought my goggles with me, but as I had not, I was obliged to do without, and this evening my eyes are all bloodshot in consequence. But I must write anyhow. Pa had a very bad night last night, but this evening, after resting all day, he feels well again. He will most probably rest all day tomorrow, so that he can take my place on Saturday, when I expect to go to Osborne for my grain at Landes'. After breakfast I shouldered the fork and walked to Williams', a mile east of Greenfield's. I had a tolerably soft snap, measuring. First we threshed a stack of "hay" as Heiser designated the millet. The result was 10½ bushels of seed. The millet had been cut before it was fully ripe, or there would have been 10 or 15 bu. of seed more. This was a decidedly soft thing, for the seed being so very small, it took a long time to fill the half-bushel. Then we threshed 51 bushels of rye, which came out very fast and kept me busy. After the rye was threshed we moved the machine, and by that time dinner was ready. They set a good table for us—chicken, potatoes, baked beans, cabbage, beets, tomatoes, coffee, etc., and it disappeared in short order. After allowing the horses time enough to eat, a stack of tangled wheat and sunflower stalks was threshed, turning out 21 bu. of rather poor grain and broken-up sunflower stalks. If the latter had been cleaned out, there would have been about 5 bushels of them. The machine men grumbled a good deal about the bad condition of the stack. The next stack—a rather small one of Jerusalem wheat—panned out well (28 bu.) and kept me very busy measuring, as did also the stack of Rio Grande, which made 31 bu. The Jerusalem wheat is the prettiest red spring wheat I have seen, and if I can get the ground ready in the spring I will sow a few acres. Williams averaged 20 bushels of spring wheat per acre. He sowed one bushel per acre. We had no fall wheat.[19] After supper I rode a short distance with Heiser, and then walked the rest of the way home. At Greenfield's they were all busy at the cane mill and evaporator. Got home before dark, and after waiting took a good wash, and here I sit in a very primitive costume—shirt and cap—no pants—writing. Who says we are not independent? (at least as regards dress,) but then we don't have many visitors, and those who do come, come in the day time.

[19] Some of the farmers in the new country were already turning to fall or winter wheat, and within a very few years almost all were sowing it.

FRIDAY, SEPTEMBER 14, 1877

At the Dugout, Kill Creek, Kansas

We had a little rain just before sunrise; barely enough
to wet the dust, but still enough to make my shoes wet
through by tramping a mile through the grass, which I have
to do before reaching the nearest traveled road. They talk
about being poor, and "making every edge cut," but when it
goes to topping cane (cutting off the seed) they just bend
the stalk down, and then one clip with a corn knife finishes
the business. The seed is not thought to be worthy of any
trouble—though when ground up into feed it sells for 80¢
per cwt. The stripping and topping of the cane is done where
the cane grows, before it is cut down. This last operation is
performed when the wagon comes for the cane. I was topping
nearly all day. We had some new molasses for dinner, and
I tell you it was good. Oh, I should have said "they was
good." Here molasses is a plural noun, and the article is
generally designated as "them molasses." Pa is all right again.
He will have work at Greenfield's all next week. We can
earn our board and enough sweet stuff to last us a year, besides paying those $9 I owe Greenfield for breaking. Came
round by the P.O. this evening, going a mile further than
if I had come directly home—only to find the mail had not
yet come in. I was disappointed for I wanted the Times that
generally comes via Bull City. Tomorrow I am going to
Osborne, hire a team, and bring my wheat from Landes'. If
I hire a team down there I'll have to take it back Sunday
morning. Then I'll take Bub along (if he arrives tomorrow
night) so that he can see how that important "city" looks.
Will drop a postal on Monday night which will most probably
reach you about Tuesday a week, if Bub arrives. He will
probably have something to say in next week's letter. I wanted

some chewing tobacco last night, but I can't go 10 or 15 cents for it when I can't get money for my work. Pa has just got through supper (8:15) and is washing up his plate, knife and fork. Now he threw the water out. Remember us to Aunty and Uncle Clauder, Aunt Addie and the girls.

SUNDAY, SEPTEMBER 23, 1877

At the Dugout, Kill Creek, Kansas

I will begin where I left off in my last letter, so here goes: Saturday morning I went by the P.O. to see if there wasn't a paper for me, and also to mail the letter. The mail carrier had not yet arrived, on his way to the railroad, so I started for town, stopping on the way at Greenfield's to give the key to Pa. Arrived in town before 11 o'clock, and after looking in vain for a team from the Creek to take my grain from Henry's home for me, I went to Joe Morrow, but his team was busy. Then to Ch. Herzog, and upon asking for his team, was informed he had sold it. So I was fast. Presently Jake Guyer drove in with a load for August Vogt, and I applied to him to take my wheat along; but he refused, for the reason that his team was in poor condition, and he would not haul a load both ways. Got ⅔ of a box of herring at Fritchey's for 50¢ and a couple of other little trifles—one of which was sugar, a very costly luxury, but one which Pa will not be without. It costs about 18¢ per lb. Well, I sat round a little while and then started for Schweitzer's, thinking that perhaps I might get his team. Just as I had made up my mind, Wils. Berger drove up in a buggy, and I hailed him to know where he was bound for. He said he was going to Morrow's, so I rode with him, and we arrived just after Nora had washed the dishes, but she fixed up a dinner for us. Then

I went directly to Schweitzer's, stopping at Getz's on the way just long enough to say "howdye"; Mr. S. was busy sowing rye, and had both teams going but I asked him nevertheless; he couldn't spare the horses, but if Monroe was willing, he might have the team and bring up my grain next day. He was willing, so I turned and went to town for 8 sacks to put the grain in, and then walked to Landes', and found only Mary and the children, Henry being in Russell County at work. But I got my grain all sacked—11½ bu. wheat and 4 bu. rye, and then we had supper, and I rested. I had been on my feet from 6 a.m. to 7 p.m. without sitting down more than two hours altogether, but my grain was ready and my team was ready, so I was happy. We had potato soup for supper—something I am extremely fond of, and Mary knew it. Slept in the bed in the granary in which I had slept when working there, with Schuyler. For breakfast we had fried eggs, and I made a good meal. Before I was done eating, Monroe drove into the yard. It was pretty cool that morning, so he came into the house till I was through. Then we loaded up and started for Kill Creek—"Bethlehem," as Gus Herzog calls my place, or, rather the three claims. We stopped in town to see whether Mr. Weinland and Geo. had arrived, and found they had not. The Glickers had sent Mr. W. an invitation to stop with them, and Mrs. G. had come to town Saturday to meet him, and Paul was to come for her Sunday and take her and Mr. W. home. After boring and "water witching" to no end, they have not succeeded in finding water. As no strangers had arrived in town the day before, we concluded our folks had gone direct to the Creek; accordingly we drove past Lapp's on the way up. When we drove into the yard, a boy squeezed out between Mr. L. and and the doorpost and came running to the wagon. It was Bub, and I tell you I was glad to see him. Spoke a few words to Mr. W. and then pushed on towards home, stopping at Snyder's on the way. After unloading Bub's box and the sacks of grain Monroe fed the horses and I made dinner—boiled corn, potatoes, fried eggs, dried beef, bread and butter and coffee. That was all, and it was not bad to take. As soon as dinner was disposed of we hitched up and went to the "Pennsylvanian's Home" better known as the "Hoette" (pronounced hoe tté by the proprietor, Don Pedro) for Mr. Brunner, but he had mashed his finger, and sent word to Ch. Herzog that he could not work. So we went to Lapp's. Mr. Weinland concluded to go to Osborne with Monroe, so he loaded his box and left. Mr. Lapp charged 40 cents for bringing Bub's box, which was just half price. As we were leaving Mr. Lapp called after us that if we wanted a watermelon we should help ourselves. So we went half a mile out of our way in order to get one. We found a bouncer fit to eat and "packed" it over home. But we had eaten three or four muskmelons, so the watermelon lay till Wednesday night, when we put away all we could, and it was something of a job, too. We did not succeed in eating it all. That was the first time I had all the watermelon I could eat this season. Why, you need not ask for them here—they are given to you, and if you take a couple without asking the folks think nothing of it. I had the keys to Pa's trunk in my pocket when I went to town, so he could not get his clothes or shaving apparatus. He put on my old blue printing office pants, and my brown Sunday coat. They fit him as well as they do me. We unpacked the box. I suppose the proper thing to do would be to write a card of thanks, so here goes: Ladies and gentlemen: At a meeting of the Kill Creek Conclave in Dugout No. 1, held Sunday, Sept. 16, 1877, it was unanimously resolved that the thanks of the

Conclave (meaning Pa and myself) be tendered to the generous donors of the articles contained in the box, and especially for the Sea Foam, cigars, smoked beef, coffee, handkerchiefs, silverware, etc., not to forget the clothes. When we came to the books and papers at the bottom, we found a couple of Monroe's Dime Dialogues. How in the world came they in that box? Pa pounced upon that gray mixed coat of Uncle George's and has worn it ever since. Before Bub had been in the neighborhood 24 hours he had three jobs offered him. Lapp wanted him to cut broomcorn, Greenfield wanted him to help in the cane, and Rook wanted him to herd, as Smith was on the sick list. Pa and I took him along to Greenfield's on Monday, and he worked with me in the fields, topping and cutting cane all the week except ½ day, when he was "roustabout," i.e., helping at the cane mill. He was very much amused to hear the folks talk about "them molasses" and being told to "take away them pummies" (pomace—crushed cane). Another queer expression I heard yesterday: "I ain't ate so many molasses this year as I did last." The grammar and King's English are horribly mangled, but I managed to live through it. On Friday Bub's hands were very sore and he could hardly do anything, so when we got home in the evening, I made up a couple of pans of biscuit and left him home Saturday to rest and get his hands well. We walk to and from Greenfield's (2½ miles) every morning and evening. His house is not very large and he has two hands sleeping there. We are more comfortable at home and don't like to leave Pa alone over night, for fear he would get lonesome, so we walk five miles a day besides doing our work. Today we did not get more than ¼ mile from home, but took a real good rest. Pa tinkered round the house and Bub and I read all day except when we were asleep. We have to be on the road before sunrise in order to get to Greenfield's in time for breakfast. I get 75 cts and board per day, and Bub gets 40 cts. I have made 9 days, Pa 2 and Geo. 5, and G. wants us to work along till the cane is all in. Pa worked for Rook since Tuesday. We are on the traveled road till we get about a mile from home; then we have to wade through grass, in some places to our knees, over the "pathless prairie," which is crossed by a couple of roads to Bull's City. They lead north, while we must go west, so they do us no good.

TUESDAY, SEPTEMBER 25, 1877

At the Dugout, Kill Creek, Kansas

While feeding the cane mill yesterday afternoon, I happened to look toward old Neuschwanger's and saw a man coming toward me who I concluded was Harry Weinland and I was not mistaken. We had a little conversation, in which he said he liked this country very much—had seen a piece of land on Twin Creek, near Glicker's that suited him; intended to start for the east tomorrow (Wednesday) a week; would stop a week in Indiana. After bidding me goodbye he went to George, who was at work in the field, and had a little talk with him before he left. Today he expected to go to Bull's City, and from there to Osborne. He found the same fault with the town people that I did—almost every one has land to sell or trade. Pa is lying on the bed. He was helping Rook haul hay, today. George is mending his shoes with store string. His hands are all right now, and he worked today and yesterday real smart. He has now made 7 days and earned 7 gallons of "them molasses," or the equivalent in work. This morning we had a right smart shower, which put us back with stripping the cane about ½ hour, but for all that we managed to strip and top enough to make 7 loads today. This morning we put away a watermelon, and I had hiccups all day in consequence. I save Bub all I can. Today we took turns stripping; I'd strip two rows and he would top as fast as I was through with it, and then he would take the fork and strip a row and I'd top it, and then take the fork again. The rows are nearly ¼ mile long. The first work we did for anybody this month was on the 8th, and from that date to this the three of us have earned our board and $19.88. We will not get any cash for our work; it will be turned over in work, potatoes, fire wood, etc., and $9 of that goes for a debt I owe Greenfield. You ought to see the watermelon seeds I have—of two kinds now, and I'll get seeds of another kind tomorrow. I have the citron melon, a green melon with yellow flesh and red seeds; and the mountain sweet, a red-fleshed melon, black seeds. The citron melon when just right, is delicious; and by the time they are ripe next fall I hope you will be with us to enjoy eating them. The seeds I now have would plant ¼ acre. And I have a good lot of tomato and muskmelon seeds. If I get all the garden seeds I am promised I can plant ever so much garden—but I am afraid some of the folks will forget me. I want you to remember to save me the seed of a first rate pumpkin, if you get hold of one. I can get any quantity of Hubbard squash seeds for the asking; and this kind of squash is mighty good eating when baked and served with butter and sugar.

WEDNESDAY, SEPTEMBER 26, 1877

At the Dugout, Kill Creek, Kansas

When I turned out at sunrise this morning it was raining right smart, and as it had been raining at 3 o'clock I knew it would be too wet to work in the cane, so I went back to bed, and we lay there till 6 o'clock. For a wonder Pa stayed in bed as long as we did. After breakfast we started for Greenfield's and by going round by Snyder's managed to get there without getting our shoes more than sopping wet. (If the writing looks as though it had been struck by lightning, you must lay it to Bub's shaking the table.) We worked in the field till about an hour before sundown, when we had supper, after which we worked at the mill. Will Paris came to help strip cane this afternoon. Pa worked for Rook half the day. He got butter at Hall's and Mrs. H. gave him a bunch of rhubarb, which he will cook tomorrow. Rook is to bring us 10 bushels of potatoes and two loads of wood on Pa's tick—that is in payment of the work Pa has done lately. Potatoes are worth 25 cts. per bushel. You remember I wrote that Wm. Paris offered us his yoke of cattle for $100 at 4 months. He sold them for $120 at 5 months, with 20 per cent interest, making the total amount $145. Several parties have tried to borrow money of me—the last was Milton Near, who wanted $60. I told him I hadn't that much to lend, and would like to have that much myself. I tell you Bub is a "great institution" with me and Pa—even if he does roll round in bed and disturb Pa, like he did the other morning, when Pa threatened to get up if Bub didn't lie still. I have only seven sore spots on my right foot, and the one on the inside of my ankle bothers me a good deal, especially when the shoe rubs. Bub thinks Syd would not like to get up before sunrise, and then work till sundown in the cane field, and walk 2½ miles home; this program to be repeated for a couple of weeks. If Dave wants a letter from me, this will be a pretty good one. There is but little to be erased. Bub thinks it is hard to understand Rook, who asked him where 'Oward was, and he did not understand who was referred to until the question had been repeated three times.

THURSDAY, SEPTEMBER 27, 1877

AT THE DUGOUT, KILL CREEK, KANSAS

The event of today was the killing of a two foot rattlesnake. We had been stripping, and Will remarked that on the sod was a good place to look for the "varmints," and I had gone ahead about ten feet. I had just put my foot down and had stripped a hill, when I heard a buzz, and, looking round, I saw a snake within six inches of my foot, and it was mad too. I gave a jump and brought the fork down with force enough to break the handle, but did not kill the snake. Then Will stuck his fork through the squirming reptile and Bub chopped its head off. It had 6 rattles and a button, and was about 3 inches in circumference. That is the closest to a rattler I have been this summer. We put away about a dozen watermelons today while at work, and did so much that Greenfield actually appeared to think he had a couple of real good hands. We went by the sun, and arrived at the house just in the nick of time to sit down at the first table. Pa did not work, but stayed home all day, and took a rest. Rook did not bring the potatoes today, as he said he would. This morning there was a heavy dew, and we got wet feet in consequence, besides having our pants wet to the knees, in front, from going through the grass. When we got to Greenfield's they had had breakfast—the first time they had breakfast before we arrived since we work[ed] there. Last night after I had gone to bed, I was disturbed by a toad so much that I got up and lit the lamp, and murdered the cause of my discomfort, and after the corpse of the victim had been passed out of the window I retired to my virtuous couch and slept the sleep of the just until the aurora of the morning warned me to paddle off to Greenfield's. I must stop writing and put several stitches in Bub's pants to keep the legs from ripping all the way up. Good night.

SUNDAY, OCTOBER 7, 1877

AT THE DUGOUT, KILL CREEK, KANSAS

I finished my last letter on Thursday a week, so I'll give the events of the last eight or ten days in a short way. Friday after closing the letter we went to work as usual. Geo. in the field and I at the mill. In the afternoon Mrs. Snyder came down with a load of cane, and then she did the feeding, while I was roustabout—carrying cane and pomace. She imposed on me, too, for every time I had the rack full of cane and the pomace cleared away, she would run off, and I had to feed the mill in addition to my other work: That was doing the work of two hands, and I got very tired. We were at work on a big job, and Greenfield wanted Will and me to work till 11 p.m. I tried to get more wages for night work than day work, but he would not give more. He was "in a box," so we helped him anyhow. I started Geo. for home when the sun was about an hour high, so he did not get lost going home. On Monday Geo. did not work, having hurt his foot, but the next day he did, and that was the last day's work he has done at the mill. He made 11¾ days, which is equal to that many gallons of molasses. I made a bargain with Morris to put in my wheat for molasses, and he did so on Thursday and Friday. The rye will not be put in till next week, as he promised Lapp to quarry rock, and next Friday he must go to Russell to fetch his wife, who expects to leave Bethlehem tomorrow. Wednesday morning before daylight there was a cold rain, and when I got up at 5, the wind was blowing cold from the north, so I went back to bed again. Turned out at 6 and had breakfast. As the wind still blew hard, I did not go to Greenfield's but stayed home and wrote to Aunt Sophia and Pattie. Pa dug the balance of the potatoes; there were 10½ bu. in all on a sunflower patch. There were about 7 bu. of eating potatoes; the balance small ones to plant next spring. Last Monday, mail night, I got your letters and the papers, and what I enjoyed immensely, Syd's package of finecut. Who says I haven't a good brother? While I am on the subject of letters, I'll answer Syd's questions. Take care of that $50. I have $60 left of that $100, and it will take some hard begging to get that away, or any part of it, except perhaps $4 to get Pa a pair of boots, which he will need. I would like to have a revolver, but the money to buy powder and shot is hard to get, though if I had the rev. I'd get the ammunition, so you may send it if you think I need it more than you do. I am not ready to get a team yet, as I have no well, and Hoot's will not furnish enough water. It is very low now. As soon as I find a team at a reasonable figure—one that I can command—I will let you know and you can send the money. Geo. would rather have woolen stockings for winter—in the summer he don't wear any. My socks are a little too short for me, as my feet have grown a good deal this summer. Don't worry about Pa's working too hard. When he don't feel like working he just loafs round the house—that is, when he is not working for somebody else. If he works for me he does as he pleases; and he actually seems to consider this ¼ section as his personal property, and occasionally bosses us round as though he was hired for that purpose. . . . Geo. don't walk in his sleep. If he should take a notion to do so, he would be waked before he had gone very far from the dugout, because the nights are real cold now, and promenading in his shirt tail is not in season. I don't think trees are hard to raise here. If we have rain enough in the spring they grow fast. As for the raspberry plants, they will come all right. You can take up some roots and make a few cuttings and pack them securely in paper. The U. S. mail will carry anything less than 4 lbs. for a trifle. But I'm off the track. About 10 a.m. Wednesday I started for

Greenfield's. When I arrived I found all hands sitting by the fire making vain attempts to get warm. I say vain, because the wind came from the north, and the furnace is on the north side of a bank. G. killed a pig, and we had fresh meat for dinner. After dinner (2 p.m.) he said we could not work because we couldn't make the sap boil when the wind blew so hard, so I went back home, and Geo. and I laid up part of the sod for a hen house. That will be part dugout, like the house. It is the third dugout we have worked on, as the potato cellar is also part dugout. We will have four dugouts when the stable is built. Thursday I worked at the mill all day. It was sundown when we had supper, so I had to go home in the dark. The moon does not rise till midnight. Mrs. G. sent a piece of pork to "Grandpa Ruede" as she calls him, weighing about 3½ lbs. It was a little unhandy to carry, but it was worth the trouble. Thursday morning we had a pretty severe frost, and my feet got real cold wading through the grass, as my shoes are out at the toes and the frost got into them at every step. I had to think of Al. Brietz's remark that "it was very pleasant to feed the mill when there was frost on the cane." I had to feed that morning, and as soon as the mill was full of cane, I'd put my hands in my pockets for half a minute and then go on feeding. Friday morning Geo. and I started for town about 7 o'clock. He was in good spirits, but by the time we had waked 5 or 6 miles he began to complain of his feet. We did not have a chance to ride, so we had to walk all the way. The river was low, so we waded it at the ford, the water being only ankle-deep. Geo. pulled off his boots, but I went through with my shoes on, as I knew they would not be any drier by pulling them off and then putting my wet feet inside them. Got to town a little before noon. Town was pretty lively as the fair had been continued a day longer than had

been intended. Took the oil can to Fritchey's, and then went
to the Farmer office. Barnhart had been unwell and was
obliged to go to the fair grounds, so he had not got the paper
up for this week. He wanted me to work, which I did, and
earned 50¢, which was more than enough to get some crackers
for dinner. After I got through setting type (which was the
first I have set in two months) and he had settled with me, he
told me to consider myself engaged to work for him from the
middle of next month for a couple of weeks, as he intended
going off. I told him I'd work, and started for Schweitzer's,
stopping at Morrow's and Getz's on the way. Mrs. M. wanted
us to stay all night, but we could not. When we got to Landes',
we found Schuyler [Landes' son] in bed, sick with diph-
theria. He has had a hard time and was not expected to live,
but is now better. Mrs. L. has just cleared the supper table,
but set out a good meal for us anyhow, after which we
plodded on our weary way to Schweitzer's. The folks were all
in bed except Monroe and Wally, but we found room in a
corner. In the morning, as Monroe had to go to Morrow's
for the fanmill to clean wheat, I put the well auger on the
wagon and we rode with him. Stopped at Landes' on the way
down, and as Henry was not home, Mrs. L. borrowed $5 to
square off the balance for my work. She said she did not
require a receipt. Told her I'd not call for the money again.
She said I need not stay away because they did not owe me
anything. I should come anyhow, and of course said I would.
We had quite a shower during the morning, but about 9
o'clock the rain ceased. As there was no other means of trans-
portation, I shouldered the auger, which consists of three
10-foot sections of ½ inch iron rods, weighing between 30
and 40 lbs., and carried it to town—2 miles. Then I proceeded to make the necessary purchases. For myself I got a

pair of boots for $3.60 (regular price $3.85) for Pa a hat, $1.35 ($1.50) coal oil, matches and shoe nails. We waited till noon for the dentist from Pleasant Valley, as Bub wanted a tooth pulled, but the D.D.S. did not put in an appearance. There was no Kill Creek team in town at 1 p.m. so we started on foot. Geo. had the hat and coal oil and the handle of the auger hung on his back, while I had the auger and tied on my back were my old shoes and a shoe brush for which Pa has wished for some time. The river was pretty cold to wade, but we had to do it. It took us till after 6 to get to the dugout with our load, and when we got there we felt that though it was only a dugout there's no place like home. Barnhart offered me 50¢ to run off the papers, but as it would have cost more than that for supper, lodging and breakfast, I declined. George's feet were pretty badly blistered, and he walked about six miles barefoot. When we got to Neuschwanger's we went in and had a little talk with the Bishop while we were eating a melon. My boots are well broken now, after walking 15 miles in them. My feet did not get blistered. We were pretty tired when we got home. Pa had supper ready, and we made the provisions disappear. He had boiled nine potatoes (fair sized ones, too) and we had a little meat and seven biscuits to help along. That supper tasted good. This morning Bub and I did not turn out till after 8, and Pa had had his break- fast. About 9 he went to Shellenberger's to meeting, leaving me to take care of Bub. It is right pleasant out of doors today; pretty strong wind. Bub's toe is pretty badly swollen, and he keeps a wet rag on it. My boots are No. 8, and a very good fit. My feet have not so much surface to cover, and I think will not get so tired as by walking in my [old] shoes. Now I am going to see if I can find a few tomatoes for supper.

Yesterday I tasted a new kind of coffee. Mrs. Greenfield

ran out of coffee—either the real article or the rye substitute—
and there she had a gang of men to be fed, and it wouldn't
be supper without coffee, so she set her wits to work, with
the result that when we gathered at the table a hot amber-
colored drink was poured into the cups and set before us. One
after another took a sip, set the cup down and demanded what
under the sun it was. The lady smiled, but refused to name it.
"It ain't coffee," said Charlie, "of that I am sure, for I know
the last was used at noon." "If you guess right I'll tell you,"
teasingly retorted his wife. Everybody took a turn, and as is
often the case, the last was the lucky winner. He noticed
several sacks of millet seed leaning against the side of the
room and hazarded "Millet." "Right," said Lida. "I thought
I'd try it, just to see what it tasted like." It was the queerest
tasting coffee any of us had ever put into his mouth, but it
"went," or the crowd didn't get any hot drink.

MONDAY, OCTOBER 8, 1877

At the Dugout, Kill Creek, Kansas

Have just finished patching the blue pants with a patch
from the remains of an old pepper-and-salt vest I found in
the box. "A hole is abominable," and here it does not matter
if you have patches of a dozen different colors on your clothes.
A great many of the folks here go in rags merely because they
have "no time" to patch their clothes. I worked at the cane
mill this afternoon; this morning in the field. After supper
I rode as far as the P.O. with Mr. Hall. Pa had just left,
and I easily caught up with him. The other night he got lost
between the stack on Hoot's place and the dugout, so I guided
him. I am a pretty good hand at that, as I am well acquainted
with the topography of the country between here and the P.O.
For the benefit of inquisitive folks I would say that when I

left Bethlehem it was with the idea that work was so plenty
and hands so scarce that the farmers would all be on the *qui
vive* to secure the first man who showed himself. But I found
that a fellow has to become acquainted before he is in demand,
and then he does not always get a permanent situation. I have
been very fortunate in securing work, but the cause is very
apparent—the crops are very heavy, and it will take a large
force to handle them. This morning Snyder as much as said
he wanted me to dig potatoes for him if I got through at
Greenfield's before the molasses is all made. Geo. was boring
for water, the result of his labors being shale. I did not get
any tomatoes last night, as the frost Thursday night killed
them. There was thin ice on standing water this morning.
Greenfield is going off in about a month with a load of molasses, and wanted me to take charge of his premises during his
absence, but I'll be obliged to go to Osborne about that time,
to work in the office. His offer was a good one: to attend to his
cows and pigs, and have the use of the milk, flour, beans, etc.,
free. All I'd have to furnish would be groceries. But when
I have no work in the office I'll have plenty to do at home
without tending to other men's stock. I must let my own work
lie at present to do other people's work. To be sure, I will
not lose anything by it; but it is not what I consider getting
ahead very fast. But then, again, I don't expect to jump to the
top of the heap at one jump. Goodnight, I'm sleepy and want
to turn in.

TUESDAY, OCTOBER 9, 1877

OSBORNE, KANSAS

Worked at the mill till about 4 p.m. when Barnhart drove
up and said he had come for me. His boy is sick. Settled with
Greenfield. The total amout for work was $21.70, from which

then was to be deducted $9 for breaking, leaving $12.70 due me. Took Barnhart round by the P.O. He was much pleased with his visit to the Creek: It was the first time he was up there. If he had not come for me, I would have been thrown out of work by Thursday, at any rate. Geo. bored a 30 foot hole today but did not get water. I hated to leave Pa and Geo., but I need the money, and $5 a week and my board is not to be sneezed at. So I went along with Barnhart to stay "till forbid." I saw a splendid yoke of oxen 5 years old, today, that I could buy for $90. They suit me better than any I have yet seen. Got to Osborne about 6 p.m. and went to Keever's, where I stay when I work here. Had supper, and as riding against the wind hurt my eyes, I went to bed early. My bed fellow grumbled because he had to sleep with me, but as I was first in bed, I stayed there. Mr. Brunner is at work for Herzog again; his finger is almost healed. It was badly mashed a couple of weeks ago.

WEDNESDAY, OCTOBER 10, 1877

OSBORNE, KANSAS

Began work about 7:30. The office was not open before. B. is on the sick list, so I have my own way in the office. It is a beautiful warm day. Roads are like a floor.

Delinquent subscribers are not lacking here, and in many cases those who are anything regular in paying up are frequently obliged to pay in trade—wheat, wood, and similar articles of barter. Settling day comes in the fall, after the threshing is done, and the Editor Barnhart often sends a load of wheat to Russell, the nearest market, to be turned into cash with which to pay the house from which he gets his patent inside. The man who freights his stuff to the railroad is invariably a subscriber, who pays for his paper in work. Wheat is worth ten cents a bushel less here than in Russell, as that is the cost of hauling. Several times I have taken pay for my work in wheat at Osborne prices, for I have to have flour. When I get my pay in this way I look up a neighbor who is willing to haul the stuff to Kill Creek, seldom being asked to pay for getting it to my place. Then I watch for somebody going to Bush's mill at Bull City where it is turned into flour, the miller taking one-sixth for his work. Neighbors help each other a great deal, because there are so few who have a team.

Everybody in town comes to the office to read the papers from the East, always two and sometimes three days old, but the latest news available. Often when court is in session, Judge Holt drops in to scan the columns of the Topeka Commonwealth, the official state paper which contains the syllabi of the Supreme Court decisions. Sometimes, if Barnhart is in a hurry to get home, he stuffs his favorite paper into his pocket, leaving the free reading room without anything for its patrons.

THURSDAY, OCTOBER 11, 1877

OSBORNE, KANSAS

I dare not leave finishing this letter till Sunday, as that would make it Thursday, before you would get it. By posting it tomorrow you will probably get it Tuesday, as it is one day ahead of what it would be if mailed at the creek. Worked hard all day in the office. I send you a paper. It has a neat puff for me in that Kill Creek article. I'd rather be at work on my claim than to be cooped up in the office. I have to force myself to go in, because it does not seem right to work in the house

after being out doors all summer. But I know that if I can get
money for my work, it will pay me to stick to it. B.'s boy will
probably be unable to work all next week; if that is the case
I'll get $8.25 for my 10 days' work. I won't work for less than
$5 a week and my board. He pays the boy $3, and if he's
worth that I'm worth $5, because I'm competent to run the
office alone. (A drummer is using Keever's pen and I must
use pencil.) Yesterday I had an awful appetite and left the
table before I was satisfied, because I would have cleared the
table. I won't get my letter on Monday, but perhaps Pa or
Bub will come down during the week and bring it. If you
have a chance, send me some socks, and have them one size
larger than I used to wear; the socks I have are too tight.
My boots are well broken now and they don't hurt my feet
like my holey shoes did. Love to all.

THURSDAY, OCTOBER 18, 1877

OSBORNE, KANSAS

Here I sit in the "office" or general loafing place in the City
Hotel. There is a crowd in the room and if this letter is rather
confused you must blame them for talking. . . . We have had
three rainy days this week, and the street is awfully muddy.
This rain is just what we want, though, for it will bring out
the grain that is sowed, and the ground that was so hard and
dry will be plowable. A good many farmers quit plowing on
account of the dry weather. Yesterday was fine, but about
7 p.m. it began to rain again. Last night and the night before
Bishop Stump of Nebraska, a Dunkard, preached in the
schoolhouse, and because I did not know what else to do, I
went to hear him, and found he was a real good hand quoting
from the New Testament. He uses the same language in

preaching as he does in conversation, which is, as regards English and Grammar, simply execrable. But it "took" with the people, and last night he had a full house, and they were attentive, too. It is probable I will have work in the office all next week. If that is the case, I will go home tomorrow or next day to get clean clothes. There are lots of drummers for different houses in St. Louis, St. Joe. and Leavenworth, passing through town. They generally—I may say always—stop here at Keever's, and that puts him in a flutter about beds. I sleep with Mr. Brunner and a blacksmith alternately. By this time the blacksmith has got used to sleeping double—at least he don't grumble when I turn in. The cover is too small for two, so we got a big buffalo robe and put it on the bed, and we are plenty warm enough.

Barnhart said if he hadn't Ham on his hands he would give me a job all winter. I never said that I would not take such a job, but I'd hate to leave Pa and George alone all winter. It is probable that I'll get a month's work in the office while Barnhart is away. That means $20 cash, and that will keep us in provisions (after what we have is consumed) for at least three months, if we do not get any work, which is extremely improbable. I have a notion to trade for Levin's corn. He has not a great deal, and I reckon I can get it, as he probably will not want it. This is an awfully dull place on Sundays as well as week days when you have no work. Mr. Schweitzer was detained on the road by the rain and did not get here till this evening. Crist left Russell on Tuesday at 10 p.m. (a drummer has gobbled the ink, so I am forced to use pencil.) De Tuck is going out on the buffalo range this winter and offered me a chance to go along, but I declined. The thing would be nice enough, but it will be awfully cold when heavy storms come up. The robes are worth about $10 when they are dressed, and it costs one robe to have two dressed by the Indians, and they are the only folks who know how to do it. Taken all in all, I don't much care to go on the range. Oh, these fellows talk and bother me! I would not have written this week if I had been home, but being away, I thought that a few lines might be welcome.

WEDNESDAY, OCTOBER 24, 1877

OSBORNE, KANSAS

As you will see, I have not yet gotten away from the printing office. I wanted to go up the creek on Saturday afternoon, but there were no teams in from our neighborhood, so I did not have a chance to ride—and another reason was that I did not know how much the river would rise. If I had gone up, and come back on Sunday, and found the river up, I would have been in a bad fix, and so would Barnhart. Talk about murky weather—why, on Saturday a week it began to rain, and until last Saturday at noon, with the exception of Sunday and Wednesday, it was raining most of the time—a steady, drip, drip, drip,—not anything like the heavy rains we had in the spring but soaking rain which no doubt will make the grain jump, as we have had several real fine days since it quit raining. Last Saturday was the primary election for county officers, which corresponds to the Northampton county convention, the main difference being that here every voter has his say in regard to the candidates, and there is very little if any chance for "ring" operations. On Tuesday night Mr. Wismer from the creek (about 5 miles from our place) was in town and did not leave until 6 p.m. I wanted to go up with him and come back today, but Frank [Barnhart] said I could go up on Saturday and stay a week or so and then come back again. I am real homesick to see Pa and Bub; this being in town I don't like. I hardly know what to do with myself of an evening. Bumming round I hate, and as there would be nothing else for me to do, I generally go to bed early. I caught an awful cold the other day, but that does not impair my appetite in the least. I am much better now, however, and I think will be over it in about a day, when I can be out in the air all day. It was nothing but being shut up in the house that gave it to me. Give me plenty of fresh air, and colds do not bother me. Today has been a splendid autumn day. If I had wished to go up the creek today I could have had two or three chances to ride to within four or five miles of home— and when Saturday comes and I really want to ride, I dare say I will not be able to find a team. I want to take a couple of pounds of beef along. I begin to feel rich. I have earned $10 already, and there will be about $3 more by the time I quit. When a fellow has only $1.25 in change to meet current expenses, and then gets a V, he begins to feel opulent. I don't break in on those $60 until I am positively obliged to, and that will not be as long as the filthy lucre lasts that I can pick up around the office, and work on the creek holds out to pay for butter and eggs. . . . I went with Mr. Glicker to hear Steinfort preach German, Sunday afternoon. We will have lovefeast and communion on the 11th of November.

WEDNESDAY, OCTOBER 31, 1877

At the Dugout, Kill Creek, Kansas

I expect to get oxen this way: I have $60 of what Syd sent before Pa came, and $10 that I earned in the office, which makes $70. Then I expect to have at least four weeks' work in the office, which will make $20 more. That will make $90, and $90 is enough to buy a yoke of cattle I know of. And maybe I'll get an X somewhere. If I do, I think I can buy cattle and a wagon for $100 cash. . . .

About the washing: Since that young one arrived at Hoot's we have done our own washing. Pa generally does it, and he is a good laundry man.

My shirts suit me first rate, but I expect I will not wear them before next summer. I haven't worn a white shirt since I left home. Wore my flannel ones almost all summer except a few weeks in August, when I wore nothing but my old undershirts (in the shirt line). . . .

I intend to keep as many pigs as I can after I get them. Just now we have not even one—and if we had, we have no place to keep it in. Pa intends to invest half of that $10 in a six months old sow, so that we can count on a litter of pigs by next spring. It will take till then to get a fair start.

Murdering toads is "ausgespielt" for the reason that they have deserted the ranch. Crickets ditto; no, I hear a solitary one chirping somewhere in the wall. I hope the frost finds him tonight.

There are no plantain leaves about. That is a weed of which Kansans (natives I mean) know nothing. Bub's feet are O.K. now. We intend to get some skunk fat; that is good for all kinds of sores, rheumatism, etc., and for greasing boots.

I am glad Ruth has had so much pleasure. She will hardly have so much fun here. I don't mean to say she cannot enjoy herself here in a much more quiet way. . . .

SUNDAY, NOVEMBER 18, 1877

At the Dugout, Kill Creek, Kansas

Syd, the monthly statement of expenses will be an interesting item to me, and as I think it would be interesting to you to know how we do, I send you a statement. It may be of interest to you to know how much it has cost us since we began to "bach" here in the dugout, so I append a list of the articles bought: Where the name of the person follows from whom we got the articles, it means that that was paid for in work. Before we began to "bach" I kept no tally of expenses.

Aug. 19	Axe	$1.50	Sept. 15	Herring	.50
	Hatchet	1.00		Nails	.06
	Matches & to-			Sugar	.25
	bacco	.20		Hauling my grain	
Aug. 25	Stove & fixtures	25.28		from Landes's	1.25
	Nails, knives,			8 sacks @ 25¢	2.00
	forks, spoons	2.47		Matches	.05
	Lamp	.75		Tobacco	.15
	Bucket	.25	Sept. 26	1 3/4 lb. butter	
	Salt	.10		(Hall)	.27
	Rice	.25	Sept. 28	10 bu. potatoes	
	Plates	.85		(Rook)	2.50
	2 bowls	.24	Sept. 29	2 loads wood	
	2 boxes	1.00		(Rook)	1.25
	Sugar	.25	Oct. 2	2 1/2 doz. eggs	
	Soap	.25		(Hall)	.20
	Coffee	.35	Oct. 4	Butter (Heiser)	.20
	Coal oil	.20	Oct. 6	Butter (Hall)	.15
Aug. 28	Flour (Heiser)	3.00		Crackers	.30
	Butter (Heiser)	.30		Oil	.20
Aug. 30	3 doz. eggs			Hat (Pa)	1.35
	(Hall)	.25		Shoe nails	.10
Sept. 1	Kettle	.50		Boots (HH)	3.60
	Pan	.35		Shoe brush	.35
	Hasp	.10		Matches	.05
	Whetstone	.05		Postage stamps	.15
	Gentian bitters	.25	Oct. 16	Butter (Hall)	.20
	Apples	.05	Oct. 17	2 doz. eggs	
	Herring	.10		(Hall)	.16
Sept. 3	2 lb. butter	.30	Oct. 21	2 lb. butter	
Sept. 10	2 lb. butter	.36		(Hall)	.40
Sept. 14	2 doz. eggs			2 doz. eggs	
	(Hall)	.16		(Hall)	.16

Nov.			Nov. 29	Bucket	.25
12-27	Butter (Guyer)	.25		Oil	.20
	Postage	.38	Nov. 30	Molasses	
	Sugar	.50		(Greenfield)	.40
	Sundries	.60			
	1 gal. molasses			Total	$60.04
	(Greenfield)	.40			

MONDAY, NOVEMBER 19, 1877

AT THE DUGOUT, KILL CREEK, KANSAS

I have 2 acres of wheat out. It is coming up nicely. Also 3 acres of rye, which was put in only last week, and is not yet to be seen above the ground. Some folks say "Don't put in any rye; it don't pay to raise it." It is a surer crop than wheat, and I want something to eat if the wheat don't grow well. Rye has been known to yield 50 bushels to the acre, but if I get 20 I will be satisfied.

TUESDAY, NOVEMBER 20, 1877

AT THE DUGOUT, KILL CREEK, KANSAS

The stone house is a thing that will be visible by next fall if I can only make the riffle—but it is hard to say now whether I can. I keep on hoping, however, and working toward that end. I must have a team to haul the stone and several other little things, before I can begin to work on it. If you were here you would see the matter in a different light. Now, Syd, don't get disheartened or make trouble in the office that will put you out—for would you want Ma and Ruth to live in a dugout? No! a thousand times no! Rather wait and work along and help me bear the burden, if such it may be termed. You and I have to "boost" the old folks along, now that Pa has no work. It will go mighty slow at times, or appear to, but will keep on hoping, and in a year or so I hope and pray we may all be reunited under my roof (in prospect) here on my farm in Kansas.

WEDNESDAY, NOVEMBER 21, 1877

AT THE DUGOUT, KILL CREEK, KANSAS

I wanted to settle with Morris for putting in my grain this afternoon, but could not find him. His bill is about $10, payable in molasses at 40¢ per gallon.

Tomorrow Pa will work at Greenfield's as the boring for water is too hard on him. I and Bub will do that. Bub has made a good start at one place, and the indications for water are first rate.

Since the 12th of September I have earned about $27—$13 of which will be cash; the balance in molasses.

TUESDAY, NOVEMBER 6, 1877[20]

OSBORNE, KANSAS

Last Thursday morning Pa waked us and then started for Greenfield's. I told Bub to go to sleep again, as it was no use to burn the oil, so we rolled over and slept till about 6:30. After breakfast, we thought we'd go at boring, but as it was drizzling pretty fast we stayed in the house. Pa came home about 10, as Greenfield said he could not work in the rain. Afternoon (we did not have dinner) we bored about 10 feet in a hole that had been begun and when we had reached the depth of 23 feet we struck shale. The indications for water are so good, however, that we intend to dig there. It is possible

[20] There is some sort of mix-up in the dates of the letters at this point, but I was obliged to copy them in the order in which they appear in Ruede's ledger book.

that in a hole 5 ft. in diameter we will be more likely to strike a vein of water than in a hole only 2 in. in diameter. It was cold, boring on top of a ridge, where the wind took us fair and square. About 5 o'clock we quit boring and made supper. Pa was working at the henhouse all the afternoon.

Friday morning I was at Greenfield's before they were fairly out of bed, and after breakfast Milton and I went to hauling hay. That was the first time I ever helped to haul hay out of the field in November. The second load we hauled in the afternoon we had to load twice. We were both on top, and in crossing a little draw, the whole thing slipped off. We came down easy—so easy that we didn't know whether we were on the wagon or on the ground. We only hauled six loads, and I got home soon after 6 p.m. The gallon of molasses I carried with me got pretty heavy by the time I had carried it 2½ miles. A gallon of sorghum molasses weighs 11 lbs. Saturday morning I shouldered the auger and struck for Greenfield's, as Mrs. Stevens was going to have the team to go to town, and I rode with her. Arrived in town about noon. Put the auger on Ed. Feld's wagon: he lives close to Schweitzer's and left it there. Stayed in town till Mrs. Stevens left for home. John Sears was in town and I told him I would go out with him. When we got to his place he invited me to stay overnight. I said "Yes." Sunday morning about 9 o'clock I went to Schweitzer's, where I stayed till Monday morning. ... Sunday night the wind blew great guns, and next morning there was ice half an inch thick on standing water. But although the wind had considerably abated, it was a very cold ride to town, where I arrived about 8:30. ... Last night I had a dream in which Ma, sorghum molasses, the printing office and I don't know what all, were inextricably mixed up. Today was election day. There was considerable electioneering. ...

SUNDAY, NOVEMBER 11, 1877[21]

OSBORNE, KANSAS

I dare say you will laugh before you get through. The way in which I have been hustled around from one bed to another this week is a caution. Monday, Tuesday and Wednesday nights I slept with a different man each night. Thursday and Friday nights I slept with Geo. Beck of Kill Creek, who is concreting the hotel for Keever. A new roof has been put on the hotel, and the second story rooms raised. Last night I went to bed in the room where I slept on Friday night, and had fairly got under the covers when Mrs. Keever came in on an errand, and I said "What's up?" She wondered who was there, and when she found out she said: "Mollie will give it to you if she knows you were in her bed!" So I had to get out. I slept on a pile of buffalo robes with Els on the floor of the common sitting room. Last night I was reading over in the office, when in walked a man holding a cigar box in his hand. I supposed at first it was somebody "setting up" the cigars, but on taking a second look I saw it was R. G. Hays, and the box was for me. I at once opened it and found all the articles safe. The corncob pipe and Havanna tobacco came into requisition at once, and I must say I have not enjoyed a smoke so much in the eight months I have lived in Kansas. The revolver, etc. were all safe. Many thanks for the tobacco.

This morning I went to preaching, and this p.m. there was lovefeast and communion at Steinfort's house. During a pause in the singing, soon after the cake and coffee had been disposed of, the Osborne Moravian Church was organized with eleven members. . . .

There was a fearful prairie fire east of town this afternoon, and most of the men in town went to help put it out. They did

[21] See note, p. 173.

not succeed, for the fire ran over the bluffs towards the North Fork. They prevented it from getting into Page's corn, however. The package was delivered today by R. G. Hays, and was investigated at once. Mrs. Keever has been very good to me, so I gave her a handful of the chestnuts, and as Mollie was looking on, she came in for another handful. I looked for a letter, but couldn't find it.

TUESDAY, NOVEMBER 13, 1877[22]

OSBORNE, KANSAS

This morning I was agreeably surprised by a visit from Pa. As soon as he came in I knew he wanted something—and he did, too. At noon I went with him and bought him a pair of boots and some odds and ends for household use—in all $4 worth—and it was spent in less time than it takes to write it. . . .

This evening we are having a pretty heavy shower, with thunder and lightning. You would not call it winter if you had been here yesterday. The sun shone brightly, and it was too warm to have fire in the office. Last Thursday we had a little snow spit—just enough to see the snow fall—but we could not see it on the ground. This morning we had a very heavy dew. . . .

I enjoyed Ruth's letter immensely, standing at ease. Pa does not intend to buy 100 pigs, as his finances are rather shaky, and pigs are worth $2.50 to $5 apiece. He may possibly be swineherd when we once get a start. There was some talk about his getting a pig last week, but he said nothing in regard to that today, so I conclude he has not got it yet. He has no place to put it in. How's that for being in too big a hurry?

[22] See note, p. 173.

He must have patience like Job—a thing I'm learning fast. I often regretted the $30 he was swindled out of, but if he had had it—well, what's the use of thinking of what might have been? I am getting ahead slowly. Before I can build I must have a team, and I am not ready to get one yet. I have no place for them, and not enough money to buy. Don't worry. I will be all right in a few months. Remember me to the aunts and cousins.

TUESDAY, NOVEMBER 20, 1877[23]

OSBORNE, KANSAS

The principal event of the past week was my going home on Saturday night. After we quit work I went to the hotel and washed my hands, and then discovered that a button was off of one wristband. Went to Mrs. Keever to ask her to sew it on. Mrs. Morrow was in the kitchen, and asked me whether I did not intend to go home. I told her no. She said: "Why, I'm going up there tonight." I replied, "Then I'm going too," and instead of getting a button sewed on, I got Mollie to pin the sleeve. Then I got the revolver and ammunition and my gloves, buttoned my coat up to the chin (I had no overcoat), and jumped into the wagon. After a little delay we started. It was a beautiful moonlight night, and right pleasant riding. Joe did not know the road, so it was a good thing for him that I went along. There was a lunar rainbow visible, which disappeared and reappeared again—that makes two, don't it? On the road we picked up a man from Crawford Co., Pa., and soon learned he was a brother of Jim Gillmore, who lives on the road to "New Bethlehem" [Ruede's claim]. He had not seen his brother for 21 years. At the P.O. I left the

[23] See note, p. 173.

Morrows to find the way to Rupert's and I struck for home
by the nearest route, over the ridge and through the big draw.
The folks were glad to see me, but not more so than I was
to be there. Slept first rate—better than I had slept for a week.
Sunday morning I went to look at the wheat, and started a
jack; pointed the revolver at it, and it made itself scarce.
We walked to the site of dugout No. 1, and I was just taking
aim at a bone that is stuck into the sod, and when about to pull
the trigger I saw a horse coming up out of the draw, just in
line with the bone; I hadn't to wait long till Lapp's head
became visible. We jumped on the wagon and rode to the
house and picked up Pa. I got my overcoat, and then we all
road to Hackerott's schoolhouse, where quite a congregation
had gathered to hear Bro. Dave Brumbach preach. His text
was too much for him. He could not expound it, and so he
ran off and preached about baptism. After dinner at Rupert's
we left for Osborne, stopping at Neuschwanger's on the way.
We arrived in town about 6 o'clock. During the evening there
was a little shower. Next Monday old man Smith, Amandus
Fatzinger and Morris' wife leave for the east. Fatzinger
would stay if he was sure his wife would come. On Sunday
it was 8 months since I arrived in Osborne. It seems like a
long time.

Huber and Berger start for the buffalo range tomorrow,
to be gone about three months.

TUESDAY, NOVEMBER 27, 1877[24]

AT THE DUGOUT, KILL CREEK, KANSAS

By this you will see that I have again been restored to the
bosom of my happy family, which was made more happy (?)

[24] See note, p. 173.

by my presence. The way it occurred was this: I had worked like a good fellow all last week, and on Saturday Frank wanted me to say for what wages I would work for him for three months. I told him I would have to go to my claim to see what work had to be done immediately and consult with Pa, and then I could tell him on Monday. It happened that Geo. came down with Hoot on that day, as the oil can was empty, so I had a good chance to ride all the way, even to my own door, as Hoot is now living on his claim, only ¼ mile from my house. He built a sod house, and as the walls are too high, the front (south) wall leaned outward and he had to prop it with heavy timbers. To return to the subject: I found I would have time to get dinner, so I took Bub along. His dinner cost me a quarter, but I could not let him go hungry. After talking over the matter of wages with Pa, we came to the conclusion that I could not work for less than $20 a month, and board. Then we went to bed. Sunday morning all three went to Hackerott's to meeting—I almost wrote "dinner," but as that is part of the program I might just as well have written it. After dinner, in conversation with John Neuschwanger, I learned that Henry was going to town next morning, so I was all right as far as a ride was concerned. Saturday night, when I unloaded, I found that the inventory was as follows: Tub, 65¢; coal oil, 20¢; and a treat for Pa and Bub, namely, a dime's worth of apples. It looked a little as though we were getting ahead when I saw the pig and chickens. That is Syd's pig. It is a sleek black sow about 6 months old. I believe she is about ¾ Berkshire. Yesterday morning I left home about 6:15 and by the time the sun rose was a mile and a half away. Arrived at Neuschwanger's in time to receive and decline an invitation to breakfast. At 8 o'clock we started for town, reaching Osborne about 11:30.

Went to the office to let Frank know my decision and terms for two months; but he had a good excuse, and did not want me. He paid me $5 and I left. Stopped to buy an axe handle and then made for home. Had to stop and rest half a dozen times on the road, and when I got home I was almost played out. Ate some nice soup, and then lay down on the bed and soon fell asleep. I don't know how long I slept, but I do know that when I waked up the ranch was deserted. Pa and Geo. had gone to the P.O. Got up and lit the lamp, and then lay down again till they came back with your letter and the papers. We had a good time reading them before we turned in. This morning there was a little snow on the ground, and the wind was biting cold. After breakfast Pa and I went to Hansen's to get some wood. The gentleman was not at home, so stayed in and round the house till he came back from a rock-hunting expedition. That was about noon, and of course we were called to the table with the rest of the family. After dinner we went down to the creek and Mr. H. showed us a large oak that had been cut and told us to get all we could, and what we could not work up we should just let lay, adding that it would cost us nothing but the labor. This he repeated several times, so as to be sure we understood him. We went to work, and in three hours had a big two-horse load ready to haul. He said we might have our winter's supply of wood (if we got it out) without paying anything for it, and we'll take him at his word. Hoot will haul the wood, sorghum, seed, etc. and take his pay in work. After the wood is down from Hansen's we must go to work at a shed for the shelter of our team (when we get one.) This will be built like everybody round here builds sheds,—i.e., set crotches where we intend to put the shed, and then put poles over them and brush on top, and cover it all with hay, which will also be put around the sides—

that will make a warm shed. About 4 p.m. Mr. Hansen came and had a talk with Pa, and wound up by asking us to stay over night. Pa did; but I could not, because there was not enough biscuit baked to keep Bub going two days. Got home about 5 o'clock. Then we went for water to what Pa calls "my puddle." It is very amusing, not to say ridiculous, to hear him complain about Snyder's boys letting their cattle drink at "my puddle." The water was quite clean this evening, and cold as ice. I put off baking till after supper; but then, finding there were enough biscuits for breakfast, put it off till morning. As Rook had promised to take a grist to mill for us tomorrow, I made a paint brush of some bristles out of the shoe brush and marked the bags "Ruede." The next thing, I suppose, will be a rush of the neighbors to have me mark their bags. I forgot to say that I used shoe blacking in lieu of paint.

WEDNESDAY, NOVEMBER 28, 1877[25]

At the Dugout, Kill Creek, Kansas

We did not turn out till 7 this a.m. About 8:30 we went for water, and had to break through an inch of ice in order to get it. Bub went sprawling round on the ice like a hog. There is a very cold wind, but the sun shines brightly, and it is right comfortable where the wind can't strike you. Rook did not come for our grist, so at 12:30 Geo. and I went to Hansen's where Pa had stayed over night. Helped awhile with the cross cut saw, and chopped some, and at 4 p.m. we left, as we had to go to see when Rook intended to go to mill. That made about a mile further for us, but it had to be done. By the time we got home it was dark. Pa stayed at Hansen's.

[25] See note, p. 173.

THURSDAY, NOVEMBER 29, 1877[26]

AT THE DUGOUT, KILL CREEK, KANSAS

This morning it was awful cold, the wind being very sharp. About 8 o'clock we went to the pond for water. This time we took the hatchet along, and we had use for it, too, for there was over an inch of ice to be cut through before we could dip up the water. The ground here is quite different from that around Bethlehem, in that when water stands it remains quite clear and pure, even in the hottest weather— only in the hottest weather there is seldom any water standing, as we don't have rain often then. A little before noon I started for Hansen's, taking Pa's scarf along, as I knew he would need it coming home. It was bitter cold, so I wrapped my cape round my head, leaving only a little place to see out. When I arrived at H.'s I found Pa sitting by the fire talking with Hansen, Hackerott and his brother-in-law, who has just arrived with his family of 12 children. Who says Kill Creek is not going to be well populated? Pa had chopped about 10 minutes and then gave it up because it was too cold. You may believe it was freezing weather when the creek, a running stream, was entirely frozen over except where the water falls over a dam. We came home, and just after we passed Hoot's house we met Geo., who said Hoot had sent word for one of us to help load wood; he would haul a load for us this afternoon. So when we considered he had had sufficient time to swallow his dinner, I bundled up again and went over. We brought a good load of oak. There are still two good-sized two-horse loads ready to haul, and that is not more than half of what Hansen says we might have. As it is good three miles to Hansen's we can only haul two loads a day. But one of his

[26] See note, p. 173.

loads is worth a dollar, because he loads high and heavy, and
then the wood costs us only the work and hauling. Pa went
right to chopping, and we put a piece of dry oak in the stove
—I tell you it makes a hotter fire than elm. That's the way
our Thanksgiving day was passed. We forgot all about the
turkey, and mince pie till we sat down to supper, which consisted of a piece of cold boiled beef, beef broth, potatoes,
biscuit and coffee, off which we made a hearty meal and were
right jolly all the evening. Pa never finds fault when Bub and
I cut up and raise cain generally, like we did when he was
finishing his letter. One of the hens has begun to lay.

FRIDAY, NOVEMBER 30, 1877[27]

AT THE DUGOUT, KILL CREEK, KANSAS

Pa and I put in ¾ of a day's work on the wood today. I did
not like to go into the house for dinner and supper; but when
they send word for you to come, and would most likely regard
it as an insult if you don't accept the invitation, there is but
one thing to do: go in and eat. We were just ready to start
for home when they called us for supper. It looks a little
like sponging, don't it, to get a lot of wood for nothing and
your meals besides? But that's the way Hansen is, and it is to
our advantage to do as he wishes. As they invited him, Pa
stayed over night. The other evening when he pulled off his
boots, Mrs. H. saw that his stockings were very poor, so she
got a pair of John's, and Pa has been wearing them several
days.

[27] See note, p. 173.

SATURDAY, DECEMBER 1, 1877

At the Dugout, Kill Creek, Kansas

Got to Hansen's about 10:30. After dinner, we went to chopping again, and by 2 p.m. had finished what we considered would be sufficient wood for the winter, besides getting a lot of poles and crotches for building a shed. When we came back to the house we found H. had killed a hog. We had spoken of getting some meat of him. As soon as the hog was dressed he cut off a piece (about 5 lbs.) and we took it into the house. Pa reached for the scales, but H. said: "No; weigh it after you have eaten it; it does not cost you more than carrying it home." So we shouldered it and left, after thanking him for all he had done for us. He wants Pa to keep school for his children if there is no school kept in the district, and Pa has a good notion to do so. H. advises us to buy a cow and wait awhile for a team. The cow will cost $25 or $30, and will give more milk than we can use. What do you say, Syd? Shall I get the cow and let the team wait? Pa says he and you came to an understanding that you were to lend him your spare cash, and I was to credit him that amount. But I prefer to owe you, as there is, to my way of seeing things, more show for you to get it back. The pig apparently belongs to me, but as you furnished the cash, it is yours. I propose to do this way in the pig business: you have bought her; if she produces, you shall have a pig to your credit every year—that is interest—and when we settle, you'll have an extra pig in place of the original, as I suppose that by the time a settlement is effected the original will have been turned into pork. There is a man on Little Medicine who has a yoke of 4-year old oxen for sale for $75. I could buy them for I have that amount now, but I believe I'll wait a little, as the chance is that I may pick up a bargain that is better. At any rate I must wait till I have a well and a shed to shelter the team.

SUNDAY, DECEMBER 2, 1877

At the Dugout, Kill Creek, Kansas

Went to meeting at Shellenberger's. Morris was there, and after meeting we settled for the plowing and sowing he did for me. For putting in my grain I paid $9.40; and the grain and hauling it from Osborne cost me $4.80; total investment, $14.20. We'll see how much I make on it. There will be cutting and threshing, and maybe stacking still to be paid for.

MONDAY, DECEMBER 3, 1877

At the Dugout, Kill Creek, Kansas

Hoot told me yesterday that if I wanted the team to haul a load of wood this a.m. I might have it, so about 7 o'clock Bub and I went for the team and brought a load from Hansen's. By the time we got home it was drizzling fast. It let up a little, so I chopped enough wood to last us a week, and then took the axe in and put it in the oven to shrink the old handle, so it could be replaced by a new one. The old handle is pretty badly split. It was a poor one in the first place, but I got it for nothing, and it did us three months' service. While we were off, Pa washed and baked. This evening Bub and I started for the P.O. about 5:30. It was drizzling and very foggy, but we counted on the mail arriving by 6, in which case we could get home by dark. Just before we reached the P.O. Levin overtook us. At the P.O. we found a number of the neighbors, with whom we talked till 6:30; but no mail came. As the P.M. concluded none would arrive, we struck for home. (Levin is stopping at Hoot's till H. gets back from the railroad. He intends to take a load of wheat—starts Wednesday a.m.) It was pitch dark and we could hardly keep the road for a quarter mile from the P.O., where it is much used; and had much greater difficulty when we got on the single

track over the bluff. For all that we arrived safe, with wet
boots, decidedly down in the mouth because we got no mail.
After July 1st, 1878, the mail route will be changed to a tri-
weekly, to run from Osborne to Mt. Ayr, about 3 miles west
of here. It will make a day's difference in the time we get our
letters.

TUESDAY, DECEMBER 4, 1877

AT THE DUGOUT, KILL CREEK, KANSAS

Very high wind. About 8 a.m. we went to the P.O. to get
our mail. It had not arrived, so we sat down and waited till
near 1 o'clock, still no mail. Started for home; had gone about
40 rods when we saw a team coming "a-whooping" on the
other side of the creek. That must be the mail! Back we
went, and presently it pulled up at the P.O. and P.M. Arnold
grabbed the pouch and hurried into the house with it. After
I had the letter I counted on, and the various papers, we left,
rejoicing. Don't laugh. If you knew how much we prize the
letters—all of us, I mean—you would not laugh at the sorry
picture we presented when we told Pa last night that the mail
had not arrived. These short days we have only two meals—
breakfast at 7 and dinner at 4. If we get hungry about noon,
we go for the wash boiler and eat a biscuit. For dinner today
we had nice soup, potatoes, corn, beef, and the usual biscuits,
molasses and coffee. Auntie's coffee is good, I can assure you.
Once in awhile I tell Bub I'd like to have one of Ma's sugar
cakes, or a roast turkey and cranberries, with two or three
mince pies to top off; he goes wild when I talk of such things
—especially when I say "don't you wish there was a barrel of
apples in the corner?" After dinner I chopped wood for exercise and then retired to the dugout and smoked all that was

left of the Durham that Syd sent me. (That is not a hint for more, for I think he has enough to look after without supplying me with the weed.) I have nearly ¼ lb. of that fine cut left, so you see I am not so hard on it as I might be. As soon as the pick is sharpened, so I can dig frozen ground, I am going to well-digging. Hoot and I are in partnership with the windlass. He furnished part of the wood and I part, and both use it. It would do Dave good to see how thoroughly we read the Times—ads and all. The letter always comes first. I don't suppose I'll get another letter through to you before Xmas. So a merry Xmas to you all. I hope it will be the only one we spend apart. By next Xmas I would like, and will strain hard, to have you all here. Grasshoppers or dry weather may, however, prevent, but please God, we'll be together in a year or less.

WEDNESDAY, DECEMBER 5, 1877

At the Dugout, Kill Creek, Kansas

Another windy day, so we stayed in the house nearly all day. Bub and I shelled corn to pass the time. About 4 p.m. Pa left for Hansen's to have a talk on the school question and to answer (for H.) a letter from a man in Iowa containing about 50 questions. Bub and I had dinner, and then sat and watched the firelight for an hour. Lit the lamp and while Bub read I got out the needle and thread, and then "stitch, stitch, stitch" till my back was nearly ready to break, mending the brown overalls with a blue patch all the way down the right leg, and a couple of "sale bills" (one white, one blue) on behind. Before I get through with these old overalls they will look like Joseph's coat—only they will be blocks instead of stripes. About 8 we turned in. Pa up at Hansen's.

THURSDAY, DECEMBER 6, 1877

AT THE DUGOUT, KILL CREEK, KANSAS

Up about 7:30. Had breakfast an hour later. Just before we sat down, Pa hove in sight with a kettle of milk in one hand and a big jack rabbit in the other. He also carried about 3 lbs. of beef drippings, but how he did it, I did not notice. The breakfast was swallowed in a hurry, and then we boys skinned the jack and put the meat to soak while Pa washed the dishes and baked. He reported that Hansen was willing to pay him $10 a month and give him his breakfast and supper, and as the gentleman said, "On ugly days he will not get away," and Bub and I will have things to ourselves. And if, by any possibility I should be called on to work in town, Bub will have to "keep bach." Tomorrow I expect to go to town to have the pick sharpened. Hope I'll have a chance to ride. This morning after getting through with the jack, I went to chopping wood, and kept at it pretty steady, till about 1 o'clock when I let Bub have the axe, and I took my turn loafing. Pa tried laying sod round the hog pen, but did not do much, as the sod was frozen too hard. Walked over to Jim's place to look at his corn and see if we could get another rabbit, but none was to be seen. I am going to trade the revolver for an old musket if I can, as the revolver is not much account for rabbits, being unfit to use shot. Hansen has a cow we could buy for $25, but I'm stuck, anyhow. If I keep a cow, I want a well of water and a shed—neither of which are on the premises. But they will be, I hope, by Christmas. We have a pretty good pile of split wood on hand—enough to last over a month; all oak. A good deal of it needs seasoning to make it first rate firewood. The pig is very tame now. We have to keep her tied, so she won't "go through" for us. Bub found a swivel somewhere, and I had a couple of rings, so we took one and drove a peg in the ground, around which the ring plays, and by fastening the swivel to the rope, prevent the rope from being twisted and tangled. This has been a beautiful day. We had half the rabbit, stewed, for supper. The hams, which weigh ½ lb. each, and the back, we have reserved for frying. It takes a good deal of grease, but it's mighty good eating. I was wishing for an onion to put into the stew, but Bub expressed his satisfaction at my not having any, alleging that that vegetable would spoil the stew. Pa wrote to G. Bishop. Bub has been wishing for the Count of Monte Cristo or something else to read.[28] I ordered the N.Y. Sun to be discontinued when the time expires.

Merry Christmas to you all!

FRIDAY, DECEMBER 7, 1877

AT THE DUGOUT, KILL CREEK, KANSAS

Started for town about 6:30. Had walked about 10 miles when Rev. Bowers overtook me, and I rode with him to town. Called at the P.O. and got Syd's letter of Nov. 18. Barnhart settled with me and wanted me to work 1½ days. Didn't take him up because the well was waiting to be dug, and wood to be hauled, and I did not know but I could have the team tomorrow. Rode back with Bowers as far as Gillmore's, 7 miles from home. Passing Greenfield's about 2:30, saw Pa and Bub picking up sorghum seed for halves. Went to see

---

[28] Bub (George) Ruede was always an omnivorous reader. At the time when I knew him, many years later, I believe he had read more books than any other man I ever knew; and he remembered what he read, for he had an extraordinary memory. Indeed, George Ruede had a powerful and brilliant mind and a keen sense of humor; and I think he might have been an important literary figure if his ambition had pointed that way. Ruth Ruede, the only surviving member of the family, is much like George in all respects.

how they were getting on and thence home to cook dinner. The pick got pretty heavy by the time I got there, and the basket for which Pa so much wished was unhandy to carry because the handle would come out. Had fried jack for dinner, and I had dinner ready when they got home. No mail tonight because the horses attached to the mail wagon broke the tongue before the driver started.

SATURDAY, DECEMBER 8, 1877

AT THE DUGOUT, KILL CREEK, KANSAS

Geo. and I had just got the sod off the place where the well is to be, when Pa brought the mail. Pick and shovel were let fall very quick, and we had a race to see which would be first to get hold of a Times, for we expected nothing else. But I got a letter after all—from Emma Chitty. Towards evening I got Hoot's team and went to Diegel's for a couple of gallons of molasses. They bought Morris' and there are still 2 gallons due me. The "beauty of Kill Creek" does not show off well during the week, slopping round in played out slippers and red stockings. Pa had been down to Jakey Gsell's for a short shovel, but did not get one. The well is too deep to use a long-handled shovel. When I took the team home, Hoot wondered if I knew a man named Fether from Bethlehem. I knew he meant John Fetter—he had come on a visit to Levin.

SUNDAY, DECEMBER 9, 1877

AT THE DUGOUT, KILL CREEK, KANSAS

John and Levin came over before I had turned out for the day. After breakfast we went to call on Jake Albright; he intends to leave for Russell next Thursday, and will start from there the following Monday. Didn't stay long. Went over to Hoot's to see about getting the team to haul wood tomorrow, and found them at dinner, so I fell in for some. Thence to inspect Levin's dugout; it is well laid up, but the sod was partly frozen, and will settle a good deal. Lapp says ours is the best dugout he has seen in Kansas, and I suppose Levin is trying to make his better.

MONDAY, DECEMBER 10, 1877

At the Dugout, Kill Creek, Kansas

After breakfast hauled a load of sorghum seed from Elick Blair's, and two loads of wood from Hansen's, which took till after 6 p.m., which constituted the day's work. There are still two loads to haul.

TUESDAY, DECEMBER 11, 1877

At the Dugout, Kill Creek, Kansas

Leveled off a place for a stable and set a couple of crotches. Pa did not feel well; I had to do the cooking, and therefore did not get much work done.

WEDNESDAY, DECEMBER 12, 1877

At the Dugout, Kill Creek, Kansas

Finished setting the crotches and laid the main cross-pieces. Had not enough poles to finish the skeleton. Sunk the well a couple of feet, while Bub sorted the corn. Pa is O.K. again. Ate a biscuit about 2 p.m. and then went to digging again, but had hardly made a dozen strokes before I struck myself on the

head with the pick. Bub yelled, "It's bleeding, How!!" and
sure enough it was! Bled like a stuck pig for a few minutes—
till I put cold water on the "contused wound," as it pleased
Bub to call it. It made my head ache, and I did no more this
afternoon for fear it would bleed again. Rook was to bring
our grist yesterday, but his wagon broke down just as he left
the mill, so we had to borrow flour of him to last a few days.
Pa proposes to build an addition to the dugout, which will be
all above ground—in other words, a sod house. Ma, will you
live in it? He proposes to floor and plaster both rooms. It will
cost about $20 for fixing up both, and then we'll have two
rooms 14 x 16 ft. If you'll live in it, we'll be ready for you
by harvest I think, and harvest comes the 20th of June, or
thereabouts. If Syd and Ruth don't want to, they need not
come directly. All of you will be welcome at any time after
the houses are up. Will you be contented in such a place?

THURSDAY, DECEMBER 13, 1877

At the Dugout, Kill Creek, Kansas

My work today consisted of making the well 5 feet deeper.
That was all I did, except making dinner. Bub chopped wood
and shelled corn. Pa washed and picked up a lot of sorghum
seed at Greenfield's, and after dinner went to Hansen's. When
he came back he had about 2 quarts of sweet milk. Geo. and
I drank nearly half. The thermometer marked about 60 deg.
at noon today.

FRIDAY, DECEMBER 14, 1877

At the Dugout, Kill Creek, Kansas

Chopped wood all day. Geo. piled it up. Pa went to Guyer's
for coal oil, and closed the bargain for a hog for $6. We'll

have butchering one day next week, for we must have meat. Rook brought our grist and a lot of cottonwood lumber and slabs. After supper I sifted out the corn meal, so we can have mush one of these evenings. Then we'll get fat (?)

SATURDAY, DECEMBER 15, 1877

AT THE DUGOUT, KILL CREEK, KANSAS

Pretty heavy frost this a.m. Geo. and I helped Hoot "snap" corn. "Snapping" is breaking off the ear from the stalk without husking it. A good deal of corn is cribbed without being husked. After dinner brought the windlass over from Hoot's, and by 5 p.m. the well was 5 feet deeper—15 feet deep now. Dug through a layer of gravel and got into a layer of hard sand. This gravel or "lime" we intend to use in plastering the house. We have had beautiful clear and warm weather all the week—nothing like what we have been used to in December.

SUNDAY, DECEMBER 16, 1877

AT THE DUGOUT, KILL CREEK, KANSAS

Went with Hoot to Neuschwanger's to meeting. Pa and Bub went to Hansen's to hear Bowers preach English this afternoon. Bub says next time he will go to hear N. There was a pretty good crowd present, in spite of the heavy fog this a.m. The sun came out by 2 p.m. Levin was at Fetter's near Bull City today. It is reported that one of Cunningham's horses gave out when they got to Dodge City, and that he and Wils Berger have returned to Osborne.

MONDAY, DECEMBER 17, 1877

At the Dugout, Kill Creek, Kansas

Cloudy and drizzling near all the morning. Went to work at the well soon after breakfast, but were chased into the house by a little shower. As soon as that was over, we went to work again. Dug through 5½ feet of gravel, very closely packed, which broke the points off the pick. Then got into sand, which was easier work. I was in the well, and the others at the windlass.

TUESDAY, DECEMBER 18, 1877

At the Dugout, Kill Creek, Kansas

At the well again. Sunk it to 25 feet and struck shale. Then we quit. We'll have to go to another place to dig now. We were not very badly disappointed, because we thought we'd find plenty shale. The chance was for water, but fortune did not smile upon us. There's 3¼ days' work for nothing. Bright and clear and warm today. Geo. and I ran round without coat or vest, and our sleeves rolled up, and did not feel uncomfortable. You need not wait till September before I can tell whether I'll have enough to bread us—I can tell that by 1st of July.

WEDNESDAY, DECEMBER 19, 1877

At the Dugout, Kill Creek, Kansas

Butchering day for us. Before we could butcher we had to get the pig. For this Pa and I went to Guyer's two miles east, directly after breakfast. Without much difficulty we caught the pig, and with a great deal less I paid $6 for it. We might

have had a larger one for $2 more, but we couldn't go it.
When we got to the creek we had some fun. Mr. Pig would
not go through the water without help, so we gave him a lift
into it twice, and twice did he emerge on the same bank from
which he had been "chucked" in. We got desperate. I crossed
with the end of the rope; Pa stayed with the pig. When I
was ready, Pa shoved him into the water and I pulled him
across hind part foremost. We got him home all right and
tied him to a post. Pa went for water, while Bub and I went
to Hoot's for a barrel (in lieu of a scalding trough), a big
dish pan and butcher knife. Then I helped carry water. That
was no fun, for we had to go ¼ mile to the pond. Pa brought
5 and ¼ buckets full. Our wash boiler lid has not arrived,
so the water took a little longer to boil. When it was hot I
got my revolver, and we sent for the "sacrifice." Twice the
cap snapped, but the third did not, and Mr. Pig fell in his
tracks without a squeal. Pa stuck him, and then we got the
water. We weighed the meat and it pulled the beam at a
little less than 100 lbs., but near enough to call it an even
hundred. We had a couple of showers during the afternoon,
one of which occurred just when we were getting the bristles
off the pig . Our boots were wet through, but we did not get
a chance to pull them off till we were done. Had fried liver
for supper. This evening it is very foggy. I must stop writing and put another blue patch on the old overalls.

THURSDAY, DECEMBER 20, 1877

AT THE DUGOUT, KILL CREEK, KANSAS

I did not find a blue patch big enough, so I used a patch
made of half a leg of Pa's old linen pants, which answers just
as well. This morning it looked as though we might have more

rain, so I did not go to work directly. I was over to Hoot's to get buttermilk, and afterwards began to dig at another place for water. I am not at all discouraged by the failure of the first well. There are men in this neighborhood who have dug 4 and 5 wells, and still have no water. Dug 3 feet. This afternoon I helped Hoot with his cellar. We did not get half done. Tomorrow I am to work for Hoot, and Saturday I must go to town. Barnhart sent word that he wanted me this morning, but as the word did not reach me till near noon, I paid no attention to it. I don't run after one day's work—if that one day is all he can give me. It takes at least a week's work to make me walk to town now. As some folks say, "We live anyhow."

FRIDAY, DECEMBER 21, 1877

AT THE DUGOUT, KILL CREEK, KANSAS

Another rainy day, or rather, drizzly. A little before 10 a.m. Hoot came over for me and Bub to help him at his well. We did not go to the timber, as the road was too soft. Took a foot of gravel out of the well, and then the water came in so fast that Henry came out. After dinner we went home, and I lay down on the bed and took a nap, from which I was awakened by Charley Hoot (Sam's boy) who came for me to help put the ridgepole on Sam's house. Hoot and Levin and I went over and found that they had two on already. Helped put on the third and then went back home. He has three ridgepoles, in order to make the roof stiffer. There were eleven of us; six would have been enough. Talking with Hoot about digging wells, etc., he told me about one new neighbor, Diegel, who has a firm faith in water witching. The well on his place does not afford enough water, so he got Don Pedro to witch for him. Don told him the water vein had been missed

by two feet on one side of the wall. To illustrate: Let this **O**
represent the well. Now the witcher says two feet on this side
is the well, so D. digs his well this shape ⬭; how's that?
One of Hoot's roosters has been fighting with the turkeys and
got whipped; then another rooster went for him and beat him
till he was nearly dead; so Hoot offered to trade with me.
Mine is not so large, but H. is satisfied, so I told him all
right. The birds have not changed residence yet.

SATURDAY, DECEMBER 22, 1877

At the Dugout, Kill Creek, Kansas

Last night after we had turned in, the water began to drip
through the roof right on the bed, in consequence of the
soaking rain and an extra heavy shower that blew up about
9 o'clock. The dripping startled me out first, and I got up and
lit the lamp to see if the water was dropping on the flour sack.
Found that all right, so I lay down again where the water
would not hit me. Presently the dripping reached Pa's end of
the bed, so he turned out and stirred Geo. and then we moved
the bed right under the ridgepole, where no drop came
through. We had to move the bran and flour to the middle
of the house. Then we managed to get about half a night's
sleep. Did not go to town today, as Hoot decided against it
on account of the rain. Took a look at my wheat and rye,
which have come out fine; this rain was what the grain needed.
A good deal of ground fell into the well, being loosened by
the rain. Didn't work a lick today.

SUNDAY, DECEMBER 23, 1877

At the Dugout, Kill Creek, Kansas

Stayed home. Pa went to Hackerott's to meeting. Cleared
off last night.

MONDAY, DECEMBER 24, 1877

AT THE DUGOUT, KILL CREEK, KANSAS

Had a heavy frost this morning. Got up before 6, and made for the postoffice to meet a team going to Osborne, if possible. Heard Rupert was going, and was on the way to his house when I saw Hansen's team coming. Waited till it came up and asked John whether I could go along. He seemed glad for company. Got to town about 11, and made my purchases, and had Bub's boots mended. Total outlay $2.65. Saw a number of my friends, and had a little talk with them. Barnhart put my name on the D. H. [dead head?] list, so I'll get the paper every week in consideration of my furnishing items whenever there are any. He wants me to come down and do three or four days' work this week. Got back to the Creek at sundown. On the way from the P.O. met Pa and Bub going for the mail. They came back without it, as Pa was hungry—he had eaten nothing since morning. The mail came in late. What do you think of digging potatoes the day before Christmas? A man down town dug some today. Got Jimmy's letter. Will have to think over it, and then answer to the best of my ability.

TUESDAY, DECEMBER 25, 1877

AT THE DUGOUT, KILL CREEK, KANSAS

Clear and bright. Frost this morning. Pa made a bedstead yesterday—a double bed with a bunk above it. He and Bub sleep downstairs, and I sleep in the garret. About 8:30 went to the P. O. and got the mail. Did not get a letter, and remarked it was queer I got none, when Sallie Meeks, the P.M.'s granddaughter, said there was a registered letter for "Rudy." Gave him a receipt for it. That letter was hugely enjoyed by all of us. There was meeting at Hoot's this a.m. Bevvy and Annie and all the other Neuschwangers were there. Bub has to do the chores. The arrangement we have is that he is to work at home for his board, and when he works for other folks he gets what he earns. He has earned about $5 since he came, but he hasn't got the money. It goes to my credit, and I owe him. If anybody wants the Immigrant's Guide, tell them to send 10 cents to F. H. Barnhart, Osborne City, and he'll send them a copy. I can't buy for everybody. After we came home this afternoon I dug the well 2 feet deeper. It is almost 6 feet deep now. There is a dance on Little Medicine tonight. Morris and Levin went. Pa went to Hansen's toward evening, as John had sent word for him to come and get some rabbits he had caught for us. Pa will most probably stay overnight. Syd, I'm ever so much obliged for the loan of those $10. If you have any more to loan, send it along, but do not borrow any money to loan to me. I am not in debt, and don't want you to go in debt on my account. I'd rather wait a little longer for a thing and pay cash for it. Then nobody can dun me or you. There are lots of men here who borrowed money and now wish they had not, and I am bound to profit by their experience. So remember, don't borrow to help me along.

WEDNESDAY, DECEMBER 26, 1877

AT THE DUGOUT, KILL CREEK, KANSAS

Went with Hoot to the timber, and by 1:30 reached his house with a load. After dinner helped him dig his cellar, and put the ridgepole in position. It was cold riding this morning. The wind was pretty sharp, and a little snow fell. Working out of doors is to me what it is to some men to get full of tanglefoot—when I get to a hot stove I get drowsy. Turned out at 5:15 this a.m. so I am very sleepy. Guess I'll go to bed, as I expect to go to town tomorrow to work a few days or a week. Work in the office strikes me just about right—when the cash begins to run short. What I earn there goes for the household expenses. Sometimes I manage to put a few dollars aside towards the team (when I get a couple of weeks together).

SUNDAY, JANUARY 6, 1878

At the Dugout, Kill Creek, Kansas

Back again; arrived last night, but expect to leave for town again tomorrow. On the 27th, when I started, snow was falling, but in the course of a couple of hours the weather changed, becoming warmer, and the walking was very bad. Arrived in town at 11:30 with my feet sopping wet. And in consequence of going off without an extra pair of socks, I had to invest a quarter. Went to work right after dinner. Sunday I spent at Schweitzer's. He offered me his oxen for $60. Told him I could not buy now, had to wait till I found water. Monday night, by invitation I watched for the New Year with the Herzogs. Supper at 10 of chocolate and "liebesmahl kuchen" with raisins in them. Got to bed by 12:15. Next night there was a dance. I got to talking with a fellow, and before I knew it, it was 1 o'clock. Didn't go to bed at all. Sat by the stove and talked till daylight. When I went to work I felt like I imagine a man does when he is getting over a spree. Could hardly walk straight. When I went to bed that night I went to sleep in a minute, and never got awake till the boss of the shanty came upstairs with the bell and rang me out.

Got $6 for my work in the office. Frank never makes a bar-
gain with me, but when I am through he asks how much
he owes me, and pays whatever I say. I was awful tired of
staying in town, but if I had known that I can't do any work
here, I'd have remained. I have got out an account of what it
has cost us since we commenced "baching." Here it is.

	August	*Sept.*	*Oct.*	*Nov.*	*Dec.*
Provisions	$ 4.75	$4.44	$3.12	$2.70	$7.07½
Household Goods and tools.	32.47	2.85	.60	1.05	1.20
Wood		1.25		1.50	
Coal oil	.20		.40	.20	.60
Clothing			4.95	3.50	.50
Stock				5.00	1.75
Sundries	1.32	1.90	1.28	1.60	3.10

The total expenses from Aug. 19 to Dec. 31, including the
pig and chickens, which we still have, was $89.31½, of which
$15.62½ was paid in work. The grain of which the flour was
made was also paid for in work—but that was before we moved
into the house, so it don't figure in this account. Then the
plowing and putting in wheat and rye was paid in work, so
that does not come in, though it amounted to $9.40. That
is a separate account.

FRIDAY, JANUARY 11, 1878

AT THE DUGOUT, KILL CREEK, KANSAS

Well, I'm home again, but tomorrow I go to town with
Hoot, as there is some business that must be attended to. The
wash boiler lid has not arrived, so Jake Getz said if I brought
the boiler he would make me a lid. I walked down last Monday in about 3¼ hours, and had hardly gotten into the office
before my coat was off and I went to work. Got through
today at noon and started for home directly after dinner.
Saw no Kill Creek team in town, so I went to the river and

sat on a stump and whistled, and in response a team came
to the ford, and I rode over half way home. I have learned
to wait since I came out. Ten months tomorrow since I left
Bethlehem. Last night I called on Mrs. Morrow and Nora.
They live in town. Had a very pleasant time. . . . This evening Hoot came over to witch for water, and showed me a
place where he claims there is a vein of water, not 20 feet from
the house. Pa & Bub will bore tomorrow, as we have the use of
an auger. I'll have to get a pair of well buckets and a pulley
tomorrow, as I don't know when I will get another good
chance to have them delivered at my door. I get awful tired
of working in town, but the cash helps me along. I have
earned $9.40 since the 27th of last month, besides board.
R. G. Hays is rushing up a house. Grugers are going to Harlan, 15 miles north of Osborne, to run a store. Fritchey "set
'em up" for writing an ad the other evening. If I gain in
weight in the future as I have in the past few months, I'll
make a man yet. I am 16 lbs. heavier than I ever was—147¾.
The last three days have been very bright, despite the predic-
tions of an old lunatic who said "9th to 13th: cloudy and
threatening. . . ."

SATURDAY, JANUARY 12, 1878

At the Dugout, Kill Creek, Kansas

Went to town with Hoot, to take the wash boiler to have
a lid put on. You see, when I got the stove and outfit, in
August, Hays & Wilson had no lids to the boilers; every
once in awhile I'd ask whether the lids had arrived, but never
got one, so Jake Getz, the tinsmith, said if I'd bring the
boiler, he'd make a lid for it. Did a lot of running round
and bought some things: A pair of well buckets, 80¢; chains

(50¢) to fasten them to the rope in order to keep the rope from being wet more than necessary; also a pulley for the rope to play through (65¢). This pulley is fastened to a "yoke" seven or eight feet above the curb and when you draw up one bucket, the other goes down to be filled. Pa wanted some small pans that could be covered with a plate, so I bought three for 55¢, and two bowls for 20¢. That was the inventory. Barnhart settled with me, and engaged me to work several days week after next. We had a bad time going to town, as it was sleeting pretty lively, but by 2 p.m. it quit, and the wind came up very cold. Called to see the Grugers. Found Mrs. G. making Christmas Cakes, of which I obtained a sample. Made the acquaintance of Mrs. Cal Reasoner, a very pleasant lady. Hoot forgot the bucket of molasses at Diegel's, so I told him I'd have to borrow of him to help us out.

SUNDAY, JANUARY 13, 1878

AT THE DUGOUT, KILL CREEK, KANSAS

Half an inch of snow on the ground this morning. Didn't turn out till 8; by the time we had had breakfast it was too late to go to Neuschwangers for meeting. Since the middle of October I have earned $37 in the printing office. Was over at Hoot's awhile this morning. Toward evening the clouds cleared off, and there was a beautiful sunset. Went to the hole in the draw that Pa dug on Friday. It is about three feet deep. They bored down and struck water. I ran a sunflower stalk down, and the auger hole was only 4 feet deep; there were about 6 inches of water in it. The misery of the thing is that it is not on my claim.

MONDAY, JANUARY 14, 1878

AT THE DUGOUT, KILL CREEK, KANSAS

Directly after breakfast Geo. and I went to boring where Hoot had said there was water. Down twelve feet and struck shale. Would have continued boring, to see how thick the shale is, but just then Geo. Lough came for the auger, and I could not tell him he couldn't have it. Went to Hoot's and borrowed a shovel; Bub and I went to the hole in the draw (not on my claim) where Pa bored and struck water. They had dug about three feet, and I dug about four more, and then had all the water we will need for the present, though I am not yet done digging wells. I intend to dig on my place till I get water. I was a pretty specimen when I arrived on the surface. What with standing in mud and water, and the dripping from the mud bucket, and striking against the side of the well, I was coated, literally smeared, from the top of my cap to the soles of my boots, which apparently weighed a ton each. I stripped off my shirt to clean up, and right where the holes in the shirt are (on both shoulders) there were lumps of mud. My face and hair were in the same fix. As Hoot wanted the shovel after dinner, I could not use it, so I took a rest. About 3 o'clock Pa came from Hansen's with a kettle of milk. Half an hour after, Bub and I went for the mail. We expected it to be in by 4, but it did not arrive till 7. There were 8 or 10 of us, and we kept things pretty lively. Got the Times and your letters.

TUESDAY, JANUARY 15, 1878

AT THE DUGOUT, KILL CREEK, KANSAS

Dug at my second well awhile this morning. After dinner brought a load of wood from Hansen's, and brought the bucket of molasses from Diegel's that was forgotten on Saturday. Went to the well in the draw this evening, and found the water waist-deep. Pa has a great notion for taking that 80 south of mine. It is not likely anybody will bother with an 80 when they can get 160 by going a mile or two further. I'm willing. When Syd comes, he can live with me till he is tired of "baching" and then live with you awhile. If Pa takes that 80, we'll rush up a sod house there instead of on my place. I intend to close the bargain with Jac. Schweitzer for his oxen (if he has not already sold them) when I go to town on Monday. Pa was helping Jakey husk corn all day. Bub was no account, owing to a severe pain in the bowels. After supper I went to Hoot's and ground a lot of coffee. The last coffee that I ground over there was on the Sunday before Christmas, according to Mrs. Hoot.

WEDNESDAY, JANUARY 16, 1878

At the Dugout, Kill Creek, Kansas

Pa went to help Jakey this morning, but came back before 10, on account of neuralgia in the face. I chopped a lot of wood, and then patched my unmentionables. This afternoon I went with Pa up on the bluffs, and discovered the n.w. corner of the section. Saw a pair of eagles on the ground, but before we got very near, they flew off. Started a jack, but did not get it, as it was out of range.

THURSDAY, JANUARY 17, 1878

At the Dugout, Kill Creek, Kansas

Looked for a stick suitable for a windlass roller, but did not find any. Pa was at Jackey's all day. About noon our new neighbor, Fred Heberlein, called. Had a long talk with him, and he used a lot of my scrap tobacco, without saying whether it was good or poor; no doubt his pipe was so foul from smoking "Old Style" that he could not tell whether he was smoking tobacco or horsehair. Pa came home with the heart and liver of a pig Jakey killed. I at once got the potatoes on the fire and fixed about half the liver and the heart, and in half an hour we had supper. The folks here, when they kill a hog, begin cooking the meat by commencing on the heart and liver, and then slice off wherever they've a mind to, and fry, piece-meal, nearly the whole hog.

FRIDAY, JANUARY 18, 1878

At the Dugout, Kill Creek, Kansas

This was a foggy, damp day, and we did no work out of doors. Pa went to Gsell's but soon came back with a kettle of milk. Hoot brought me five bushels of corn, and Bub and I shelled it Pa laid up the cobs back of the stove to dry out. Paid 20¢ per bushel for the corn. About 2 p.m. Pa wanted dinner, so I got some together, and afterwards we went to look at the 80 south of my claim. By going to the top of a bank we could see the whole tract. Graybill, the latest comer, has gobbled my job at Hoot's—helping Henry gather corn. He wants Henry to help with his house. There are three vacant 80s joining my claim. They are all rather rough.

We live in what Lish Gregory calls "Sod Town," which is built along both sides of the road west from J. A. Fritsche's place on Kill Creek to the present east line of Mt. Ayr township. "Pennsylvania Avenue" is three miles long and all the people who live along this road are either recent arrivals from the Keystone State or came originally from there, and finally landed in Kansas after living in several other states. Some of these settlers are great wanderers, and I have no doubt many of them will go on farther west when this country is well settled.

The houses along this road are big or small in proportion to the ability of the owner to procure rafters—usually split rails —in sufficient number, or a ridge log that will make a house more than 16 or 20 feet in length inside. Some of the roofs sag, because the walls have settled unevenly or because the rafters have bent under the weight of the sod roof. The rafters are always put in green, because the settlers have no inclination to wait for them to season. To get a place to live is the prime consideration with a man who has to live in a canvas-roofed wagon until he can provide a more comfortable place for his family.

SUNDAY, FEBRUARY 3, 1878

OSBORNE, KANSAS

I am here yet, and expect to stay till the end of the week, as Barnhart expects to go to Kansas City on business, to be gone a week.

I came down two weeks ago tomorrow, and saw Schweitzer about buying the oxen. He said he would keep them till the 1st of March if I could not get ready for them before. He appeared to be a little anxious about the money, but calmed down when I told him I would pay cash down.

We have more fun than a little here at Anderson's. The other night we had a railroad conductor here, and he had been telling stories for awhile when Fritchey came in. The R.R. man had not been talking for about ten minutes, but we all called for him to finish his story, and he began a fresh one, though the way he began made Fritchey think he had interrupted the story. Our man finished his story, and that reminded Fritchey of one. Everybody was anxious to hear it, so he cocked up his legs on a chair and began spouting; he had just fairly launched out when the heads began to drop till the whole dozen had their heads down or leaning against the wall, apparently asleep. Fritchey did not seem to notice this peculiar state of affairs until somebody snored. He stopped talking, but as the objectionable noise was not repeated, he began again—but before he had got a dozen words out, there was such a chorus of snores that he could not hear himself talk. He remarked that "this must be a d—d sleepy crowd"; which upset the gravity of the audience and awaked them at the same time, and such a side-splitting laugh as we had at his expense I have not enjoyed for a long time. He got "mad enough to chaw the whole lot," as he afterwards told somebody. He looked toward the door as though he would like to leave; a stranger was leaning against it, so he had no way except to laugh with the rest. He was the worst beat man I ever saw. It was a "put up job" on him. We afterwards sold Frank Leebrick on the same thing—snored him into silence.[29]

A young druggist named Heberhart, from Madison, Ind., is coming here to set up in business in about a month. The Grugers intend to move to Harlan, 15 miles north of here, in a few weeks. R. G. [Hays]'s house is under roof, and this week the plasterers will begin work.

Land hunters are quite plenty, and a good many places are sold. Government land is being rapidly taken up, if report is to be believed.

Neither Pa nor Geo. has been in town in the last two weeks,

---

[29] These pioneers were generally much given to practical jokes.

and I'm kind of homesick. It's a good thing, though, that I have work here, as I could do no work out of doors. I'll make $14.50 this trip. I bought 6 bu. wheat from Frank for $3.90; 4 bu. at 70¢ and 2 bu. at 50. That will make enough flour to last a couple of months. . . .

Next Sunday the New Evangelical church on Kill Creek will be dedicated. I suppose there will be an awful crowd present.

It's almost a year since I left Bethlehem, and I feel as though I had lived here all my life.

Ira is very well satisfied here. His mother thought it would be a good idea for him to farm with me; it would be well enough, only we are 12 or 14 miles apart, so that plan is not practicable.

We had about 3½ inches of snow on Tuesday, but the sleighing was not much, because there are only one or two who have even an apology for a sleigh and nobody has a cutter, so those who came to town rode in their wagons.

TUESDAY, FEBRUARY 12, 1878

At the Dugout, Kill Creek, Kansas

Arrived last night, after being absent just three weeks, during which I earned just $14.50. I missed half a day by going on Monday; that's why the bill was not $15. Yesterday morning about 10 o'clock I began watching for teams and about noon Dave Meeks came along, so I asked him to take some things up for me. He said he would, so I got my stuff together at the printing office. There were 6 bushels of wheat I had bought of Barnhart at the price he paid to people who had brought it in on subscription—70¢ for fall wheat, and 50 for spring wheat—which made the bill $3.90. Then there was part of a gallon of coal oil (the can leaks badly), a barrel, tobacco bucket, shovel, and the wash boiler I brought to town some time ago to have a lid put on. I had to pay him a dollar to go round by my place, and it is no further that way than by the other road. When F. H. B[arnhart] came back from Kansas City on Saturday evening he complimented me on the good paper I got out last week. Today it is 11 months since I left Bethlehem. Graybill has changed the numbers of his filing and taken the 80 south of me—so Pa will have to take the one on the east. . . .

Answers to Syd's questions:

I think we will have plenty of work on my place for two, and if not, there is generally something to do for others. Barnhart will be very apt to call for help occasionally, especially if he knows one of us will be sure to come, and we can always be ready (except in harvest or threshing time) to help him and make a little cash, which is mighty handy. Don't worry about being a drag on me. I won't say "Ready" till I have a place for you to live in and see that the wheat will be enough; and of that I have good prospects. As for the winter—why, I expect it will be like this winter—work at home and once in a while work in the office. I don't feel a bit doubtful but that we'll have enough to eat, and have a place to live in. You can't imagine how glad I felt when I saw by the letter that you had made up your mind to come.

WEDNESDAY, FEBRUARY 13, 1878

AT THE DUGOUT, KILL CREEK, KANSAS

As it was drizzling or snowing all day, we stayed in the house.

THURSDAY, FEBRUARY 14, 1878

AT THE DUGOUT, KILL CREEK, KANSAS

Same sort of weather as yesterday. Pa wanted to go to see how Don Pedro was getting along, so Bub and I fixed up and went with him. I went to take a look at the old wagon Jakey has in charge, which can be bought for $15; concluded the price was too high. I know of one for sale down town, and intend to try for that. Got three Times today. Graybill had sod broken to lay up his house. And now they say Snyder wants the 80 east of me for Addie. Well, I don't care. Let her have it. We can be just as happy and contented on 160, can't we, as on 240? I think Pa is getting too old to run a farm. We boys would have to do all the work anyhow, and I'd rather have the family all together. If we all work together we can improve our 160 and make it produce more than if we only half work it and put in the other half of the work on another piece of ground. The main objection to pre-empting is that a man is obliged to reside on his place all the time; and anybody who wants to can put a homestead over his pre-emption and cause him trouble by making him contest the homesteader off. . . .

FRIDAY, FEBRUARY 15, 1878

AT THE DUGOUT, KILL CREEK, KANSAS

Ford's well auger has been at Shellenberger's for some time, and as we heard he was done using it, Bub and I went for it but arrived just in time to see a man drive off with it. So we had our walk (8 miles) for nothing. Scared a jack on the way home. Graybill and Hoot were laying up sod on G.'s house. Sam Hoot has a pair of oxen; one Texan, thin as a board—the other Cherokee, with warbles, i.e., worms

in the flesh under the skin. Our neighbor Fritsche has returned with a yoke of cattle. Pa has given up the idea of taking a claim. He expressed himself as being very indifferent
about it, so I told him not to take one. By all working together on my claim we can make it pay us better wages and
more profits than two-thirds of the men who have twice or
three times as much. The curse of this country is land-grab-
bing. Few men are satisfied with one claim; they must have
a pre-emption, homestead and timber-filing, and between the
three they have so much work they don't know which end
they stand on. This week we have really done no work, as
the weather has been very unfavorable. I would not like to
live in Graybill's house, as I think it will settle very much.
The sod is very wet and rotten. We can eat corn bread
(Johnny-cake is what they call it here) as well as the old
settlers. The hens lay now, and we get milk at Jakey's so
that we have corn bread about every other day for breakfast.
Fried pork, cornbread and molasses, and coffee are good
breakfast. Geo. and I think so. Expenses last month amounted
to $7.97½, divided thus: Well outfit $2.55; household goods,
75¢; provisions 67½¢; corn $1; rails for hog pen, $2.14;
sundries 86¢. This month the bill already foots up over $10,
but there is wheat sufficient to make flour to last two months.

SUNDAY, FEBRUARY 24, 1878

At the Dugout, Kill Creek, Kansas

I reckon I'll have to give a history of last week, as it was
a very interesting one for me. On Monday we turned out
about 5:30, and by 6 I was on the road to Osborne. The sud-
denness of my departure was caused by a conversation I had
with Hoot in reference to having the use of his team for a

couple of days to haul hay for a shed in which to put my team when I brought it from Schweitzer's. He said if I'd get the oxen I might put them behind his straw stack till I had a shelter for them, and might water them at his well until I had a well dug. So I concluded that as I could have the use of his team for only one day, I had better take up his offer and do my own hauling. I had just crossed my east line when I met August Fritsche on his way to mill. Requested him to bring my grist. He said he did not know me. Told him who I was, and he said he would bring it as far as Sam Hoot's. I could not make him understand where my dugout was. Walked to Harry Humphrey's five miles from town, and rode with him the rest of the way. Arrived in Osborne about 9:30 and went to see Watson & Gillette, who had a wagon for sale. The price was $40. That was $10 more than I had. Then to Herzog's to see what Charley wants for his wagon. He was not home, but I got my dinner by waiting for him. He wanted $50 so that was no go. Back to W. & G.'s to see if they would not come down. But they would not. Next tried Ed Humphrey. He would sell for $30. As that was the highest figure I could go, I went to see the vehicle. Found the tongue was broken, as well as the hind bolster, and the box was not much account. I closed the bargain because I could hear of no other wagon for sale. Then went to Sears. John wanted something to read, so I took him the Phantom Ship. When I came near the house I saw Mrs. S. looking out the window and saw she did not recognize me, as I was shaved clean. Knocked at the door, and walked in and bid her "Good evening." Then she knew who I was, and we had a good laugh at her for not recognizing me at once. Had supper and then went to Schweitzer's. Talked awhile and then paid him for the oxen—$60. Turned in about 10. Next morning after breakfast Wally went out and yoked the oxen for me, and I started for town. When I got there Ed Humphrey had the wagon at the blacksmith shop, getting it repaired, and wanted to back out of the bargain. I had heard of another wagon for sale for $15 so I borrowed one of Ed's horses and rode about 4 miles from town to see the owner and the wagon but could find neither. I wanted to get a wagon offered to me for $15 or $20, so I could back Ed down on his price, but he saved me the trouble. I did not let him off very easy. Priced all the wagons I could hear or think of, but could not get a satisfactory price. At last I came across C. G. Paris and asked him whether he knew of a wagon for sale. He replied that he had one. How much? $35. Make it $30 and I'll take it. He argued about ten minutes with me, saying he'd take $30 and never ask me for the other V. Told him I did not do business on that line; that I had $30 to pay for a wagon, and I wanted a receipt in full, that I would not go in debt for even $5. Could apparently make no impression on him, so I went up town and bought a chain, and started for home without a wagon. I had not got out of town before he called me back, saying he'd take $30. So I tied the oxen, paid him and got a receipt. Then I again started for home Got to the river, and after a little trouble succeeded in riding across on ox-back. After poking along for 2½ hours, I arrived at Paris' house. The wagon was not there, and I lost an hour getting it. Did not get home till 9:45, and found Pa and Geo. in bed. Tied the cattle to the wagon and threw them a bunch of hay, and then went in to have some supper (I had eaten nothing since breakfast) and read your letter and one from Ad. Turned in at 11. Wednesday was rainy. Didn't haul anything, but tied the oxen at Hoot's straw stack, and stayed indoors all day. Thursday was clear, so I borrowed Hoot's hay rack and Pa and I went for a load. Put on as much as we thought the oxen could pull and started for home. Had gone half a mile when we got stuck in a prairie dog hole, and had to get help to pull out. Threw off part of the hay and got as far as Fritsche's where, in going up a rise, the oxen suddenly geed off and upset hay, wagon and everything. Took them off from the wagon and fixed up things again, and finally got home with about half the hay we started with. Since then we have hauled hay on the wagon box and it goes much better. We pile it up pretty high and tie it on. There are two or three more loads to haul, and by the time it is all up we will have a pretty good stable. The cattle mind me pretty well now, and I am getting used to walking two miles an hour alongside the wagon. Today we all went over to Hoot's to meeting. Was at Graybill's to dinner. Mrs. Graybill offered to do our washing if I would furnish the tub and rubbing board (so I furnished the articles) and half the soap. That will let Pa off from washing. Bub was down town yesterday and bought a curry comb, so now we can get the dirt out of the oxen's hides. I have something less than a dollar, and Pa has a whole dollar in cash, but we are happy anyhow. I'll have to trust to Providence to put work in my way to raise about $20 to buy a breaking plow, hoe, fork and rake, and timber for the new sod addition we intend to put to the ranch. I had those 6 bushels of wheat ground; the miller takes off 1/6 for toll, so that from 5 bushels of wheat I got nearly 200 lbs. of flour. From about $4 worth of wheat I got about $6 worth of flour. That grist panned out better than any I have yet sent to mill. I am the Kill Creek correspondent of the Farmer, and am on the D. H. list of that journal.

TUESDAY, FEBRUARY 26, 1878

AT THE DUGOUT, KILL CREEK, KANSAS

Brought a little load of wood from Hansen's this morning, and afternoon went to Greenfield's for our half of the sorghum seed Pa and Geo. picked up. It made a good big load. Talked with Levin awhile. He was hauling a load of rails to make a hog pen, and remarked that it was very unhandy to have to wait till somebody was ready to let him have a team. I concurred with him in that opinion and remarked that until a man had a team to haul things when he was ready, he had no idea what a good thing it was. A good many remark that "Billy" is rather a small ox, but I always tell them "That's better than no team." I'm satisfied, even if I can't haul a very big load. Today I was guilty of investing a dime in a plug of tobacco—the first I have bought in four weeks. I have used very little of the weed in that shape for sometime. Oh, well, I have still 70¢ and that will last a while yet.

WEDNESDAY, FEBRUARY 27, 1878

AT THE DUGOUT, KILL CREEK, KANSAS

Hauled a load of wood this a.m., and after putting away some of the necessaries of life, Pa and I went to Geo. Lough's to attend a meeting of the voters of this school district, which was called to discuss the question of building a school house. There were 15 present, of whom 9 were residents of Sod Town. All the business could have been done in 1½ hours, if there had not been so much side talk, such as "How much spring wheat did you sow?" and other questions of equally great importance in the discussion of the question before the meeting. Bailey Taylor offered to make a gift to the district of two acres of land, but it was, after a good deal of wind being used, rejected, as the land lies in a low place. As Sam Hoot remarked "The mosquitoes are so awful bad in them draws!" Dick Benwell's offer of two acres was accepted. The lot lies at the intersection of two section roads, high up, and is a beautiful site for the house. One of the delegates from Sod Town (Sam Hoot) wanted four acres, on the four corners, one for the house, another for a place to stack hay for the preacher's horse (when somebody comes to preach in the house), a third for a hitching ground, and the fourth for a play ground for the children. But that was not the reason Dick's offer was accepted. After a good deal of talk it was decided to build a stone school house, and papers were circulated to see what those present would do toward helping to build the institution. Everybody promised to work; nearly everybody signed for 6 days—some included their teams. In all there were 81 days' work promised. Then a paper for cash subscriptions was circulated, and $18 pledged. Pa and I each gave 6 days' work, and Pa was put on the building committee along with Hackerott and Heberlein. About the things to bring along: You had better make an inventory of all the possessions of the family that are portable, and send it for us to select from, and then we can tell better than by depending on our memory.

THURSDAY, FEBRUARY 28, 1878

At the Dugout, Kill Creek, Kansas

Graybill and I went to Hart's, 3½ miles north, for the prospecting auger, this morning, and spent the afternoon in boring, but did not get any water on my place. Pa was off looking after the affairs of the school building committee. Expect to bore all day for water tomorrow.

FRIDAY, MARCH 1, 1878

AT THE DUGOUT, KILL CREEK, KANSAS

Geo. and I bored a 28 foot hole this morning and struck shale. Just then it began to rain pretty fast, so we quit boring and stayed in the house all day. Towards evening I yoked the cattle and took them over to Hoot's, but they would not drink. This failure to get water does not discourage me in the least. I am getting used to being disappointed when I prospect, and bore as much to see how far it is to shale as for water. When I do strike water, I expect it will be a surprise to me. I don't want to go to the east side of the claim where I am almost sure to get water, because the prettiest building site is right where I am, on the s.w. corner. Hoot says he will pick me out a place to bore. I'll try again. In fact, I'll keep on boring till I do strike water. No prospect for clear weather tomorrow.

SUNDAY, MARCH 10, 1878

AT THE DUGOUT, KILL CREEK, KANSAS

All last week, except Saturday, I worked in the quarry, getting out rock for the schoolhouse. On Tuesday night when I came home, Pa announced that he and Bub had been boring and struck water at 8 feet in the "old dugout draw," near the south line of the claim. Of course I was very well pleased with the news. I'll have to build another sod house. I'd have to do so anyhow. Last Monday Bub and I bored a hole 40 feet deep and did not strike either shale or water. The rods were all in the hole, so we had to stop. If I'd had another 10 foot rod I'd have bored still further. On Friday Chris and I dug in the trench for the foundation of the schoolhouse. A little before noon a high wind blew Stanfield's stovepipe down, and the sparks set fire to his stable, burned that and his stacks, and then the fire swept the prairie for miles. The wind, fortunately for us, kept in the s.e. and the fire did not come within two miles of our place. If the wind had shifted, my stable, hay, etc. would have been burned, and I'd have no feed for the oxen. That high wind blew all the hay off the stable, and when I got home I found it a wreck, so I stayed home yesterday and fixed it up. Pa and Geo. were at Hansen's Friday for a couple of hens Mrs. H. gave Pa because they wanted to set —but they don't seem to want to now. They brought 37 eggs with the hens, because Mrs. H. told Pa she'd give him the hens and eggs to set. I set a hen Friday night. We have 8 hens and a rooster now. Last night Hoot's and Graybill's families and we three went to Rupert's to hear Bro. Dave Brumbach (Dunkard) preach, and particularly to see Mrs. Morrow, who I knew would be there. Franz Huber has returned from the buffalo range, black and dirty. The wind tanned him very much. Today Pa and I went to Neuschwanger's to meeting. Got home about 4 p.m. Total expenses for February were $105.01, divided as follows: oxen, yoke and chain, $61.25; wagon $30, household goods and tools $4.50; provisions $4.30; oil 30¢, sundries $4.41.

MONDAY, MARCH 11, 1878

AT THE DUGOUT, KILL CREEK, KANSAS

About 7 a.m. took the cattle to Hoot's for water and then hooked them ahead of the horses, and Henry and I took the road to the river at a point about 6 miles north to get a load of sand for the school house. The man on whose place we got the sand said he wished a whole lot of folks wanted to build and would haul the sand off his claim, so he could get to the soil, which is about four feet below. We filled the box full. It was a pretty tough pull, but when it was delivered we found we had as much as two other men together had brought. Reached home by 3 p.m., when we unhitched and fed the teams and gave them a chance to rest while we had dinner, after which we took the sand to the schoolhouse site. When the load was off our day's work was done. I walked all the way, and part of the way was pretty painful walking, for Billy trod on my foot; and when an ox is pulling hard his tread is pretty heavy, I can assure you.

TUESDAY, MARCH 12, 1878

At the Dugout, Kill Creek, Kansas

Tonight it is a year since I started for Kansas. First thing this morning was a call on H. J. Brunner to get permission to take rock out of his quarry to wall the well after it is dug. I intend to get the curbing all down before I dig the well, so that I can wall it up directly. He gave the desired permission, and I went to getting out rock about 10 o'clock. By night had 4 or 5 loads ready to haul.

WEDNESDAY, MARCH 13, 1878

At the Dugout, Kill Creek, Kansas

At work in the quarry this morning. Hauled 4 loads of rock this afternoon. I'd like to have the old hatchet when I wall up the well, but as I can't I'll have to use the new one. When I'm in town I don't visit anywhere much—never at Steinfort's—sometimes at Joe Morrow's. Of all the women in town I like Mrs. Morrow the best. She treats me more like a son than any woman about here. You talk about "getting out on a pleasant day." Why, we're out every day except when it rains, and that is decidedly the exception. We're having beautiful weather now. There was another big prairie fire today, but it was over a mile west of my place, and did not come any nearer.

THURSDAY, MARCH 14, 1878

AT THE DUGOUT, KILL CREEK, KANSAS

At the quarry this a.m. Mr. Brunner wanted us to put up his sod house—just laying up the walls. But I don't know when Frank will want me at the office, and I don't undertake anything that must be done in a certain time without knowing I can do as I promise, so we did not take the job. After dinner when I went to yoke the cattle, Bub got the bellyache and so was disabled. I hauled 4 loads. You ought to see the difference in the appearance of the cattle. They are getting to look right sleek since they have all the fodder and hay they can eat. They have improved in appearance a good deal in the last four weeks.

FRIDAY, MARCH 15, 1878

AT THE DUGOUT, KILL CREEK, KANSAS

This morning went to digging the well. Got down 5½ feet, and then found the gravel etc. was too heavy to throw out of the hole. After dinner I went to Gsell's to see whether Levin could let me have the windlass. He said I might. The bucket was at Sam Hoot's. Yoked the cattle, and with Pa for passenger and assistant went to Sam's for the bucket and to Levin's for the windlass, coming round by my place for several articles we will need tomorrow in digging, or, rather, in getting the dirt out. Set the crotches and fixed everything so we can go to work in the morning. Bub had bellyache all day, and was unfit for work. Yesterday morning when we came from the quarry we met John Sherley from Osborne, with three Eastonians, looking for H.J.B[runner]. It cost those fellows about $50 each to get to Osborne. They bought tickets along the road, instead of buying through tickets at once. I'm going to town the beginning of next week, but when I'll get back I couldn't say; maybe next day—maybe in a couple of weeks. I'd like to get about five weeks' work, so I can put up the other house, and buy a breaking plow and several other necessary articles. There are five ox teams in this immediate vicinity: Fritsche, Snyder, Rook, mine and Sam Hoot's. Of the lot Fritsche's are the finest. Rook's are the biggest-framed, but there is not much flesh on their bones. I'll be awful glad when you get here; it will save lots of postage stamps and time now used for writing letters—not that I don't like to write, but this week there was so little to chronicle.

SUNDAY, MARCH 24, 1878

AT THE DUGOUT, KILL CREEK, KANSAS

I have to begin with the 16th. That was Saturday, Bub's birthday. Went to work on the well and took out 110 buckets of ground. I went through three feet of shale and struck water in gravel below the shale—plenty of water. The well is about 12 feet deep. We quit before sundown, because Pa and Bub got obstreperous and refused to work any longer. The water came in very fast, and it made me feel good, though my boots were full of water all the afternoon, and my old overalls were torn to shreds. I wanted to save them to show you how I patched them, but they were so very poor that I pulled them off and let them lie by the well. Now Mrs. Gray-bill wants them for patches. Sunday we went to Hackerotts to meeting. There was 4 feet of water in the well, and that had to be baled out on Monday morning before we could begin laying up the wall. Bub and I dipped the water out, and then Pa and Bub let down stone and I laid up the wall, all but about a foot by sundown. Tuesday morning Bub and I finished the wall and took borrowed things home. Wednesday morning I went to town. Took the coal oil can along. It was four weeks since I had been in town, and I was pretty sure of getting work. Went to the office and had not talked with Frank ten minutes before he told me to go to work. Stayed till last night and earned $3. Bought a hay fork and came home, arriving at 9 p.m. Found the folks in bed. Picked up a lot of corn on the road. I hate to see corn wasted that way. It drops off the wagons and gets ground into the dirt. I intend to get one of Joe Morrow's new style breaking plows. They are a tip top invention. Went to Shellenberger's to meeting today. My wheat begins to make a good show now. All the fall grain looks better now than it did this time last year. A year ago Monday I jumped off Geo. Shipton's wagon at Keever's in Osborne, and Friday a year ago I saw Kill Creek for the first time. I have gone into summer costume—shirt, overalls and boots; no coat, vest or socks. Set another hen.

SUNDAY, MARCH 31, 1878

AT THE DUGOUT, KILL CREEK, KANSAS

On Monday Bub and I hauled a couple loads of rock to fill in round the well on top of the ground, so that in wet weather it will not be muddy. Pa brought the mail and the $5. I'm ever so much obliged. I had just 15¢ left when I went

to work in the office. Now I have about $1.50 more than the
$5 you sent, and by this time next week I expect to have
enough to buy a plow. Tuesday I walked to town and Wednesday went to work in the office. Got through yesterday noon;
earned $3. Brought a hoe and iron rake home, which rejoiced
Pa, who has been wishing for such a rake since last summer.
The expenses last month amounted to $6.28. Wednesday and
Friday were real cool and rainy; on Friday the thermometer
marked 1° above freezing, but the peach trees are not hurt.
They were all blooming last week. Brought some side meat
along—8¢ per lb. One chick has come from the first setting.
Eggs are only 5¢ per dozen.

MONDAY, APRIL 1, 1878

At the Dugout, Kill Creek, Kansas

Pa went off this a.m. to have a petition signed for issuing
school district bonds to the amount of $106. The other peti-
tion was for $250, which was about $150 more than we could
draw—the amount being proportioned to the taxable property
(real estate) in the district, and there are only 240 acres of
taxable land in this district.[30] Bub and I made a watering
trough, and got three rails ready to put up at the well; the
rails are tied at the top, and the tripod has the pulley hanging
from the apex. After dinner we hauled more spall stones for
round the well. The "heel flies" troubled the cattle very much
the last few days, and they tore loose and ran off; today I
greased their heels, which seemed to relieve them. Our water
is perfectly clear and rather softer than Hoot's. Last Monday
16 emigrant teams passed the P.O. in one train, and there is

---

[30] Land was not taxable until the government had finally given a deed
to it, and only a few of the oldest settlers here had yet received deeds.

not a day that we don't hear of, if not see, emigrant teams. Tomorrow I go to town to work Wednesday and Thursday, if not longer.

SUNDAY, APRIL 21, 1878

AT THE DUGOUT, KILL CREEK, KANSAS

It's so long since I wrote that I hardly know where to begin, but I reckon you'll make some allowance, seeing that I am home only from Saturday morning to Tuesday noon, and therefore don't have much news to tell. Friday afternoon Frank paid me $2.50 for three days' work, and I happened to catch Wismer's team, so I had a ride half way home. Refused an invitation to remain over night and almost got lost between the church and home. I did not want to go past Neuschwanger's, and then got off my road in the dark, but finally got home about 10 o'clock. The first bit of news was bad. The sow was dead—$5 and the feed lost. Yesterday we took another hen off the nest. She had 10 chicks from 12 eggs. Now we have 37 chicks and 9 old fowls. This last brood is nearly all white and feather-legged. Another hen is sitting on 15 eggs. She will come off in a week. I lose very little time going to and coming from town. I generally leave home sometime Tuesday morning, and so far have always got back by Friday night. Since March 20 I have earned $13.75, of which I have saved $3 towards buying a breaker. Those $5 you sent and the $1 Bub gave me puts me within $4 of the cost. Then I'll need a monkey wrench and file to keep the plow sharp. That will be another $1.50. The death of the sow made me feel a little blue, but that was something I couldn't help, and the fit soon wore off. I expect I'll have three days work every week till harvest. I need it, too, for I must build that house, and that can't be done for nothing. But you need not worry about my finances. I'll pull through all right, only it will take a little time. Was over to see Mrs. Brunner this morning. She is quite well contented. As I was coming home I met Franz Huber driving over to see Levin. He had Nora Morrow, Mary Lapp and Ida Wolf in the wagon with him. To-morrow I am to help Chris at his well. John Fickardt bought a yoke of cattle for $100 soon after he arrived, and last Wednesday he started for the railroad to sell them. He and John Stadijer and Billy Everard had each taken a homestead about 10 miles N.W. of Osborne, but they got notice that the land had been taken up in February. So now John S. and Billy talk of buying a claim on Twin Creek. Jule Feufstueck was offered a span of horses, harness, wagon, 300 bu. corn, a lot of wheat and rye, farm tools, etc., and 160 acres of land with 16 acres of fall grain on it—all for $700. He has written for the money. I counted the Bethlehemites in the county that I know. There are 66. Last Wednesday we had a pretty heavy shower, and one can see the difference in the wheat. Down town we had a pretty heavy hail storm. Very little fell here on the creek. The tide of emigration is a little slower, but still they come, from all parts. Saw H. E. Weinland and Emma Kues on Friday. Emma didn't recognize me. No meeting in this neighborhood for three weeks. Neuschwanger has gone to Mc-Pherson Co. to conference. Was at Hoot's for eggs last evening, but their hens are on a strike, and they had only two dozen "zum Oshtera."[31] Pa has gone to Wismer's on a visit, and we will probably not see him till some time tomorrow. Last night I tried to put the staple in the yoke so as to give Billy the advantage, and in pounding it in the staple broke. A job for the blacksmith. The assessor put down my property at

[31] "Zum Oshtera"—for Easter.

$72. That will bring the taxes between $2 and $3. The cattle were assessed at $45, wagon $10, household goods $10. How do you like the Farmer? Do you get it regular? The expenses for provisions for three months averages $2.47 per month, or about 20¢ per week for each of us; and we have meat and flour for three weeks on hand. The total expenses, leaving out the team ($91.50) for three months were $27.76; that includes tools and odds and ends. Spent a pleasant evening with Mrs. R. G. Hays last week. Hardly know what to do with myself evenings when in town. Even if there is some sort of circus in the hall, I don't go, because I don't care for them; and then, too, I have better use for my quarters. The boys laugh at me, but I'm used to it and don't mind it. We have about an acre in potatoes, and still have about two bushels to plant, and no ground to plant them in. Bub has 10 chestnut and one peach tree started. Several of the former are two inches high. The wheat and rye look nice. Frank gave me a potato weighing 17 oz. and I made 21 sets of it and planted them yesterday. The pile of manure got on fire two weeks ago, Friday, and Pa covered it with ground to prevent its blowing round, and to smother the fire. Yesterday I opened it to get some ashes to put into the potato bed, and the blamed thing began to smoke and in a few minutes would have been in a blaze if I had not thrown more ground on it. The death of the pig gave Pa the blues. The school bond question was decided Wednesday, in favor of bonds to the amount of $106. Two or three of the raspberries are growing; also a couple of the blackberries. I set out 9 soft maples, that F. H. B[arnhart] gave me, last Saturday, and they are all growing, along the draw where the well is. The new house will be about 100 steps north of the well. I have as good, if not better, water than the neighbors. Have planted a few dozen hills of sweet corn. Jim has a pony team now. He was going to have a "horse team" and seemed offended when I asked whether he called his pony a horse. The. Fogel intends to begin work on his house tomorrow. What are Ruth's directions? I want that photo of her, as I am sure she don't look like the one I have. Mrs. Brunner wouldn't have known who I was if Bub hadn't told her, so you will probably not be able to say exactly when you see me.

MONDAY, APRIL 22, 1878

AT THE DUGOUT, KILL CREEK, KANSAS

Graybill employed Bub and me to help at his well. It is the one Bub and I dug last fall before Chris took the claim. The hole has been partially filled by the gravel falling from the top, and he had only a small place to dip water. He had to go down and dip every time his wife wanted to wash. He dug the well 9 feet deep, and when he got through digging I offered to lay up the wall. He was glad I offered, as he said he had never seen a well wall in process of construction. (I did not tell him I had never seen a well walled out till I laid up my wall. If I am green, I don't let 'em know it.) Walled it to his satisfaction. I went in barefoot, because my boots wouldn't stand any more water. By the way, Cal Brendle does stretch the long bow in his letters, as any one who lives here can tell. I have not heard of a single wolf being killed in the country since I'm here. The balance of the "plenty of game," such as he calls game, is not quite as plenty as might be supposed from reading his letters. We have a hearty laugh over his letters, being as they are, written by one who has seen only the easy side of Kansas life. About the time he gets to farming (if he ever gets that far) his father will not find his letters so interesting to the public, as I am afraid they will contain too many $ marks. He don't seem to be a very go-ahead boy.

SUNDAY, MAY 26, 1878

AT THE DUGOUT, KILL CREEK, KANSAS

I have not written for a long time, and I reckon a letter will be appreciated, so I'll give you a short one. Yesterday a week, as Pa or Bub probably wrote, we began breaking. Such a time as we had, learning to get the grasshopper to go into the sod and remain there I hope never to have again. By this time the thing works all right, but the cattle skip the furrow so often that Bub has to walk alongside. But we get the sod turned. Tuesday I was out by 5, and we got the plow running by 6. Had ½ acre broken by 10:30, when we unyoked, and after having something to eat, I walked to town. Didn't have much work in the office Wednesday, and Thursday I didn't do 3 hours work though I was paid for a day. Friday I was at the press all day, and I was tired when 6 o'clock came. Remained in town till yesterday a.m. when I got a ride from the river to Fritsche's. Got home by 12, and at 2 started the plow. Quit an hour before sundown, because Bub has not recovered from his walk to town Thursday and corn planting on Friday, which tired him very much. I have 10¢. Had to get a pair of shoes for myself a couple of weeks ago, and last week, a pair for Bub—hence the low state of my finances. The shoes cost $2.25 per pair. Fritchey threw off 25¢ because I got two pair. Got a pair of iron bow keys for the yoke: the wooden ones dropped out and broke so often, and then the bow fell out and the yoke would slip way back on Sam's back-bone, leaving Billy in a bad fix, especially when the yoke fell off of Sam. These bow keys will not slip out.

Herman Glicker is out here again. He "beat" his way to Chicago, where he got a ticket for the balance of the way. He intends to remain here. John Stadiger bought a place three miles east of town for $700. I guess he'll go to Bethlehem for his family as soon as he has the business settled. I laid out $6.65 for provisions this month. A cwt. of flour, $2.60; ham, 22½ lb. at 9¢, $2; are the principal expenses, but the flour will last a good while. On the 20th Feb. we had 200 of flour out of 5 bu. wheat and that flour lasted us till the 17th of this month. We used a good deal of cornbread—at least I did —about three days in a week. Like it better than wheat bread, and can live on it better. We sold 4 bu. potatoes at 50¢ per bu. Pa paid for 10 bu. in work at the rate of 25¢ last fall. We now have about an acre of potatoes and 2 of corn planted. Tomorrow we expect to finish breaking inside the wheat, and on Tuesday begin breaking for a garden back of where the new house is to be. I want an acre there for garden. The rye looks fine—it is over waist high. Lots of rye in the wheat, which is a little over knee high, with full heads. Took a hen off the nest on Tuesday with 12 chicks. The red hen left 15 eggs, after sitting a week, and is running with a motherless brood. Graybill has over 100 chicks, and the other day he caught seven prairie chicks just hatched and put them under a hen he has in the house, with the hope of taming them.

SATURDAY, JUNE 8, *1878*

At the Dugout, Kill Creek, Kansas

Got home from town about noon. This was the 12th week I worked in town for a couple of days each week, and I have earned $30.50, of which I have about $3 left. Next week and the week following I will be home—maybe longer. In Au-

gust Frank is going to York State, and then I'll have from 4
to 6 weeks work. I want to earn enough next winter to buy
a horse, and then I'll sell the cattle and buy another horse,
because I know Syd will not like the cattle. We'll get ahead
faster when Syd will be here, because he or I can work in the
office whenever Frank wants us, and the other can run the
farm, so we will always have a little cash. We are going to
have a fine young lady for a neighbor. Her name is Sabina
Miller. Her stepfather, Schwaup, has taken the claim north
of Jim. I got acquainted with her at Keever's this week. When
I got to town Tuesday I discovered an "Art Gallery" below
Fritchey's, so I had a type taken for you. Pa thinks it is a
better picture than likeness, but a majority pronounce it a good
likeness.

SUNDAY, JUNE 9, 1878

At the Dugout, Kill Creek, Kansas

Went to Neuschwanger's to meeting. They had communion
and feet washing. Some of those present at Sunday school were
frightened off by a black cloud that blew up. Rode home with
Hoot. Yesterday I got a piece of sewing wax from Mrs. Hoot.
I wanted to borrow a piece, but she gave it to me.

MONDAY, JUNE 10, 1878

At the Dugout, Kill Creek, Kansas

Very heavy dew this morning. Did not begin breaking till
about 7 o'clock. Quit at 11 and went to patching my blue shirt.
After dinner planted a few rows of corn and then went to
breaking again. Part of the sod is very rotten and I could do
better work with a stirring plow, but there is a big patch of

blue joint that would take four horses to pull a stirring plow through. Pa went for the mail, but did not reach the P.O. as Laura Hoot had brought our mail. . . . I was sure there was a letter at the P.O., so I went for it. Grandpap said there was a registered letter. Many thanks for the money. What's the matter with Syd? I never wrote for him to stay back, and I reckon on having him here when you come. I want him too. So don't let me hear about his hanging back till spring. Many hands make light-work, even if it does take much provisions. Broke a little more than ½ acre today.

SUNDAY, JUNE 16, 1878

At the Dugout, Kill Creek, Kansas

Broke out a good piece on Tuesday, and had just turned the oxen out to graze when Dave Bleam drove up with his buckboard and told me Barnhart wanted me. He had discharged the tramp (Harry Watson) because he was no account—something I discovered at once when I worked with him. There was no saying NO, so I went in and donned my "town suit," jumped into the vehicle, and rode as far as Dave's house, where I had dinner, and then walked to town. Frank was married that afternoon to Miss Emma Eckman, and cigars were plenty for Ham & me the balance of the week. Earned $3.50. Understood him to say I might stay home this week, but he said he wanted me, and that if I charged him harvest wages he'd have to pay them. That will be about $1.25 and board per day. We had rain every night except Monday night. Tuesday and Wednesday evenings I kept hotel for Keever. Did not get to sleep till midnight, and as the house was full, I had to sleep on the floor. That, however, is nothing to me now, as I have slept on the floor so much since I am in Kansas that I don't mind it. Steinfort is cutting a good deal of wheat for people round town. . . . The river was up pretty high yesterday and came into the wagon box when we forded. Lapp and I rode to within a mile from his place. Had supper there and then pushed on home where I arrived about 8:30.

MONDAY, JUNE 17, 1878

At the Dugout, Kill Creek, Kansas

Went to meeting at Hoot's yesterday morning. It was a dreary day, rainy. There was not a very large audience. Pa surprised me when Deacon Shellenberger said "Weiter platz und freiheit"—by making a few remarks. After dinner Bub and I went with a load of folks to S.S. [Sunday school]. In fact, Sam took the whole S.S. with him. Afterwards I went to Johann's and stayed there all night by invitation. This morning I went over to the old gent's to get the cradle, as I could get nobody to cut my grain with a machine. . . . This afternoon about 2 I got home with the cradle, and as the rain had about quit and the wind came up and dried the grain, about 3:30 I began cutting. Cut about ¼ acre before night. Pa and Bub handled the rake and bound it, taking alternate sheaves.

TUESDAY, JUNE 18, 1878

Osborne, Kansas

Turned out about 5, and as soon as the wheat was dry enough went to cradling. Pa tied it awhile and between us we got ½ acre cut by noon. Then I started for town. It was awful hot, too. Took it easy and got to town about 6. The folks up on the creek all have four horses to their machines. The river is high and I had to cross on the ferry boat. I am very stiff in the legs from the violent exercise this morning and walking 15 miles after noon. We had a regular "blacksmith" at work in the office, and he beat Keever out of a week's board, and Mrs. Korb ditto, and today he lit out after taking an old pepperbox revolver belonging to somebody else. I reckon I'll find my wheat all in shock when I get home as Pa and Bub were just wild to do the work. The rye will not be ready for ten days. Send my photo album with Col. Bear.

SATURDAY, JULY 13, 1878

AT THE DUGOUT, KILL CREEK, KANSAS

Home again for a couple of days. I made $9 this last trip to town. Went down last Tuesday a week, and after a little talk with Col. Bear, went to the office and Frank told me to go to work after dinner, because Thursday was a holiday. Worked right along, and Thursday all day. Thursday morning about 2 o'clock I got awake, and hearing a terrible noise somewhere in the neighborhood (I slept in the garret at Keevers) I went up on the roof and saw a light in the room over the office, and presently heard somebody call off the figures for a dance, when the mouth organ struck up the music, and they had a regular hoedown. I did not wait to hear any more, but went back to bed.

There was a big celebration at Bull City on the Fourth, but $1 was more than I could afford to throw away for a day's fun, so I did not go.

I have $10 toward the house, and the other $10 will not be long coming. If Frank goes to Iowa the coming week, I will probably be able to add $5 or $6 to the pile.

I wanted to stack my grain today, but Jim has the wagon, so I will probably get at it Monday. Tuesday I must go to town again. I was fairly homesick this week—tired of town. There's no rest for me anywhere but here, and here but very little. But it's home and my mind is at rest even if I am at work. . . .

Today Bub and I were leveling off the place for the new house, though I suppose it will be a couple of weeks before we get to laying up the sod. . . .

MONDAY, JULY 15, 1878

AT THE DUGOUT, KILL CREEK, KANSAS

Up before 5. After breakfast yoked up and hauled and stacked the wheat. It made only two loads. The rye will make three, but they will not be so large. Col. Bear, Mrs. B., R. G. Hays and his wife stopped here on the way to Bull City. It has cost us for provisions an average of 30¢ per week apiece for the six months ending July 1. Since the 20th March I have earned $49, and since last October a little over $100. I can see where part of it is; the balance has been eaten. Pa don't mind the heat today, because there is a pleasant breeze stirring—almost too much for stacking.

TUESDAY, JULY 16, 1878

OSBORNE, KANSAS

Started for town about 6. Bub went along to see Col B[ear] and Rob Rieser. Left Bub at R. G. [Hays]'s and I went to Joe Morrow's for dinner. John Rupert took Bub along home this evening. Had a heavy shower about 7 p.m., which freshened things nicely.

FRIDAY, AUGUST 7, 1878

OSBORNE, KANSAS

The shorter the time till you come, the harder it is to get a letter started. I was kept here ten days the last trip, and got home Friday evening. Saturday we hauled a lot of sod. Pa and Bub had the stable walls partially laid up, and we hauled enough sod to finish them. When it got too hot to work the cattle, Bub and I went to work laying up—Bub carrying sod for Pa, while I carried all I laid. Geo. thought it went faster when I helped, to which Pa assented, saying that of course it did when I laid up twice as much as he. Sunday night I could not sleep. About midnight a heavy thunder storm set in, and it rained three hours. Such lightning I never saw before. It was one continuous sheet. The big draw had about 7 feet of water in it at daylight. I did not sleep over two hours that night, and was out of doors before the sun was up. Sam had pulled up his picket pin during the night, but had gone only as far as to where Billy lay, and laid down aside of him. The sod was too soft to be handled. Chris got me to fetch a sack of flour from Sam Gillmore's. Snyder would like to get hold of my oxen, but would not like to give more for them than $30, I suppose. He can't have them. Finished the stable walls. After dinner I laid up all the sod that was over at the house. Yesterday morning went to Lapp's and rode with him as far as Mahaffey's on the river, which was too high to ford, though it had fallen 5 feet in as many hours. Kill Creek was bank full; so was Little Medicine. Crossed the river in a boat and walked 6 miles to town. When I arrived I told Frank I intended to stay home next week, as I wanted to finish the house and do the threshing. He said I could not, as he was going to Iowa; he started this morning, so here I am till Friday a week. . . . I'll write full instructions when

I let you know the house is finished. I'm going to board at Joe Morrow's. I have to wait too long before I get my meals at the hotels, and besides, I can gain 50¢ per week by boarding myself. I have been doing my work when I was through working for other people. I hope another year will be better for me. The next month's work I get here will be a big lift towards buying a horse or cow. Pa has $5 towards buying a cow, that G. Bishop sent to pay for experimenting on gumbo. . . .

SUNDAY, SEPTEMBER 1, 1878

At the Dugout, Kill Creek, Kansas

I reckon I'll have to give you some instructions in reference to coming, as you seem to be bent on coming anyhow. I can be ready for you in three weeks if things work right this week.

We all went over to meeting at Hackerotts this morning, having heard that Mennonite services were to be held there. Word is always passed round the neighborhood several days in advance. On arriving in sight of the house it seemed as if there was something unusual on the program, as there were more teams in the yard than we generally see at such times. Getting closer, we heard someone speaking indoors, and found that Lutheran services were in progress. The room was nearly as full as it could be, but we managed to find place. The preacher wore a black surplice and white tie, which are not often seen in this part of the world, and attract notice on that account. The service was in German and very long, but that did not tire us, for we were all used to rather long sermons. At the close of the sermon a child was presented for baptism, and the baby surely received enough names to choke it to death: Clara Katerina Henrietta Johanna. About 11 o'clock the Lutherans vacated the room and the Mennonites took possession. Mr. Yoder, the Mennonite preacher, preached a very disconnected sermon in English, at the close of which Bishop Neuschwanger made a few remarks in German. After dinner Bub and I went to Garman's to eat watermelons and Pa soon followed to help us. When melons are about he is the last man to say no. About 2:30 Bill hitched up and took the whole crowd to Hoot's, where Yoder delivered his farewell sermon to the Kill Creekers, as he expected to start tomorrow morning for his home in Nebraska.

MONDAY, SEPTEMBER 2, 1878

At the Dugout, Kill Creek, Kansas

To work about 7:30. Put the rafters in position and began filling between them with sod. It took a good deal of time to set the rafters, because the ridge pole is not straight. After dinner Bub and I hauled four loads of sod and then put the boards on the roof. We put them all on, getting through about 8:30. Pa went to Aug. Fritsche's to take care of the premises by sleeping there. F. has gone to Russell with a load of wheat, and will not be back till Wednesday.

TUESDAY, SEPTEMBER 3, 1878

Osborne, Kansas

Couldn't sleep last night after I got to bed, and about 2 o'clock dressed and went over to the straw stack. There I slept all night. Took the overcoat along to cover with. Up about 6. Pa came from Fritsche's just about the time I concluded to get up for the day. After breakfast Bub and I began laying sod on the roof. By the time half was laid we found we would need a couple of loads more, so we yoked up and hauled two loads. Then I quit. Bub was to work at it this afternoon and finish. I walked to town this afternoon. Pa says we never before did as much work between Friday night and Tuesday noon. I don't expect to get home until Friday a week. A year ago last Wednesday we moved into our present residence. Then Pa thought that in two years would be time enough to think about having you here. Now he is as anxious to see you as I am.

[From this point the narrative takes the form of a diary.]

The threshing was done Aug. 14th, Henry Hoot taking charge of the business. The wheat yielded 28½ bu. and the rye 33 bu., which was put into straw until the old house was vacated. During September I worked in the office, getting home very late. Pa and Geo. finished the new house and cut the corn fodder. On the 28th September we moved into the new house, after having occupied the dugout for 13 months. Joe L. Weber paid us a visit before we moved. He got sick from eating watermelon, which, added to the remaining effects of the fever which he got in the Arkansas Valley, made him very miserable. I went back with him to Osborne. Ma's letter of Sept. 22 made us all happy. The sale of goods in Bethlehem was over; they were stopping at Aunt Addie's, and would leave for Kansas on the 30th. I was at work in town when Ma arrived. The Farmer Office had been removed into the second story of Baldwin and Wilson's drug store, and I was on the watch for the hack all the afternoon. When it arrived I was ready to assist her in alighting at R.G. Hays'. It was a rainy day and the roads were bad. Ma stayed at Hays' till Sunday morning, when Ira Stout brought us home. Carl Brendle came along to see the country. At Greenfield's we picked up Syd and George, who were out exploring. Syd arrived on the 4th of October, having come out with Houser, of Paradise Creek, bringing the baggage. By dint of some persuasion, he got Houser to bring him through in a day. I went back to town with Ira. Syd also went, on a visit to Ira. He worked in the office for me that week, while I plowed for wheat.

Tuesday, Oct. 8, and Wednesday, the 9th, were the dates of the memorable Indian scare, and many people left their homes and fled to Osborne. We did not go. A man informed me he had been told by one who had come from Russell that day, that there were 6,000 Indians between here and Russell. But I didn't believe it. Bill Garman and Fogel went to the Saline to see the red men, which they did not succeed in doing.

The most probable clue to the cause of the excitement was obtained from a gentleman we met at the Covert post office, who had ridden from Hays City since Sunday morning. He states that, in view of the known fact of the Indians having crossed the Kansas Pacific Railroad some distance west of Hays City, it was thought advisable by some of the citizens of that town to appraise the settlers on the Saline adjacent to that place of the *possible* danger of a raid. The warning was taken as an alarm, which has spread with growing exaggeration down the valley. The gentleman of whom we speak has ridden down the Saline from Hayes City, and has seen no Indians.

Got my wheat in by the end of the week. Syd came home Sunday. On the 11th October he homesteaded the 80 north of my place. He said he came for a three months' loaf, so he and Geo. went fishing every day till they were tired of that and everything else.

This year (1878) I broke about 6 acres, making my farming land for 1879 11 acres. The crops turned out pretty well. We had about 50 bushels of sod corn, and same of potatoes. And bread stuff sufficient for a year. Bought seed wheat of Fritsche, who also did some plowing for me. Sowed 6 acres in fall wheat and 3 acres in rye.

Index